Being Apart

Being Apart

THEORETICAL AND EXISTENTIAL
RESISTANCE IN AFRICANA LITERATURE

LaRose T. Parris

UNIVERSITY OF VIRGINIA PRESS   *Charlottesville and London*

THIS BOOK IS MADE POSSIBLE BY A COLLABORATIVE GRANT FROM
THE ANDREW W. MELLON FOUNDATION.

University of Virginia Press
© 2015 by the Rector and Visitors of the
University of Virginia
Printed in the United States of America on acid-free paper
First published 2015

9 8 7 6 5 4 3 2 1

Library of Congress Cataloging-in-Publication Data

Parris, LaRose.
   Being apart : theoretical and existential resistance in
Africana literature / LaRose T. Parris.
      pages   cm
   Includes bibliographical references and index.
   ISBN 978-0-8139-3812-7 (cloth : acid-free paper)
   ISBN 978-0-8139-3813-4 (pbk. : acid-free paper)
   ISBN 978-0-8139-3814-1 (e-book)
   1. African literature (English)—Black authors—
History and criticism.   2. Caribbean literature
(English)—Black authors—History and criticism.
3. American literature—African American authors—
History and criticism.   4. African diaspora in
literature.   5. Pan-Africanism in literature.
6. Passive resistance in literature.   7. Existentialism
in literature.   8. American literature—African
influences.   I. Title.
PR9340.5.P37 2015
820.9'96—dc23
                              2014044779

For the Ancestors

CONTENTS

ACKNOWLEDGMENTS

The seeds of this work were planted during my childhood, as I grew up in a remarkable family during a charmed time. My parents immigrated from the island nation of Jamaica to the Bronx, with their infant children in tow, just as cries for civil rights became a unified call for Black power; their Black nationalist worldview made them right at home in New York City's progressive community. As a young girl, I was in awe of my parents and family friends because they were fully engaged in activist work, committed to creating a more equal and just society. Fortunately my mother and father saw their roles as parents as indivisible from their work as activists, and in that capacity they taught us two invaluable lessons: the life of the mind is wondrous and fulfilling, and the struggles, triumphs, and gifts of our ancestors will inspire us for the rest of our days. Each weekend our parents had us recite written reports on Toussaint L'Ouverture, Harriet Tubman, Marcus Garvey, Sojourner Truth, and many other great freedom fighters. In those days there was no name for our extra homework; now it is called homeschooling. My parents also avidly collected Malcolm X's recorded speeches and Robert Nesta Marley's roots reggae albums. With their revolutionary voices filling our home, they stirred us to imagine a world of African diasporic unity and true equality within the human family. Therefore I must begin by thanking my parents and first teachers, Dulcie and Canute Parris, for blessing me with the love of knowledge and for awakening my political conscience.

During the early stages of this project, several dedicated and generous scholars were instrumental in mentoring me. I am truly grateful for the guidance of Robert Reid-Pharr, Ammiel Alcalay, and Peter Hitchcock, who read drafts of this manuscript when it was still in its infancy. Without their expertise and insights, I would not have been able to shape the work into its current form. During this same period, I also had the good fortune to take a class with the historian, poet, and critic Kamau Brathwaite. This was an amazing intellectual and creative experience, for it made the writing and revising of this book possible. Thank you so much, KB.

Several colleagues at LaGuardia Community College provided encouragement and read early drafts of chapters over the years. I would like to thank Justin Rogers-Cooper, Sandra Sellers Hanson, Noel Holton Brathwaite, Demetrios Kapetanakos, Allia Abdullah-Matta, Kimberly del Busto Ramirez, and Charity Scribner for their unwavering support. I would also like to acknowledge the Research Foundation of the City University of New York for awarding me two PSC-CUNY grants, one in 2011 and the other in 2012. These grants afforded me the time and mental space that was needed to reconceptualize the project.

I am also grateful to Kurt Young and Itibari Zulu for publishing an excerpt of chapter 3 in the November 2011 issue of the *Journal of Pan African Studies*.

When I attended the 2012 Modern Language Association convention in Seattle, I was fortunate to meet Cathie Brettschneider, the humanities editor at the University of Virginia Press. I would like to express my sincere appreciation for her immediate interest in the project. I am also grateful to the entire editorial staff at the Press, and to the Modern Language Initiative editors Tim Roberts and Judith Hoover for their great attention to detail in the final stages of the manuscript's preparation.

In June 2014 I gave a presentation on this project at the annual meeting of the Caribbean Philosophical Association (CPA). This was truly a life-changing experience. Presenting my paper and participating in so many rich, stimulating discussions gave me the drive to complete the work during the summer of 2014. The CPA members' brilliance was equaled by their warmth and kindness. I would like to thank all of the members for this experience, but in particular Jane Anna Gordon and Rosario Torres-Guevara for giving me the platform to present my work and for welcoming me into this unique intellectual community.

I must also express my heartfelt gratitude and appreciation for my family. Dulcie Parris, La-Verne Parris, Nicholas Parris, Michel ZhuParris, and Ahnjili ZhuParris have given me unconditional love and support for my entire life. Over the past three years, however, I could not have done *any* of this work without them. Their unfailing generosity and belief in me gave me the determination to complete the manuscript, in spite of a demanding teaching schedule. I must especially thank my twin sister, La-Verne, who read the entire manuscript several times; her guidance and patience were truly invaluable. Like my family, there are several friends who have been in my life for more than a decade and who were excited about this project when it was a mere glimmer of an idea. I am thankful to Rosa Garcia, Prentis Goodman, Jimin Han, David Singleton, and Jorge Soriano for their heartfelt encouragement.

Finally I would like to thank Lewis Gordon. Without his pioneering work in the field of Black/Africana existentialism, this book could not have been written. His genius as a philosopher is matched only by his generosity of spirit, and I am truly blessed to have benefited from his mentorship.

Introduction

> To be recognized as human was to be accorded an authentic kind of
> historic being. On the other hand, to be dismissed on raciological
> grounds as bestial or infrahuman was to be cast outside of both culture
> and historicality. . . . Recognizing the extent of this pattern . . . and
> the legacy of its claims upon academic historiography . . . is another
> necessary step toward appreciating how the idea of history as a narrative
> of racial hierarchy . . . helped to undo modernity's best promises.
>
> —Paul Gilroy, *Postcolonial Melancholia*

During Western modernity,[1] the eighteenth- and nineteenth-century
proliferation of literary productions by enslaved and free Africans must
be understood for its historical, philosophical, and epistemological
import, as African people's interventions into Western discourse became
a form of theoretical resistance to their enslavement, subjugation, and
marginalization. Attendant to the birth of modern philosophy's natural
rights doctrine was the coterminous rise of Eurocentrism and racist discourse;[2] this ideological confluence represents the cultural and epistemological dualism of modernity that eighteenth- and nineteenth-century
Africana writers ardently contested. Africana writers delineated philosophical racism as an epistemic progression born of seminal historical,
geopolitical, and socioeconomic forces; for European conquest, Western imperialism and colonialism, the European slave trade and Western
chattel slavery irrevocably shaped the power dynamics among Europeans, Africans, Asians, and Native Americans through the subjugation of
non-Western "others" and the capitalist/hegemonic domination of Europeans and European Americans. Enlightenment discourses of scientific
racism instantiated a protracted attack on African people's humanity and
historicality, which acted to set Africans apart from the human family

and radically alter their place in Western historiography. The African's re-creation into the ahistorical, bestial Negro slave became central to Western slavery's ideological and economic survival. Thus the European slave trade in Africans catalyzed a radical negation of African human identity since

> the construct of Negro, unlike the terms "African," "Moor," or "Ethiope" suggested no situatedness in time, that is history, or space, that is ethno- or politico-geography. The Negro had no civilization, no cultures, no religions, no history, no place, and finally no humanity that might command consideration. . . . The creation of the Negro, the fiction of a dumb beast of burden fit only for slavery, was closely associated with the economic, technical, and financial requirements of Western development from the sixteenth century on. (Robinson 81)

The African's mass enslavement in the West necessitated a complete reconfiguration of African identity that existed outside of logical time, history, and culture. The African's distorted character came to be embodied in the figure of the Negro, the enslaved beast of burden whose presence came to define the boundaries of Enlightenment racial science, while establishing the perimeters of subhumanity and the anti-African trajectory of Western hegemonic discourse. It is within this historiographical, philosophical, and political context that I theorize the literary productions of enslaved and free Africans and their descendants during the nineteenth and twentieth centuries.

The writings of Phyllis Wheatley,[3] Olaudah Equiano, Ottabah Cugoano, Benjamin Banneker, Toussaint L'Ouverture, David Walker, and others present eloquent, philosophical attacks on the tenets of scientific racism and the selective endowment of freedom and natural rights to Europeans and European Americans during the eighteenth- and nineteenth-century intensification of chattel slavery in the West. Collectively these Africana writers' works stand as the first direct challenge to Enlightenment discourses that manipulated the construction of racial categories to rationalize the degradation of various racial groups (Keita, *Race and Writing History* 165). As such, their works "mark the emergence of an alternative epistemology" (164) that critiques the theoretical foundation of Western civilization's hegemonic symbolic order (Gordon, *Existence in Black* 3). This representative order of Western hegemony is reflected in the empirical and sociopolitical foundations of Western philosophy and expressed in the canonical works of prominent white American and European Enlightenment thinkers. For instance, the ideal of egalitarianism theorized by John Locke (among others) verifies that racist suppositions became intrinsic to the West's ethical and political foundations. In Lockean terms, egalitarianism could only be practiced by and extended to "rational" beings. Since Enlightenment thinkers like Locke deemed Africans bereft of rationality—the distinguishing feature between men and beasts—they did not consider Africans human persons capable of realizing the rights of man.[4] Apprehended thus, racist thought is at the very core of the West's most lauded doctrines of liberty, equality, and fraternity; it is not a conceptual aberration that somehow arose to destabilize liberal society. And, as I review in chapter 1, eighteenth-century Enlightenment thinkers' formulation of freedom and natural rights did not occur in a theoretical vacuum. The reality of the European slave trade and the inhuman bondage of chattel slavery provided Western thinkers the physical evidence with which to transform the abstraction of freedom into its more concrete textual and oral articulations. As Angela Davis, Orlando Patterson, and Toni Morrison ask, what highlighted freedom and liberty more than the stark actuality of African captivity and enslavement? (Davis 132; Morrison 38).

The solidification of philosophical racism is apparent in the eighteenth- and nineteenth-century Enlightenment writings of David Hume, Immanuel Kant, Thomas Jefferson, and Georg Hegel. While many of their European and American contemporaries contributed to the growth of racist discourse, several critics have effectively argued that these four may be considered preeminent proponents of scientific racism because of their status as philosophers, their noteworthy derision of African humanity, and the far-ranging influence of their work.[5] Their works present a loaded existential proposition for people of African descent because these Western philosophers categorized Africans as subhumans, lacking the very self-conscious awareness of Being that nineteenth-century Africana thinkers were fiercely committed to exploring and articulating. The irony is thick, for Being and Freedom, paradoxically, become primary points of exploration in all of Frederick Douglass's nineteenth-century autobiographies.[6] Given Africana people's defining yet disputative relationship to Western discourse, we must situate eighteenth- and nineteenth-century Africana writers within their proper theoretical and dialogic context since their writings refute Western epistemologies that situated African people outside of both history and humanity.

BLACK VINDICATIONIST HISTORIOGRAPHY

Jefferson's castigation of Wheatley's poetic verse in his *Notes on the State of Virginia* (1785) marks the beginning of a sustained ideological movement, initiated to oppose the rhetoric of African subhumanity prevalent in European and American Enlightenment texts. The Black vindicationist tradition,[7] or "what came to be called 'vindicating the Negro'" (Drake 32) arose in response to racist discourse and became one of the most significant intellectual and polemical developments in the articulation of the abolitionist cause; the proliferation of Africana letters; and the birth of a collective Black nationalist, Pan-African diasporic consciousness during the eighteenth, nineteenth, and twentieth centuries. The vindicationists' rhetoric of African achievement, ingenuity, and race pride inspired enslaved and free Africans and sympathetic Europeans and European Americans to radically alter the commonly held Western view of the degraded African.

In the late eighteenth and nineteenth centuries, Black vindicationists staunchly defended the Negro's struggle for freedom, equality, and human dignity; hence they addressed a constellation of related ethical and political themes in their oral and written manifestos. They refuted denigrating Western stereotypes of Africans, stressed their people's membership within the human family, and extolled the virtues of African civilization and culture. To inveigh against chattel slavery's immorality, the vindicationists disproved theories of innate African moral, intellectual, and spiritual lowliness that undergirded the system's three-centuries-long existence. And although they differed in their philosophical and programmatic approaches, the renowned vindicationists Edward Blyden, Martin Delany, and Henry Highland Garnett exhorted colonization of Liberia or emigration to the Caribbean, Central America, South America, and Canada as racism's intractability in thought and praxis seemed insurmountable in nineteenth-century Western society.[8]

To meet their historiographical aims, Black vindicationists, including the abolitionists David Walker and Frederick Douglass, initiated studies of ancient Western and African history. They cited the classical works of Herodotus, Homer, and Diodorus, among others, to substantiate their argument that an ancient African people, the Egyptians, had provided the cultural foundations for classical and, later, modern Western civilization. The vindicationists' references to late eighteenth- and early nineteenth-century French sources, however, proved even more indispensable to the related discourses of abolition, colonization, and African historiographical restoration. The writings of the French explorers Dominique-Vivant Denon, Henri Gregoire, and Constantin-François Volney presented scientific proof to the world that Egypt was in fact an African civilization and that "the African in America was descended from Africans who had raised one of the grandest civilizations of ancient times" (Keita, *Race and Writing History*, 25, 26).

Blyden's *A Vindication of the Negro Race* (1857) disproved the Hamitic thesis of African racial inferiority through a deliberate analysis of the Hebrew Bible. Moreover Blyden's later works, *The People of Africa* (1871) and *Christianity, Islam, and the Negro Race* (1887), earned him scholarly accolades and distinctions, one of which was his election as a fellow to the American Philological Association in 1880. *The People of Africa* is one of the earliest Africana texts to use the written accounts of the ancient Greeks to highlight the classicists' own descriptions of the ancient Egyptians as an African race that laid the foundation for Greek culture, arts, and sciences.[9] Later vindicationists such as George Washington Williams, W. E. B. Du Bois, Carter G. Woodson, and other Africana intellectuals during the late nineteenth and early twentieth centuries continued the historiographical work that Walker, Douglass, and Blyden began. In their intervention into ancient historiography, these Africana thinkers attempted to offset the academy's predominant narratives of African ahistoricality as well as racist thought's hegemonic manifestations within nineteenth- and twentieth-century American society as a whole. Racist thought was manifest in the disciplines of history and social science, just as it was in articles and editorials (in both northern and southern periodicals) supporting the American school ethnologists' racist polygenetic claims (Stanton 144, 152, 155–56, 169). Thus the Black vindicationists' struggle was manifold. In their battle to win recognition from white American scholars within the field of historiography, they fought the entrenchment of racist discourse within academia, while also working to reach a wider audience among the general public. Theirs was a Sisyphean mission, for as much research as they had amassed and as many books as they had authored on the African's centrality to Western civilizational development their intellectual legacy has never been widely acknowledged. This conundrum is reflected in the reception and legacy of George Washington Williams's 1883 work, *A History of the Negro Race*.

Like Walker, Douglass, and Blyden before him, Washington presented his thesis that the ancient Egyptians were an African people and the pioneers of Western civilization. This assertion did not diminish his work's credibility among European American critics. On the contrary, A. L. Chapin's review in the March 1883 edition of the *Dial* claims that Williams's text presents "timely and valuable light for the study of this problem" and that it "will well stand a comparison with books of history from the pens of white men."[10] In spite of this approbation, Williams's work was not widely distributed; rather its dissemination was restricted due to the dictates of a segregated nation, read mainly in Negro primary scho0ols, colleges, and universities (Keita, *Race and Writing History* 49; Bruce 693). Williams's work, along with those of the early twentieth-century vindicationists Du Bois and Woodson, created a theoretical shift in African and Western historiography that would be furthered a century later by African-centered and Afrocentric scholars (Keita, *Race and Writing History* 52–57, 68–69). Nevertheless the vindicationists' legacy remains largely unknown with barely "any mention of over a century of [their] work" (West and Martin 311) since their scholarship was dismissed as racially chauvinistic.

The absence of Blyden's, Williams's, Du Bois's, and Woodson's historiographical contributions is extremely problematic, given that the European American historian Martin Bernal's *Black Athena* (1987) offered the same thesis that the vindicationists had presented over a century ago. In *Race and the Writing of History*, Maghan Keita cites the critic Molly Levine's praise of Bernal's text as groundbreaking, declaring it the first work "to fully integrate [a] survey of theories . . . into a sociology of knowledge": what knowledge reveals about society, how knowledge is structured and produced, and knowledge's uses in various social settings (42). These specific aspects of Western knowledge production and dissemination are precisely what the vindicationists elucidated in their nineteenth- and early twentieth-century discursive interventions. Their writings refuted false claims of inherent African servility and ahistoricality, thereby restoring balance to the false civilizational binary of European achievement and African degeneracy. With their scholarly productions, the vindicationists revealed the biased workings of Western knowledge production, but instead of garnering recognition for promoting objectivity within the discipline of history, they were seen as advancing a particularly racist and chauvinist agenda. Bernal himself makes this point: "Certainly, if a Black were to say what I am now putting in my books, their reception would be very different. They would be assumed to be one-sided and partisan, pushing a Black nationalist line and therefore dismissed" (qtd. in Keita, *Race and Writing History* 31). Such has been the Black vindicationists' troubling theoretical bequest. Recalling this travesty in Western academe, Keita underscores that "it is the height of dereliction to entertain such a . . . discourse, without the . . . critical examination of the intellectuals of African descent who spoke to this very issue and preceded Bernal by . . . a full century or more. The absence of recognition and analysis of their thought makes the exercise of deciphering the sociology of knowledge and its relation to race well nigh impossible, and certainly ahistorical" (44). Keita's assertions are indisputable, for a thorough examination of the "sociology of knowledge" in African historiography in the United States shows that the works of Douglass, Blyden, Washington, Du Bois, and Woodson were dismissed with impunity, never granted the serious scholarly attention that Bernal's *Black Athena* was one hundred years later (43).

The protracted erasure of nineteenth- and early twentieth-century vindicationist scholarship discloses the workings of the sociology of knowledge and the politics of knowledge propagation in American society on three crucial counts. First, the vindicationists' absence in mainstream studies of African historiography confirms that Western knowledge production is fixed on a Eurocentric axis in both content and authorship. Second, this legacy of exclusion reveals that historiographical knowledge is then used to maintain Western chauvinism in historical studies, in the realm of academic inquiry writ large and— given the hegemonic features of Western historical discourse—within American society as a whole. Third, the vindicationists' persistent elisions in American historiographical records ensure the perpetuity of a hegemonic, historiographical narrative that, in turn, perpetuates the related myths of African ahistoricality and an anathematized Africana intellectual tradition.

The pages that follow attest to the historical, philosophical, and epistemological import of Africana thinkers' resistance to their assigned ontological[11] marginality and perceived intellectual immateriality. It is this disavowal, this utter renunciation of which the vindicationists and the Africana thinkers discussed in this study were and still are keenly aware. The consciousness of their people's exclusions from the historiographical, sociopolitical, cultural, and intellectual history of the West is what has moved these thinkers to reinvigorate Western theory and simultaneously create new systems of knowledge. I proceed from the vindicationist tradition to argue that the entrenchment of racist and Eurocentric thought in Western discourse was initiated in three interrelated conceptual projects: the erasure of ancient Africa's role in the development of classical civilization; the transmogrification of the African into the bestial Negro slave; and the denial of chattel slavery's import to the growth of modern Western capitalism and empire. This is the tripartite crux of African negation in Western discourse. This is *being apart*.

THEORETICAL ENGAGEMENT

Being apart refers to the historical, ontological, and epistemological peripheralization of African people and Africana knowledge production in the West during the eighteenth, nineteenth, and twentieth centuries. Categorized as subhuman, ahistorical beings whose four centuries of slave labor were deemed negligible to modern capitalist development, Africans have been historically disregarded by Western discourse, due to the influence of three modern thought systems that have bound various forms of racist and Eurocentric thought to the Western canon: Enlightenment discourses of scientific racism, Hegelianism, and Marxism. Prevalent in Enlightenment racist thought are the first two aspects of anti-African Western discourse: the African's transmogrification into the subhuman slave and the related excision of ancient Africa from the narrative of Western historical development. These facets of African negation are refuted in the writings and speeches of Walker and Douglass, as chapter 1 shows.

Although Western radical theory does not possess the egregiously racist doctrines of Enlightenment and Hegelian thought, Marx's blind spot toward the global import of what I have termed the African diasporic proletariat[12] is tied to the third aspect of African negation in Western letters: the denial of chattel slavery's centrality to the birth of modern capitalism and empire. While Marx himself acknowledged chattel slavery's import to the growth of capitalism, he rather myopically relegated Western slavery's economic import to the category of primitive accumulation without fully recognizing chattel slavery's considerable role in the unprecedented capitalist accumulation of the (pre)industrial era (Bogues 78–79). In this regard Marx's focus on the European proletariat's role in the movement of history and class struggle is Eurocentric rather than blatantly anti-African. I address Marx's oversight in chapter 2 in my analysis of Du Bois's *Black Reconstruction* (1935) and C. L. R. James's *The Black Jacobins* (1938) for two principle reasons. First, as Sylvia Wynter has observed, Marx crystallized the economic conflict between the ruling and laboring classes, but "he had overlooked the ontological aspect of the opposition between them" ("On Disenchanting Discourse" 217). Second, as Hannah Arendt has noted, the impact of historical materialism on Western thought and culture in the modern era remains as enduring as that of scientific racism.[13]

In their theoretical opposition to scientific racism's entrenchment, Douglass and Du Bois challenged Eurocentric histories and made significant advances in the field of African historiography. Their works argue that African people's degraded status, as chattel, was a clear inversion of their ancient ancestors' lot as the progenitors of Western civilization. Douglass's and Du Bois's awareness of African people's paradoxical position in the West seemingly led to their meditations on Being and Freedom a full century and several decades before existentialism's rise to prominence on the European continent. Douglass pondered these determinant facets of human existence during his captivity in the South and continued to do so when he escaped bondage in the North. Neither Douglass nor Du Bois was a self-proclaimed existentialist. Rather, as the philosopher Lewis Gordon has averred, Douglass, Du Bois, and many other Africana and European thinkers (David Walker, Anna Julia Cooper, Toni Morrison, Angela Davis, Søren Kierkegaard, Martin Heidegger, and Fyodor Dostoyevsky) may be classified as philosophers of existence since their works theorize "an existential dimension among other dimensions and [they] may not have formally defined themselves as existentialists" (Gordon, *Existentia Africana*, 16; Gordon, *Existence in Black*, 2).

Douglass and Du Bois pondered questions of existence specifically because Western thinkers had declared African people ahistorical and subhuman, which served to rationalize their enslavement, colonization, and subjugation. The very Western hegemonic order that had normalized African peoples' removal from the tide of history and the human family had also effectively replaced their Egyptian forebears' African racial heritage with those of Europe and Asia.[14] In addition to this multifaceted epistemological assault, Douglass and Du Bois witnessed the myriad ways ideological racism also functioned during and after the chattel slavery era to demean their people socially, politically, and psychologically. It became a matter of course for them to meditate on Being and Freedom since their people had been besieged in thought and praxis for three centuries—the entire duration of modern Western thought's existence. Douglass's and Du Bois's writings clarify that

if one is nearly everywhere told that one is not fully a human being, but
one finds oneself struggling constantly with human responsibilities—
over life and death, freedom and lack thereof. . . . the moment of
theoretical reflection demands . . . engagements with ontological
questions of being—for example, essence, necessity, contingency, and
possibility—and teleological questions of where humanity should be
going—for example, liberation, humanization, and freedom. (Gordon,
Existentia Africana 28)

This awareness, this dreadful clarity of their people's condition in the
West, catalyzed Douglass's and Du Bois's unique insights into the ways
that humankind could actualize its greatest principles of individual
and collective liberation, human progress, and true freedom, justice,
and equality. These philosophical insights became the most persistent,
resonant themes in their writings.[15]

Contextualizing Douglass as a philosopher of existence presents significant canonical and academic implications, for his autobiographies—
detailing the physical brutality, social dispossession, and psychological
horrors of Western chattel slavery—are not required reading in most
world history and philosophy survey courses, yet Aristotle's *Politics*
remains a core text. In stark contrast to Aristotle, Douglass does not
hold the "natural slave" as indispensable to the establishment of political society. Douglass experienced life as another man's chattel; as a
result he dedicated his life to critiquing Lockean proponents of natural
rights for their adherence to liberal ideologies that simultaneously ven-
erated the humanity of Europeans and their descendants in the Americas while repudiating that of Africans and theirs. Douglass penned his
life story on three separate occasions so that he, a slave reborn as a philosopher,[16] could testify to the inhuman violence endemic to the chattel slave system and upon which it was built. In *Narrative of the Life of
Frederick Douglass (1845)*, his moving apostrophe to the sailboat is not
easily forgotten. Douglass poses two quintessentially existential questions as he ruminates on the veracity of God's existence and the nature
of his Being as a slave. Addressing the enviable sailboat, he laments,
"You are loosed from your moorings, and are free; I am fast in my
chains, and am a slave. You move merrily before the gentle gate, and
I before the bloody whip. . . . O God save me. . . . Let me be free. . . . Is
there any God? Why am I a slave?" (293–94).

A century before French existentialists declared God's inexistence
and during the same period that the German proto-existentialist
Nietzsche declared God dead, Douglass disputed God's existence in a

world where chattel slavery had already existed for over three hundred years. Consequently, in each of his three autobiographies, Douglass poignantly mines the human nullification of chattel slavery to recount his infamous battle with the slave-breaker Edward Covey. In *My Bondage and My Freedom* (1855) he equates his Freedom with his human existence. What is more, he states that denying his individual subjectivity and succumbing to the intersubjectivity of the master-slave relationship made him "nothing": "This battle with Covey . . . was the turning point in my *'life as a slave.'* It rekindled in my breast the smouldering embers of liberty . . . and revived a sense of my own manhood. I was a changed being after that fight. I was *nothing* before; I WAS A MAN NOW. . . . It recalled to my life my crushed self-respect and my self-confidence, and inspired me with a renewed determination to be A FREEMAN" (186). Douglass intentionally describes this fight as the "turning point" in his life as a slave, for after defying Covey he reclaimed his personhood and his inalienable right to exist as an autonomous individual. He was no longer another man's property but a free man and historical agent who actualized his right to a liberated existence. In his struggle with Covey, Douglass reclaims his very Being, for, as he states in his own words, "I was *nothing* before."

As Cynthia Willet and Lewis Gordon have effectively argued, Douglass analyzes the greater philosophical implications of his battle with Covey, ultimately developing an existentialist theory of self that fully illustrates the contest's ontological implications (Willet 166–68; Gordon, *Existentia Africana* 16). His struggle is an existential triumph. In his victory over Covey he reasserts his subjectivity, thereby reclaiming his existence as a human being, no longer living what Orlando Patterson has termed the "social death" of a slave. Despite the existential implications of Douglass's victory and the inherently interdisciplinary nature of his works, the persistence of Eurocentric thought and praxis in Western academe prevents students and teachers alike from appreciating the multivalent import of his writings. Douglass's autobiographies, speeches, letters, and articles reveal the breadth and depth of his philosophical reflection, committed scholarship, and progressive mission. Certainly his entire oeuvre foregrounds the great import of his intellectual work to the development of Western thought and letters in American society.

Like Douglass before him, the twentieth-century historian, sociologist, and philosopher of existence W. E. B. Du Bois presents his seminal theory of double consciousness in *The Souls of Black Folk*

(1903), decades before the advent of existential thought in Europe. Yet Du Boisian double consciousness is rarely interpreted as a proto-existentialist theory of bifurcated subjectivity, even though Du Bois's formulation of double consciousness was published more than two decades before the term *Existenzphilosophie* was coined (Heinemann 1). Du Bois's classic work explicates an impenetrable system of racial oppression under which Negro Americans were forced to live during and after Reconstruction. He utilizes interdisciplinary methods to initiate a careful analysis of the Negro American consciousness through the historical context of Reconstruction-era disenfranchisement. Ostensibly beginning with a sociopolitical analysis of Negro American dispossession, he enriches his study with the question of individual subjectivity through the metaphor of the Veil and the related concept of double consciousness: "The Negro is . . . born with a Veil . . . in this American world—, a world which yields him no true self-consciousness, but only lets him see himself through the revelation of the other world. It is a peculiar sensation, this double-consciousness, this sense of always looking at one's self through the eyes others, of measuring oneself by the tape of a world that looks on in amused contempt and pity" (215).

For the Negro American of Du Bois's era, "the world that looks on in amused contempt and pity" is one where political disenfranchisement, socioeconomic exploitation, and Ku Klux Klan vigilante terror constitute the material conditions and lived reality that, in turn, spawn a bifurcated consciousness: one half Negro, the other half American. This was a conditional citizenship that afforded no true citizenship rights, for during this period in American history, the designation *Negro American* was an oxymoron. If one were a Negro one could not truly be an American who enjoyed every right of citizenship that defined the American ethos. Du Boisian double consciousness, or "looking at one-self through the eyes of others," represents a true crisis of consciousness for Negro Americans: a uniform, autonomous sense of Being could not exist in a society steeped in the codified tenets of scientific racism. Thus double consciousness represents a twin sense of Being, one part defined by institutional racism and racist stereotypes of Negro identity, and the other defined by the self. One part American, one part Negro, no parts reconciled. Two decades after the publication of *The Souls of Black Folk*, Du Bois's theory of bifurcated ontology is seemingly echoed, albeit in a much lengthier phenomenological tome, in Heidegger's *Being and Time* (1927). Heidegger's concepts of being-in-the world and being-for-others offer striking similarities to the societal alienation and self-alienation of Du Boisian double consciousness.

Douglass, Du Bois, and many other Africana thinkers have written works of great philosophical import, yet the enduring legacy of racist thought has led these thinkers' intellectual productions to be marginalized or negated. Through Douglass's and Du Bois's circumscribed canonical and disciplinary influence within the academy, we may grasp that Western discourses of racism are founded on "general concepts [that] stretch across any number of discursive orders acquiring new interpretations. . . . The more general the expression . . . the more malleable and pliant it tends to become" (Goldberg 3). One need only recall the nearly imperceptible movement from Kant's declaration in *Observations on the Feeling of the Beautiful and the Sublime* (1764) that "this fellow was quite black from head to foot, a clear proof that what he said was stupid" (61), to the twentieth-century best-selling text of scientific racism, *The Bell Curve* (1994). Richard Hernnstein and Charles Murray recycle Enlightenment racist thought, thereby reiterating the fallacy of feeble-minded, culturally deprived people of African descent (Jorgensen 236–37). Yet *The Bell Curve* was seemingly published because of the general ignorance surrounding the three-centuries-long Africana intellectual tradition of literary and philosophical discourse, which conveniently serves as the primary substantiation for Hernnstein's and Murray's argument. From the eighteenth-century works of Kant to the twentieth-century work of Hernnstein and Murray, it becomes clear that racist thought has not only disparaged Africans throughout the diaspora, but it has also led to the protracted and systematic devaluation of their scholarly productions. This fact is reflected in Toni Morrison's observation, "Because we . . . are seen as a discredited people, it is no surprise, then, that our creations are also discredited" (qtd. in Christian 283).

It follows that this study identifies Eurocentric thought as one of the West's most defining hegemonic discourses. In this regard I employ Antonio Gramsci's and Louis Althusser's definition of hegemony to describe the predominant Western thought system that is grafted upon every aspect of society and culture through institutional, cultural, and political dissemination and the conscious and unconscious complicity of the general populace. I then use the Althusserian construct of the ideological state apparatus in chapter 3 in my discussion of Frantz Fanon's *Black Skin, White Masks* (1952), and chapter 4 in my discussion of Kamau Brathwaite's nation language theory, to denote the social institutions that maintain hegemony: the educational system, the church, the government, and popular culture in general. Western hegemonic discourse, then, refers to specific tomes of the Western canon and to the ideations of racism delineated therein.

In my consideration and exploration of Freedom, I have been influenced and greatly inspired by those Africana scholar-activists whose commitment to the actualization of Freedom has determined the scope of their work. Toni Morrison, Kamau Brathwaite, Angela Davis, Paul Gilroy, Lewis Gordon, and Cedric Robinson use interdisciplinary methods to explore historical, literary, and philosophical expressions of Freedom that encapsulate the Africana experience. Indeed explorations of Freedom among nineteenth- and twentieth-century Africana thinkers reflect the immediacy of liberation struggles among a people whose enslavement defined and challenged Freedom's very conceptualization (Davis 130). As the literature of a formerly enslaved populace, Africana literature reveals the theoretical shortcomings inherent in Western conceptualizations of Freedom. Freedom should not be considered a static ideal or abstraction; rather it should and must be perceived as a dynamic process of individual and collective actualization. The enslaved African forebears left us this very lesson.

Chattel slavery's nearly four-hundred-year existence led legions of enslaved Africans to grasp the immediacy of their Freedom, and this apprehension was constant irrespective of their physical bondage. If they had not grasped the irrefutability of their Freedom, they would not have rebelled on slave ships and on the plantations, or even risked their lives as fugitives in the numbers that they did. Cedric Robinson notes the existential dimensions of the Africana liberationist impulse in his incisive analysis of slave rebellions. He urges readers to consider the comparatively small number of white casualties as evidence that the slave rebellion "was not inspired by an external object. . . . It was the renunciation of actual being for historical being; the preservation of the ontological totality granted by a metaphysical system that never allowed for property in either the physical, philosophical, temporal, legal, social or psychic *senses*" (168). Chattel slavery was systemically structured on reducing thinking, feeling human beings into objects, into other men's property. Insurrection became a way for enslaved Africans to reclaim their humanity within a philosophical and socioeconomic system that consistently denied it; therefore the number of slain white victims was not an indicator of their victory. Triumph lay in their determination to defy subjugation, reassert their agency, and manifest their Freedom. Enslaved African forebears like Queen Nanny, Cinque, Mackandal, Boukman, Toussaint L'Ouverture, Denmark Vesey, Gabriel Prosser, Gullah Jack, Nat Turner, Frederick Douglass, Sojourner Truth, and Harriet Tubman rebelled to achieve physical liberation and assert their agency, just as thinkers like Walker and Du Bois fought to assert their epistemological agency by stressing their people's centrality to the movement of Western history, culture, and thought.

Given that Africana literature in the West has proliferated under philosophical, political, and socioeconomic conditions that normalized African people's enslavement and dismissed their literary productions, it is necessary to analyze Africana works "in ways that foreground their politicized history" (Lubiano 647). Such an informed critique necessitates a thorough analysis of not only history and philosophy, as we have seen, but also Marxist and existential theories. This is essential, for *Being Apart* offers a theory and philosophy of Africana literature in which the precepts of Marxism and existentialism are vivified, simultaneously presenting themselves in the lived reality of enslaved Africans.

PHILOSOPHICAL CONVERGENCE

In *Marxism and Form* (1971), Fredric Jameson contends that the commonly held assessment of Sartre's *Critique of Dialectical Reason* (1960), as a textual reconciliation of Marxism and existentialism, is inaccurate. Jameson avers that Sartre's work does not attempt to reconcile these two thought systems specifically because "there can be no contradiction" since they present "two wholly different types of reality" (208). According to Jameson, Sartre's *Critique* was not written to overturn the aphorism that "Marxism is a way of understanding the objective dimension of history from the outside; existentialism is a way of understanding the subjective individual experience" (208). Instead Jameson maintains that Sartre's "search for a method . . . does not take the form of a reconciliation of contraries, but rather a kind of unified field of theory in which two wholly different ontological phenomena can share a common set of equations and be expressed in a single linguistic or terminological system" (208). According to Jameson, Sartre's aim in *Critique* is to present a method of theoretical unity in which two different ontological phenomena—one of historical objectivity and the other of individual subjectivity—may share similar concerns and be articulated within the same lexical schema. Though Jameson provides Sartre's own lived experience in the French proletariat society of the 1920s as an example of this synthesis (207), an earlier, more striking example may be found in the lived experience of Douglass and others under the chattel slave system.

The material conditions of enslavement and subjugation led Douglass to ponder the meaning of his existence within a socioeconomic and ideological system designed to annihilate his self-identification as a human being. His lived reality as human chattel intensified his will to assert his Freedom and agency by rebelling against Covey and escaping to the North. This convergence between Douglass's material reality as chattel and his subjective reality as a liberated agent exemplifies Jameson's contention that two different ontological phenomena—one of historical objectivity and the other of individual subjectivity—may be experienced and articulated at once. Douglass's experience supports Jameson's contention that "a lived synthesis of the two systems exists," for enslaved Africans had actualized and vivified the fusion of these conceptualizations in their quest for liberation in the sixteenth-, seventeenth-, eighteenth-, and nineteenth-century slave rebellions during the Middle Passage, in escapes from the cotton and tobacco plantations of the South, and from the sugar cane plantations of the West Indies and Central and South America. So in order to examine Africana literature's relation to critical theory in a comprehensive manner, it is necessary to demonstrate how the collective struggle of Marxian materialism and the individual subjectivity of existential Freedom converged on the field of lived experience in enslaved Africans' defiance during chattel slavery. I explore this philosophical convergence further in chapter 2 in my discussion of Du Bois's *Black Reconstruction* and C. L. R. James's *The Black Jacobins*, two highly interdisciplinary revisions of traditional Marxian thought.

ON INTERDISCIPLINARITY

The preceding pages have confirmed Africana literary discourse's intrinsic interdisciplinarity; it is both a field of study and a process of intellectual inquiry that necessitates engagement with works of history, philosophy, and literature. While some critics may prefer to maintain disciplinary territoriality by relegating literary theorists to the field of textual analysis and leaving the philosophy of literature solely to philosophers (Lyon 682–84; L. Mackey 677), this work of literary theory probes Western philosophical discourse in order to situate Africana literature within "the context of philosophical thought system[s]" (L. Mackey 677) and to "analyze the logical foundations of the 'practice' of [Africana] literature" (Lamarque 8), in order to meet two related objectives: to highlight the ineluctable convergence of historical, philosophical, and cultural themes in nineteenth- and twentieth-century Africana literary productions and to demonstrate Africana thinkers' counterhegemonic challenge to Western philosophical negation or erasure.

Engaging with Africana literary discourse and Western philosophy in this manner exemplifies Arabella Lyon's river metaphor of interdisciplinarity between literary theory and philosophy. Lyon's symbolic image of the river—in contrast to that of disciplinary territoriality outlined by Clifford Geertz, Susan Stewart, and others (Lyon 681–83)—reveals the manner in which "philosophy and literary studies [share] networks of aims, actions and structures of association" (682).The mutuality of thematic intent and action between philosophy and literature is plainly evinced in the eighteenth- and nineteenth-century slave narrative's focus on ameliorating the African image in the collective Western consciousness, just as it is in the vindicationists' historiographical attestations of ancient Egypt's African cultural roots. This convergence of issues and thematic content confirms that literature embodies the "history of ideas and philosophy" since "literary history parallels and reflects intellectual history" (Wellek and Warren 111). Equally reflective of this discursive confluence is the eighteenth-century English Enlightenment novel, which became a literary medium for controversial topics and simultaneously presented factual information within its fictitious framework. As Edward Said has also shown, later nineteenth-century British and French novels served as discursive Trojan horses to promote the interrelated ideological agendas of empire and slavery (Outram 16; Said 62–67).

Western critics of all affiliations have commonly noted the intertextuality between literary discourse and philosophy in the eighteenth- and nineteenth-century writings of Africana, European, and European American authors.[17] However, some critics still labor under the misapprehension that Western philosophical thought is somehow inapplicable to the Africana experience.[18] This is the inevitable result of existentialism's and philosophy's axiomatic pairing with Western thought and culture (Gordon, *Introduction to Africana Philosophy* 1–3).

TWENTIETH-CENTURY EXISTENTIAL THOUGHT

Existentialism's focus on the facticity[19] of human agency and freedom rendered it germane to Western culture as alienation seemingly peaked in the societal disillusionment after World War II (Heinemann 3, 12–13). The events of the Jewish Holocaust presented a dreadful reality; consequently the French existentialist precept that humankind dwelled in a godless universe offered the only rational explanation for the Shoah. Only cruelty born of human agency could explain the genocide. Nevertheless in the annals of history, state-sponsored ethnic cleansing was not unique to the society and culture of twentieth-century Germany. The Jewish Holocaust's antecedents lay in the genocide of native peoples throughout North America, the Caribbean, and South America during Europe's fifteenth- and sixteenth-century quest for New World empires; as European empire expanded in Asia and Africa the number of its victims increased as well. Aimé Césaire reminds us that the Jewish Holocaust was the direct result of this brutal legacy: "People . . . say: 'How strange! But never mind—it's Nazism . . . and they hide the truth from themselves, that it is barbarism . . . but that before they were its victims they were its accomplices; that they tolerated that Nazism before it was inflicted on them, that they absolved it, shut their eyes to it, legitimized it, because, until then it had been applied only to . . . the Arabs of Algeria, the coolies of India, and the blacks of Africa" (14–15). The widespread shock of the Jewish Holocaust was the fact that the unchecked racist practices of Western domination had imploded and led to the extermination of European racial, religious, sexual, and political minorities as well.

To be sure, disillusionment characterized European society after World War II; nonetheless empire's collapse in Africa and Asia presented another seminal global shift. The events of Third World decolonization led the French and French colonial Marxist intellectuals Sartre, Césaire, and Fanon to respond politically and philosophically to the French-Algerian War of the mid-1950s and early 1960s. These Marxist thinkers forcefully mined existentialism's political implications for the contemporary decolonization movement, and at the center of their anti-imperialist inquiries was the state of the colonial subject's consciousness. Césaire, Fanon, and Sartre used existential philosophy to delimit colonial subjects' subjectivity, recontextualizing their psychological transitions from colonial dependency complex to liberated consciousness (Le Sueur 227–54). Fanon, the subject of chapter 3, surpassed his predecessors in his application of existentialism, dialectics, and psychoanalysis to diagnose the colonial subject's initial self-alienation and eventual self-emancipation. Despite Césaire's, Fanon's, and Sartre's more radical application of existentialism to the liberationist ideologies of Third World decolonization, existential thought is still primarily associated with European culture. This seemingly inevitable blind spot toward the philosophical dimensions of Africana writers' works reveals the contradictory position of Africana thinkers within Western society.

THE PARADOX OF THE AFRICANA SCHOLAR

Being apart must also be understood as a causative, paradoxical condition, for how can Africana scholars incontrovertibly prove their contributions to Western thought when canonical discourse, without fail, erases or debases their intellectual productions? As I have shown, the fact that three centuries of Africana, European, *and* European American scholarship on Africana contributions to Western development have still not thwarted widely held theories of innate African ahistoricality and inferiority speaks to the intractable nature of Western racism. This troubling reality shows that Africana thinkers (and African-centered discourse) occupy a conditional position in the West, for they remain tied to the very Western culture that disparages their people's achievements and negates their epistemological relevance. This irony is made painfully clear in the earlier discussion of the nineteenth- and early twentieth-century Black vindicationists. It also presents itself in the case of James's *Notes on Dialectics (1948)*.

In *Notes on Dialectics*, the Trinidadian socialist and philosopher devotes an entire study to explicating Hegelian dialectics' fundamental import to cultivating a teleological understanding of the modern labor movement. James lauds Hegel's philosophical innovation in *Science of Logic*, asserting that the genius of Hegel's dialectical theory is the fact that it is "a new way of *organizing* thought. Not of thinking. But of knowing what you do when you *think*" (13). For James, Hegel's definition of an extant intellectual tendency as a specific philosophical method is groundbreaking, for it marks a shift in Western theory. It is this theoretical shift that compels him to praise Hegel as "very wise" and as a "maestro"; he also describes Hegel's dialectical process as "marvelous" and "lovely movement" (13, 19, 21, 41). Only when critiquing Hegel's World-Spirit—the organizing principle upon which dialectics rests—does James pause in an otherwise deferential critique. He characterizes the World-Spirit as funny (56), an amusing addendum to an otherwise ingenious philosophical system.

While *Science of Logic* was originally published in 1817, Hegel furthered his World-Spirit concept in his 1837 work, *Lectures on the Philosophy of World History*. In this latter text he decries the African continent

as an ahistorical void and its people as subhuman beings lacking the
very higher-order consciousness that separates humans from animals.
It is quite clear that James was a close reader of *Science of Logic* and,
given the breadth of James's philosophical expertise, it is highly improb-
able that he was ignorant of Hegel's *Lectures*. Therein lies the paradox:
by virtue of James's identification as a radical theorist he was compelled
to address Hegel as the originator of the modern dialectical process, yet
he avoids discussing Hegel as a preeminent nineteenth-century thinker
who also rather seamlessly wedded anti-African historical discourse to
the Western canon. Hegel staunchly declared African people, including James, bereft of the very humanity and intellectual capacity to
think, let alone critique his body of work. In short, it would have been
anathema for Hegel to imagine the Afro-Trinidadian James produc-
ing his groundbreaking *Notes on Dialectics*—a text that has also been
described as one of the most difficult and important works ever presented to an American Marxist audience (Buhle 92).

It is important to note that James's evolution as a thinker occurred
during a seminal, transformative epoch in world history. Like many
scholars of the postwar period, James confronted the immediate reality
of the collapse of Nazism and totalitarianism in Europe and the fall of
European empire in the Third World. These distinct yet related geopolitical events became the basis for profound philosophical analyses of
racism and hegemonic power as thought systems and social practices
(Gilroy, *Postcolonial Melancholia* 39). James's particular investigations
included applying Hegel's dialectical system to the duality of oppression and resistance inherent in labor and Third World decolonization
struggles, irrespective of Hegel's racism.

Thus the paradox of Africana scholars is as ineluctable as their African ancestry and as inextricable as their connection to Western culture and society. For over three centuries they have labored to earn
their rightful place at the meeting ground of Western history, philosophy, and canonical discourse. They have toiled ceaselessly and produced influential works of historiography, philosophy, and literature,
yet only those specializing in ethnic studies will have the opportunity
to appreciate the breadth of this intellectual bounty. This injustice may
be corrected, of course, as scholars of conscience continually expose the
historical fallacies that have been accepted as truths. Their sustained
agitation will then cause the seemingly omnipotent discourses of hegemonic power and canonized racism to become specters within them-

selves. The road is long and seemingly without end, yet this is where I begin, just as so many before me have also begun.

Throughout this work I use the terms *African, Africana, African diasporic,* and *people of African descent* adjectivally in some cases and interchangeably in most cases. *African American* refers to those of African descent living within the United States; *Africana* and *African diasporic* describe people of African descent throughout the diaspora, and these terms also describe their literary productions. I use the terms *Black* and *Negro* (in either lower or upper case) to maintain the authors' original usage as well as their contemporary terminology. I also use the term *Third World*, to denote what is now referred to as the Global South for the same reason. *European* and *European American* describe those Western thinkers whose works do not necessarily promote white or European racial superiority, while the terms *white European* and *white American* denote those Western thinkers whose works do (Allen 9–14, 17–21).

I use the terms *African American oral tradition, orature,* and *vernacular* interchangeably. Similarly I use the terms *America* and *American* in the hemispheric sense of "the Americas" to connote the United States and the Caribbean. These terms appear frequently in my discussion of Kamau Brathwaite's nation language theory in chapter 4.

To narrow the study's focus, I selected primary texts by African American and Caribbean thinkers. Several secondary texts by writers from the African continent are prominent in chapters three and four; however in the future I anticipate expanding the study to include a similarly detailed analysis of primary works by these, and other, African thinkers.

This study is not definitive. Nevertheless I have attempted to provide a careful analysis of Western history, literature, and philosophy that foregrounds the manner in which Africana thinkers have asserted their historical, philosophical, and epistemological agency to resolutely contest the Eurocentric, hegemonic nature of Western discourse.

CHAPTER ONE

Being Apart

*The Enlightenment, Scientific Racism,
and Chattel Slavery*

> Africa . . . was the Old World of prehistory: supposedly lacking
> language and culture, the Negro was increasingly taken to occupy
> a rung apart on the ladder of being, a rung that as the eighteenth
> century progressed was thought to predate humankind.
>
> —David Theo Goldberg, *Racist Culture*

The Age of Reason[1] is generally hailed as the West's triumph over the provincialism of religious fervor in the eighteenth century through mastery over science, economics, and civil government. As the epochal representation of modernity's maturity, it is also considered an unparalleled sociocultural and political moment that established connections among ideology, science, industry, and society toward the common goal of "'the mastery over nature'" (Kennington 392). The Western subject's dominion over nature is reflected in the highly influential scientific and anthropological classifications of *Homo sapiens* initiated by Linnaeus in *Systema Naturae* (1737). Yet while the eighteenth century witnessed the domination of science and empiricism over religious and spiritual dogma, it is important to note that eighteenth-century European thinkers like Linnaeus replaced a specifically religious hierarchy with a divinely inspired natural hierarchy in the schema of the Great Chain of Being (conceptualized two centuries earlier), which ordered all living and spiritual beings along a continuum, from God and the angels to the lowest of animal creatures.[2] It follows, then, that during an era when Western thinkers were preoccupied with establishing and maintaining dominance over the natural world these same theorists would gravitate toward a geopolitical corollary to this form of mastery, one that extended beyond local European borders and simultaneously provided a collective sense of identity and purpose for the Western subject. Enter the modern configurations of race and nation, both of which arise concomitantly in the eighteenth century to provide Westerners with the sense of inhabiting a shared linguistic and cultural collectivity distinct from the non-European racial others who were becoming enslaved and colonized (Hudson 256; Goldberg 4). Given the advent of these ideological, cultural, and sociopolitical developments, it seems curious that the Enlightenment is rarely viewed as an era synonymous with subjugation. Yet if one were to examine the thematic connections between the Enlightenment's narratives of universal egalitarianism and the rising episteme of scientific racism that emerged simultaneously, a more accurate accounting of eighteenth-century developments emerges:

> Subjugation perhaps properly defines the order of the Enlightenment: subjugation of nature by human intellect, colonial control through physical and cultural domination and economic superiority through mastery of the laws of the market. The confidence with which the culture of the West approached the world to appropriate it is reflected in the constructs of science, industry, and empire. . . . The scientific catalog of racial otherness, the variety of racial alien, was a principal product of this period. The emergence of independent scientific domains of anthropology and biology in the Enlightenment defined a classificatory order of racial groupings. . . . In cataloging racial aliens, however, Enlightenment science simultaneously extended racial self-definition to the West: Western Europeans were similarly classified on the hierarchical scale moving upward from dark-skinned and passionate Southern Europeans to fair-skinned and rational Northerners. The catalog of national characters emerged in lock step with the classification of races. (Goldberg 29–30)

The nations of the West believed that their growth, development, and expansion were due to an implicitly multivalent Enlightenment imperative: the domination of Western man and science over the physical environment, the subordination of other races to Europeans and European Americans, and the expansion of Western economic wealth and influence both domestically and abroad. At the same time, however, it must be noted that Europeans also created intraracial distinctions among various ethnic groups on the European continent. This practice of transforming regional cultural differentiations into racial ones began during the Middle Ages, when various immigrant populations dominated Europe's mercantile classes and various labor forces became identified with specific immigrant or ethnic populations, as European society transitioned from feudalism to capitalism. As capitalistic endeavors grew, so too did the tendency to racialize various ethnic, linguistic, and cultural groups (Robinson 26).

THE GENEALOGY OF SCIENTIFIC RACISM

To fully understand how Enlightenment discourses of scientific racism established their seemingly intractable positions in the Western canon, it is necessary to emphasize that their ideological antecedents were established four centuries earlier, in the late fifteenth century, on the Iberian peninsula. Western thought and praxis already had a long and evolving tradition of racialism, or categorizing racial characteristics and "others," which was then used to rationalize a social system built on using these classifications to construct the notion of European (white) racial superiority and dominance and its vital corollary, non-European inferiority and subjugation. Xenophobic proscriptions against non-Christians in fifteenth-century Spain and Portugal led to exclusionary practices that, while initially founded on religious grounds, may also be characterized as racist in their stigmatization of Jews as racially and biologically impure others. The Spanish and Portuguese aversion toward religious and racial others is also the result of Iberia's own subjugation and colonization at the hands of African Moors who ruled the region for almost seven hundred years (from the eighth century until the Reconquest of the late fifteenth century). More specifically, the Spanish and Portuguese reclaimed native sovereignty in the late fifteenth century through alternating trends of ethnic cleansing, expulsion, and military campaigns. Wresting political and sociocultural control from African Muslims gave these Europeans a newfound sense of national identity, thereby emboldening them in their own imperial and colonial undertakings outside of Europe—in Africa, the Americas, and Asia. These imperial territories became the testing ground for Europeans' transplanted theories of racial categorization that began with Jews and Muslims. In the late fifteenth century, the new others became enslaved and colonized Africans and the nearly exterminated Native Americans.[3]

Fifteenth- and sixteenth-century Europeans' search for the biological and environmental causes for such notable differences in physical characteristics and cultural mores among Native American and African peoples led to the development of two contrasting yet equally problematic evolutionary theories: monogenesis and polygenesis. The former theory held that mankind had evolved from one common human ancestor, the biblical Adam; however, according to this line of thinking the non-European races had degenerated to their current "inferior" state due to climatic differences and their living outside of Europe's temporal zone. Polygenesis, the more egregiously racist theory, emphasized that separate and distinct evolutions had occurred for the different human races, and specifically that Africans and Native Americans had evolved from pre-Adamite man, a subhuman strain of *Homo sapiens* that developed before the biblical Adam and his descendants in Europe (Bernasconi, "Who Invented the Concept of Race?" 18–21; Popkin 81–82).

In addition to these scripturally based, quasi-scientific evolutionary theories, Western conceptualizations of racial others were also heavily influenced by popular travelogues written by explorers, traders, and slavers. These texts influenced eighteenth-century thinkers like Linnaeus and Kant and legitimized European stereotypes of Africans and racial others based on their physical characteristics. These racial dissimilarities were then transformed into coherent hierarchical systems based on "objective" (racial) science.[4] While some of these travel writings recounted great racial variation among the different nations, these were largely ignored; those that reinforced stereotypes of barbaric racial others were embraced for their instantiation of Europe as the peak of human civilization and national diversity (Hudson 250–52). So what we see developing in the West from the fifteenth through the nineteenth centuries is three hundred years of textual accounts legitimizing the concept of European racial superiority, largely founded on religious and racial resentment and discrimination toward Jews and Muslims in the fifteenth and sixteenth centuries; biased travel writings principally used to alternately titillate[5] and intimidate Europeans, thereby inspiring ignorance and fear toward Africans, Asians, and Native Americans in the sixteenth and seventeenth centuries; and quasi-scientific theories of evolution buttressed by the growing fields of anthropology and biological classification during the seventeenth and eighteenth centuries. This explosive and divisive mix of xenophobic religious antipathy, prejudiced travel reportage, and racial categorizations—now legitimized by science, philosophy, and the belletristic tradition during the eighteenth and nineteenth centuries—created fertile ground for the propagation of

European racial chauvinism within the Western canon and the collective Western consciousness.

Duly convinced of European racial superiority, Western thinkers embraced subjective opinion masquerading as science for irrefutable fact, especially claims addressing matters of human achievement determined by racial groupings. These historical, cultural, and ideological developments in the eighteenth century primed Western thought for the development of a specifically racist discourse that could easily accommodate the most salient and compelling features of such varied sources on racial difference and differentiation, which would justify the European slave trade and Western chattel slavery. Thus it seems inevitable that the eighteenth century would give birth to scientific racism, given the four-centuries-long development of racialist and racist discourse that had already laid the foundation for more extreme views of European racial superiority and, in particular, African inferiority. Four centuries of theorizing on the African's assumed inability to attain civilization and culture had reached its peak in the eighteenth-century scientific concept of race.

It is no wonder, then, that by the time of the Napoleonic expeditions in Egypt, in the late eighteenth and early nineteenth centuries, French scientists would initially identify the ancient Egyptians as an African (Negro) people and then, within a generation, revise their findings to conclude that the founders of Western civilization who constructed the grand pyramids and monuments could not have been the racial ancestors of the enslaved, degraded Africans in the West (Du Bois, *World and Africa* 118; Keita, "Africans and Asians" 4). Constantin-François Volney, who initially described the Egyptians as a Negro people, then later capitulated to the dominant anti-African discursive trends of his day, best evinces this historic reversal. In his 1783 reportage Volney laments the paradoxical plight of enslaved Africans in the West: "How we are astonished . . . when we reflect that to the race of negroes, at present our slaves, and the objects of our contempt, we owe our arts, sciences, and . . . when we recollect that, in the midst of these nations, who call themselves the friends of liberty and humanity, the most barbarous of slaveries is justified; and that it is even a problem whether the understandings of negroes be of the same species with that of white men!" (*Travels* 82–83). Numerous critics and historians have remarked on the gravity of Volney's ruminations on the plight of enslaved Africans at the hands of Republican Westerners.[6] Nevertheless it is Hume's footnote in "Of National Characters" (1741) that ignited a theoretical flame in racist thought, razing the significance of Volney's observations on the reversal of fortune experienced by African people under the chattel slave system. The transmogrification of the African, a pivotal contributor to Western development, into the brutish Negro slave became a legitimized, defining, and enduring feature of Enlightenment discourses on race. By the late eighteenth and nineteenth centuries, the African was effectively set apart from Western humanity, viewed as a subhuman, perceived as a being apart.

Thus the subjugation-based order of the Enlightenment, and its dehumanization and dehistoricization of the African, may also be read as a Western hegemonic imperative, for the influence of a dominant racist ideology in which the West was positioned as *the* center and ideal model of civilization came to define Western science, anthropology, geopolitics, and economics. These symbiotic ideations of Western hegemony, racial subjugation, and African dehumanization may be found in the writings of Hume, Kant, Jefferson, and Hegel.[7] Hume's influential footnote in "Of National Characters"; Kant's writings in *Observations on the Feeling of the Beautiful and the Sublime* (1764) and *Physical Geography* (1800); Jefferson's *Notes on the State of Virginia* (1785) and Hegel's *Lectures on the Philosophy of World History* (1857) are canonical Enlightenment texts that advanced racist thought in the eighteenth and nineteenth centuries. It may also be argued that their racist views furthered the related projects of modern Western nationalism and Western-centered historiographies because of their propagation and consumption through print culture.[8] This convergence of ideology, sociopolitical reality, and European and Western national chauvinism is best reflected in the infamous footnote to "Of National Characters," which spawned several textual responses and theoretical addendums, including Edward Long's *A History of Jamaica* (1774).[9]

HUME'S FOOTNOTE AND JEFFERSON'S THEORETICAL RESPONSE

There is some disagreement among critics as to whether or not Hume's footnote is reflective of his philosophical position on the institution of chattel slavery;[10] however, most are in agreement that the footnote (and its well-documented revision) indicates Hume's firm commitment to the furtherance of anti-African racist thought. Many critics are confident that the footnote provided empirical justification for theories of inherent European racial superiority.[11] Richard Popkin best states the case for the footnote's position of infamy in critical race analyses of Western philosophical thought:

> The position Hume set forth seems to have been based on an implicit polygeneticism. . . . From this, he derived his racial law, which was to have great impact on Kant and on some of the American racists of the time. The anti-racists . . . and the American abolitionists had to struggle against the authority and influence of Hume's claim. . . .
>
> Hume's reputation and status as an empirical social scientist made his prejudicial observation a crucial part of the intellectual battleground on racism in the latter part of the eighteenth century, and gave the supporters of extreme bigotry a serious leader of the Enlightenment to appeal as their theoretical ancestor. (254, 266)

Hume's prominence as an empiricist who professed the existence of distinct species of men (possessing separate evolutionary histories) transformed his subjective opinions on racial inequality into immutable fact. Eighteenth- and nineteenth-century debates on slavery seemingly turned on the polygenetic, Eurocentric views he expressed. With Hume as an ideological forebear on whose work several thinkers would expand and extrapolate, eighteenth-century philosophical racism established itself as a growing field of discourse shaped by a noticeable intertextuality (Eze, *Race and Enlightenment* 6–7; Popkin 254). Here is Hume's footnote in its entirety:

> I am apt to suspect the negroes, and in general all the other species of men (for there are four or five different kinds) to be naturally inferior to the whites. There never was a civilized nation of any other complexion than white, nor even any individual eminent either in action or speculation. No ingenious manufactures amongst them, no arts, no sciences. On the other hand, the most rude and barbarous of the whites, such as the ancient GERMANS, the present TARTARS, have still something eminent about them, in their valour, form of government, or some other particular. Such a uniform and constant difference could not happen in so many countries and ages, if nature had not made an original distinction betwixt these breeds of men. Not to mention our colonies, there are Negroe slaves dispersed all over EUROPE, of which none ever discovered any symptoms of ingenuity, tho' low people, without education, will start up amongst us, and distinguish themselves in every profession. In JAMAICA indeed they talk of one negroe as a man of parts and learning; but 'tis likely he is admired for very slender accomplishments, like a parrot, who speaks a few words plainly.[12]

Ironically Hume's position on white European racial supremacy rests on his reputation as an empiricist—a philosopher putatively trained in documenting and conceptualizing truths based on irrefutable factual evidence. The Jamaican about whom he writes so disparagingly is Francis Williams, one of the first persons of African descent to graduate from Cambridge University in 1758 (Immerwahr 485). Hume was well aware of Williams's intellectual achievements at the time he wrote the footnote; nonetheless he was prone to such generalizations even when faced with contradictory evidence and explained this intransigence in his own philosophical writings (Popkin 259). If Hume had been a skilled empiricist rather than "a lousy empirical scientist" (Valls, "'A Lousy Empirical Scientist'" 130) who willfully ignored local evidence of African and Caribbean achievement, he would not have based his suppositions on the prejudicial travel writings of his day (Popkin 255; Eze, *Race and Enlightenment* 6). The content of his footnote, and its subsequent substantiation by Kant and eighteenth- and nineteenth-century pro-slavery advocates,[13] has led critics to theorize the Enlightenment as indicative of an era during which "the number of discussions about the causes and the varieties of mankind took a quantum leap . . . because of the growing interest in the social sciences, but more . . . because of the need to provide justification for the social, political, and economic domination of Europe over the colonial empire, and the use of Africans to exploit these lands" (Popkin 252).

Seen in this light, Hume's philosophical position on the institution of chattel slavery becomes virtually irrelevant. His comparatively brief footnote was singularly embraced as the empirical and philosophical rationale for slavery and imperialism's very existence and entrenchment within the sociopolitical and geopolitical workings of eighteenth- and nineteenth-century Western society. As such, it is my contention that his singularly polemic annotation may be viewed as initiating the modern epistemology of scientific racism since it led to marked proliferation of racist thought within the larger Western canon. Hume's status as a prominent empiricist lent further legitimacy and veracity to an ideological system principally founded on Western suppositions, stereotyping, and false claims of innate African inferiority. This thought system lent philosophical and ethical legitimacy to the institution of chattel slavery while furthering the discourses of institutional racism that would become defining features of the late eighteenth, nineteenth, and twentieth centuries. Indeed it is quite clear that the creation of the subhuman, ahistorical Negro slave was imperative to the merging of anti-African racism and Western discourse. The bestial African had to exist so that the unbridled exploitation of slave labor could continue to feed the burgeoning capitalist economies of the West. The African was effectively transformed into the ahistorical Negro from whom

> not even the suspicion of tradition needed to be entertained. In its stead was the . . . slave, a consequence masqueraded as an anthropology and a history. The creation of the Negro was obviously at the cost of immense expenditures of psychic and intellectual energies in the West. The exercise was obligatory. It was an effort commensurate with the importance Black labor power possessed for the World economy sculpted and dominated by the ruling and mercantile classes of Western Europe. The Atlantic slave trade and the slavery of the New World were integral to the modern world economy. (Robinson 4)

Black labor power under chattel slavery defined Western economic growth from the sixteenth to the nineteenth century. As Eric Williams and Theodore Allen stress, the enormous capital gains from triangular trade financed England's banking, insurance, iron, railway, and steam engine industries, thereby stimulating the country's entire economy. In the United States, New York banks reaped significant profits from credit extended to cotton belt states for the production and export of cotton crops, which "amounted to nearly $750 million, constituting more than half the value of all United States exports."[14] For Western economies to prosper, chattel slavery became the cornerstone of modern capitalism; thus it had to be systematically justified through a well-developed body of thought that documented African people's existence as distinctly separate and subordinate to that of Europeans and European Americans. Chattel slavery's four-hundred-year existence rested on the historical, epistemological, and ontological negation of the African. In this regard the Enlightenment writings of Hume, Kant, and Jefferson, and later Hegel, provided the formal, discursive means to sanitize chattel slavery and perpetuate the capitalist exploitation of the enslaved.

The European Enlightenment's influence on the development of American Enlightenment thought and discourse should not be underestimated,[15] for the Age of Reason's celebrated yet dichotomous principles of natural rights and property rights shaped eighteenth- and nineteenth-century American society. What is more, the influence of Hume, among other Scottish philosophers, on the development of Jefferson's philosophical thought is particularly striking (Anderson 89n13). On the one hand, America had been founded on the epoch's revolutionary ethos of liberty, equality, and fraternity; yet the Founding Fathers, and Jefferson in particular, codified their adherence to the Lockean edict of rational man's innate right to property (including slaves) by including provisions in their own Declaration of Independence (Diggins 207–8, 210, 212, 215, 219). Though the word *slaves* does not appear in the nation's founding document, *chattel* by definition includes slaves. Jefferson is esteemed in the collective American consciousness as one in a group of preeminent liberators of the American people, yet in his contradictory position as slaveholder and American freedom fighter one may easily apprehend the growing influence of Hume's anti-African empiricism and the solidification of scientific racism by the late eighteenth century.

Like Hume before him, Jefferson declared the subjugation of enslavement as concrete proof of the African's inherent inferiority rather than making the more logical deduction: that the reality of Africans' enslavement was the cause of their inferior condition. The following passage in Jefferson's *Notes on the State of Virginia* presents the author's adherence to Hume's racially flawed empirical method: "Will not a lover of natural history then, one who views the gradations in all the races of animals with the eye of philosophy, excuse an effort to keep those in the department of man as distinct as nature has formed them" (133). Here Jefferson himself notes the overwhelming influence and significance of philosophy on the individual's interpretation of differences among various racial groups.

Yet according to John Diggins, Jefferson was unable to square the Declaration's emphasis on universal human equality with his acceptance of African inferiority since

> the Negro's "fundamental equality" . . . could not be confirmed by the empirical criteria of the Enlightenment. . . . Conceiving equality as an empirical proposition, he looked to the natural world to confirm an idea that actually had its origins in the moral world. . . .
>
> The reason why America's revolutionary ideology did not necessarily lead to abolition . . . is that the doctrine of equality bravely announced in the Declaration could easily be refuted by what Jefferson's eyes confirmed: that there were great differences among men and that God or nature had cruelly distributed human talents unevenly. (225–26)

While Diggins is correct in his distinction between Jefferson's moral and physical interpretations of the enslaved African's condition, his critique does not fully consider the overwhelming influence of racist thought[16] and Hume's empiricism on the faulty deductions supporting Jefferson's proposition that "God or nature had cruelly distributed human talents unevenly." Jefferson was attached to an empirical method that failed to address the very real existence of African American achievement. This is reflected in his inconsistent comparisons between Roman slaves and African American slaves and his disparagement of Phyllis Wheatley's literary achievements.

In an attempt to further his argument, Jefferson makes incongruous (empirical) comparisons between slaves under the Roman Empire and enslaved Africans in the Americas (131–32). First, he announces that he could never "find a black had uttered a thought above the plainest narration" (130). Then, immediately following, he proclaims, "In music they are generally more gifted than the whites with accurate ears for tune and time" (130). Here Jefferson admits to African artistry that surpasses that of whites, yet he follows this admission with his now infamously disparaging remarks about the unprecedented poetic accomplishments of Wheatley: "The compositions published under her name are beneath the dignity of criticism" (130). He willfully chose to ignore Wheatley's linguistic and lyrical prowess, and his inability to apprehend how the dehumanizing and oppressive chattel slave system itself instantiated the Africans' "distinct" and "inferior" nature reveals that his attachment to the "scientific" laws of race actually crippled his empirical faculties—in much the same manner that these beliefs prevented Hume from acknowledging the accomplishments of Francis Williams. And though Jefferson's text does not mention the African American mathematician, astronomer, and almanac-maker Benjamin Banneker by name, Banneker's scientific contributions and his famed letter to Jefferson, questioning how Americans' inability to understand the emancipation of slaves as identical to America's recent liberation from British colonial rule, offered Jefferson irrefutable proof of black intellectual achievement (Gates and McKay 153; Jorgensen 234). Following Jefferson's deprecation of enslaved Africans' intellectual and creative abilities, on the next page of *Notes* he contrasts the Roman slaves as "the rarest artists," claiming that their membership in the white race allows them to excel; their nature (as whites) not their condition (as slaves) produced their intellectual endowments, as opposed to the "inferior" nature of Africans that prevents them achieving similar creative and intellectual distinctions (131).

Although Jefferson seems to make a comparative historical analysis between Roman slaves' and African slaves' artistic abilities, it is marred by the bias of logical fallacies rooted in racist thought. How could Jefferson claim that blacks were *superior* to whites in musical talent and then immediately proclaim that Roman slaves of the white race were the rarest of artists? If he had been following the rules of logic, he would have deduced that black slaves were superior musicians to white slaves; therefore Roman slaves could not have been the rarest of artists. Thus one may argue that Jefferson's ideals of equality and liberty did not hasten abolition because his subscription to racist doctrine prevented him from viewing enslaved Africans as equal, rational human beings. This is evident in the faulty comparisons he makes in the sections of *Notes* cited earlier and in his application of Hume's anti-African empirical deductions,[17] which led the former president to reach his specious conclusion on white superiority and black inferiority. As Jefferson's statements attest, the overarching power of racist thought in the late eighteenth century and the first half of the nineteenth century must be highlighted. Indeed critics have effectively argued that Enlightenment racial science and the modern concept of race had reached a political fever pitch in the 1780s and 1790s (when Jefferson was governor of Virginia and later secretary of state) due to the confluence of two related historical developments: British and French parliamentary debates on abolition and the fearsome reality of the Haitian Revolution.[18] In his letters to St. George Tucker (an advocate of gradual emancipation), Aaron Burr, James Madison, and Rufus King (U.S. minister to Great Britain), Jefferson decries the looming threat of Haitian insurrection and its potential to catalyze the same liberationist impulse in enslaved Africans throughout the Americas. The only solution, according to Jefferson and other supporters of African colonization, was to transport enslaved Africans back to their native land (Dubois and Garrigus 162; Jefferson 134).

In the pages immediately preceding the section of Jefferson's *Notes* cited earlier, there are several paragraphs in which he adds his voice to the growing late eighteenth-century debates on racial hierarchies and essential, or "natural," racial differences. He begins this section of "Laws" by addressing the question of future emancipation and the potential enfranchisement of enslaved Africans in the American union. Equal citizenship for blacks, he argues, is impossible because of insurmountable political differences between the white and black races that will inevitably lead to race war (128). Additionally he insists that there are other differences,

> which are physical and moral. The first difference which strikes us is that of colour. Whether the black of the negro resides in the reticular

membrane between the skin and the scarf-skin . . . whether it proceeds
from the colour of the blood, the colour of the bile . . . the difference
is fixed in nature. . . . And is this difference of no importance? Is it not
the foundation of a greater or less share of beauty in the two races?
Are not the fine mixtures of red and white . . . preferable to the eternal
monotony . . . that immovable veil of black which covers all the emotions of the other race? Add to these, flowing hair, a more elegant sym-
metry in form, their own judgment in favor of the whites, declared by
their preference of them, as uniformly as is the preference of the Ora-
nootan for the black women over those of his own species. (128)

Jefferson's fixation on the biological origins of Africans' dark skin color,
as well as his contradictory insistence[19] on the superior aesthetic value
of white skin, reflects two trends in contemporary eighteenth-century
thought. In his description of the plain difference between white and
black skin, he echoes the opinions of the European thinkers Georges
Buffon and Kant, who explained the African's dark pigmentation
through the hypothetical presence of black bile or iron deposits below
the skin. Jefferson's claims for the universal aesthetic superiority of
white skin were also influenced by the manner in which racialized discourse influenced the resurgence of classical beauty standards, embodied in fair skin and straight hair; moreover classical aesthetics also used
this standard of acceptable beauty to ascribe ontological value to individuals. It is quite evident that Jefferson equates what he (and other
eighteenth-century thinkers) perceived to be the "absence" of beauty
in blacks to an inherent ontological negation that persists among Africans due to their ascribed subhuman status. Thus he claims that orangutans prefer black women to females of their own species because of
what he and others believed to be Africans' ape-like disposition. However, where Jefferson ascribes superior moral value to whites one may
see a specifically Kantian influence, since Kant used his extensive writings on anthropology and physical geography to theorize skin color as
indicative of a permanently fixed moral and rational quality (Goldberg
30; Eze, "The Color of Reason" 218–21).

Simply put, Jefferson was both unable and unwilling to concede the
theoretical similarities between the actualization of white American
freedom from British colonial rule and the liberation of enslaved Africans from chattel slavery because his belief in scientific racism blinded
him to the enslaved Africans' humanity. Scientific racism's negation of
African humanity and its insistence on the absence of ontological worth
among Africans presented a philosophical problem for nineteenth-

century Africana thinkers. David Walker, who refuted Jefferson's *Notes on the State of Virginia* and its claims of African subhumanity, used his *Appeal* to condemn the entrenchment of nineteenth-century racist thought and its necessary tethering to chattel slavery. Throughout his *Appeal* he warns that white Americans firmly believed it their birthright to be served and enriched by enslaved Africans, since they deemed Africans subhuman due to their dark skin and other African racial characteristics (4, 5, 7, 12, 26, 27). Walker's admonitions are borne out in works of Enlightenment thinkers that preceded him. So influential were Western thinkers like Hume, Kant, and Jefferson in their philosophical treatments of the African character and their rationales for African enslavement that the institution of slavery has come to be almost exclusively associated with people of African descent, more than with any other racial or ethnic group. The exclusive yoking of slavery to the African represents a twofold problem. First, Enlightenment philosophies are not generally perceived as furthering discourses of racial difference that were established as early as the thirteenth century (Robinson 13–16). Second, the institution of slavery is not perceived as one of many cultural developments in Western history; instead it is understood as the distinct lot of the African: "There is scant sense that the universality and rationality of enlightened Europe and America were used to sustain and relocate . . . an order of racial difference inherited from the premodern era. . . . In this setting, it is hardly surprising that . . . the history of slavery is somehow assigned to blacks. It becomes our special property rather than a part of the ethical and intellectual heritage of the West as a whole" (Gilroy, *Black Atlantic* 49).

As we have seen, Western antipathy toward Africans and their enslaved descendants in the West had roots prior to and during the Early Modern period. The link between the image of the savage African and eighteenth- and nineteenth-century Western anti-African racism becomes clear, as the African came to represent the quintessence of the slave. Consequently nineteenth-century Africana abolitionists like David Walker challenged the erasure of enslaved Africans and their ancestors from the narrative of Western development. Walker's *Appeal* presents its own subversion of Western thought because in fighting for enslaved Africans' physical liberation he also sought to prove their existence as human beings and historical agents, possessing historical and ontological value. To do this he invoked the ancient civilization of Egypt as clear proof of African humanity, historicality, and civilization.

WALKER'S DISCURSIVE INSURRECTION

With America's confirmed status as a slaveholding society in the early nineteenth century, several African American abolitionists addressed the nation's pretense at democracy and its willful betrayal of its founding egalitarian principles. Walker's *Appeal in Four Articles; Together with a Preamble, to the Coloured Citizens of the World, but in particular, and very expressly, to those of The United States of America* (1829) was not the first document written by a free northern African American to challenge the hypocrisy of America's selective commitment to social egalitarianism among white males, and Jefferson's claims in particular; however, it was the first published document to name the former president and the title of his only published book in an impassioned treatise (Hinks 176–79). Lengthy refutations of Jefferson's claims constitute the first half of Walker's classic proto-Black nationalist text.[20] Modeling the structure of his *Appeal* on the U.S. Constitution, with a preamble and four articles, Walker initiates his ideological intervention by highlighting the glaring inconsistencies at the heart of this slaveholding nation's founding document. Some critics have argued that Walker's text should receive more attention than it has, based on its emphatic philosophical and text-based exhortation that Americans failed to extend Enlightenment ideals of equality to enslaved Africans. Others have argued that the document's primary significance is its seemingly prescient articulation of Black nationalist ideology.[21]

Both interpretations raise important points about the *Appeal*'s significance as a physical document and its foundational import to more contemporary liberationist struggles. However, analyzing Walker's *Appeal* through the critical lens of Heideggerian historicity and a Sartrean existentialist theory of history allows for a broader understanding of its repudiation of scientific racism and its use in rationalizing the capitalist exploitation of chattel slavery. In the preamble and first two articles Walker refutes three central claims of scientific racism: the prevailing notion that enslaved Africans' ancestors, rather than being the progenitors of Western civilization in Egypt, had only been recipients of the West's civilizing project through the bondage of chattel slavery; the Western image of the subhuman enslaved African; and the polygenetic theory that Africans had come into existence through their own separate, subhuman evolution.

Walker, a free African American from Boston, begins the preamble with a unifying rallying cry that announces the text's comparative his-

torical analysis of slavery in ancient and modern times; it is one that
Walker furthers in Articles I and II:

> My dearly beloved Brethren and Fellow Citizens. Having travelled
> over a considerable portion of these United States, and having in the
> course of my travels taken the most accurate observations of things
> as they exist—the result of my observations has warranted the full
> and unshaken conviction, that we, (coloured people of these United
> States;) are the most degraded, wretched, and abject set of beings that
> ever lived since the world began; and I pray God that none like us ever
> may live again until time shall be no more. They tell us of the Israel-
> ites in Egypt, the Helots in Sparta, and of the Roman slaves, which
> were made up from almost every nation under heaven, whose suffer-
> ings under those ancient and heathen nations, were, in comparison
> with ours, under this enlightened and Christian nation, no more than
> a cypher—or, in other words, those heathen nations of antiquity, had
> but little more among them than the name and form of slavery; while
> wretchedness and endless miseries were reserved, apparently in a
> phial, to be poured out upon our fathers, ourselves and our children by
> *Christian* Americans. (1)

Walker's invocation of ancient slave systems serves two discursive functions: first, he identifies himself as a student of history who has surveyed
the texts of Josephus and Plutarch (1) and fully grasps the fact that systems of slavery have existed since the dawn of human civilization; second, he outlines the principal difference between modern enslavement
and ancient systems of servitude as the wretchedness, endless miseries, and dehumanization of chattel slavery. Walker furthers this line
of argumentation on Western slavery as an aberrant and more vicious
strain of enforced servitude than any other in history through prefa-
tory remarks that decry the greed and wanton lust for wealth among
American slaveholders: "In the United States of America . . . the labour
of slaves comes so cheap to the avaricious usurpers, and is . . . of such
great utility to the country where it exists, that those who are actuated
by sordid avarice only, overlook the evils" (3). He steadfastly proclaims
that the greed of slaveholders precludes any moral concerns about the
cruelty of the system in which they partake. What further condem-
nation of America's growing capitalist economy, built on the backs of
African slaves, could he offer?

  While the preamble presents Walker's scathing assessment of America's slavocracy, it also issues a challenge to his enslaved comrades to
fully consider the harsh reality of their abysmal condition in bondage,

reminding them that he entreats God in his desire "to awaken in the breasts of my afflicted, degraded and slumbering brethren, a spirit of inquiry and investigation respecting our miseries and wretchedness in this *Republican Land of Liberty!!!!!!*" (2). His desire to rouse his enslaved brothers and sisters to a heightened sense of consciousness about the nature of their oppression at the hands of whites is the *Appeal*'s first articulation of the need for unified black resistance. The preamble's next section also forces readers to consider the damaging ways in which racist thought had rationalized Africans' enslavement by creating the notion of their perceived subhumanity based on their racial characteristics: "Who can dispense with prejudice long enough to admit that we are *men*, notwithstanding our *improminent noses* and *woolly heads*, and believe that we feel for our fathers, mothers, wives and children, as well as the whites do for theirs" (4–5). Thus the preamble establishes the historical and ideological trajectory of Articles I and II by decrying the unprecedented inhumanity of Western chattel slavery through its links to racist thought and capitalist exploitation and its necessary dialectical response—a call to arms for the enslaved to initiate their own liberation.

Article I opens with a list of the races and tribes of peoples who have fallen under the boot heel of colonialism and slavery (and were eventually liberated), reminding readers that these varied nations of people were nevertheless always considered human. But not so for the African:

> My beloved brethren:—The Indians of North and of South America— the Greeks—the Irish, subjected under the king of Great Britain—the Jews, that ancient people of the Lord—the inhabitants of the islands of the sea—in fine, all the inhabitants of the earth, (except however, the sons of Africa) are called *men*, and of course are, and ought to be free. But we (coloured people) and our children are *brutes* ! ! and of course are, and *ought to be* Slaves to the American people and their children forever ! ! to dig their mines and work their farms; and thus go on enriching them, from one generation to another with our *blood* and our *tears* ! ! ! ! (7)

Furthering his case for the historical aberration that is chattel slavery, Walker is emphatic in his disdain for American slavery and the related racist doctrines that placed the African apart from the rest of humanity, a form of historical and ontological alienation that was initiated for the sole purpose of justifying the slave's degradation to ensure the wealth of white America. In like manner, Sterling Stuckey contends that "[Walker's] criticism, stated with contempt, is a sustained attack on those using others for financial gain to purchase comfort for themselves and their families. Walker's cry was at bottom one of hatred of the spirit of capitalism as well as of slavery and racism" (121). This anticapitalist and antiracist sentiment is clearly evident in the *Appeal*; however, Walker's pamphlet furthered the abolitionist cause on both ideological *and* material grounds. He did not detest capitalism, slavery, and racism as discrete systems; he saw them as facets of one insidious hegemonic triumvirate that attempted to destroy the humanity and liberty of his people. Therefore the *Appeal* skillfully contextualizes the necessary connections among chattel slavery, scientific racism, and capitalism to reveal "the unique brutality of American slavery . . . in terms of the ideological machinery used to explain to both blacks and whites why blacks were enslaved in republican America" (Hinks 200). Peter Hinks is quite correct in his assertion that Walker's refutation of Jefferson's assault on African humanity in *Notes on the State of Virginia* is "fundamentally ideological" (201). Nonetheless Walker's discursive response to Jefferson's claims also shows that Walker apprehended the gravity of the historical moment and thereby used his *Appeal* to assume historical agency—much like Jefferson himself—and leave his mark on the subject of Western slavery for perpetuity. Therefore Walker's agential act, and the *Appeal*'s theoretical resistance, may be thoroughly interrogated through elements of Heideggerian (phenomenological) historicity and Sartrean existentialist historiography.

For phenomenologists like Husserl and Heidegger, to exist as a human is to "be" in time. Temporality is the abstract yet concrete field upon which human existence is measured, apprehended, predicted, and defined. The present moment, then, acts as an immediate vista that simultaneously facilitates interpretations of the present and the past: "The Now is a vantage point from which we survey the past and the future. To exist humanly is not merely to be in time but to encompass or 'take it in' as our gaze takes in our surroundings. . . . this temporal grasp, in varying degrees of complexity and explicitness, makes us both participants in and surveyors of the temporal flow, both characters in and tellers of the stories constituted by it" (Carr 95). The "now" of the late eighteenth and early nineteenth centuries in Western history, as noted earlier, is widely recognized as the pinnacle of modernity's maturity—a time during which abolitionists challenged chattel slavery's ascendance and intensification on both moral and philosophical grounds. Both Jefferson and Walker were crucial characters and narrators in the history of slavery who concomitantly gazed upon slavery's past during ancient times as a social institution and its present within the context of the Enlightenment's epistemological developments. Though both men used the history of slavery in antiquity to respectively justify and denounce its modern manifestation in the Americas, equally revelatory and prescient are John Adams's and Walker's comments about the future value (and veneration) of Jefferson's *Notes on the State of Virginia* in times to come. Adams remarked that Jefferson's pages on slavery were "worth Diamonds. They will have more effect than Volumes written by mere Philosophers" (see Cappon, *Adams-Jefferson Letters,* qtd. in Diggins 206). Even though Walker found Jefferson's views on enslaved Africans morally repugnant and historically and ideologically specious, he conceded the lasting impact of the former president's passages on slavery: "See this, my brethren!! Do you believe that [Jefferson's] assertion is swallowed by millions of the whites? . . . See his writings for the world, and public labours of the United States of America. Do you believe that the assertions of such a man, will pass away into oblivion unobserved by this people and the world? If you do you are much mistaken" (15). Jefferson's stature as an American statesman and philosopher has, generally, gone unquestioned. Solely based on his statements about slavery in *Notes*, Adams proclaimed that the impact of Jeffersonian thought would surpass that of philosophers, and nearly half a century later Walker himself was in tacit agreement. Walker was exceedingly conscious of the future impact Jefferson's *Notes* would have; therefore he continued to challenge Jefferson's position on African inferiority and enslavement through scriptural and historical accounts.

In Article I, Walker critiques American slavery by asking readers to recall that even the ancient Egyptians did not degrade their Israelite slaves by declaring them less than human, a charge that Jefferson so boldly defended in his *Notes*. Walker dares his readers:

> Show me a page of history, either sacred or profane, on which a verse can be found, which maintains, that the Egyptians heaped the *insupportable insult* upon the children of Israel, by telling them that they were not of the *human family*. Can the whites deny this charge? Have they not, after having reduced us to the deplorable condition of slaves under their feet, held us up as descending originally from tribes of *Monkeys* or *Orang-Outangs*? . . . Is it not heaping the most gross insult upon our miseries, because they have got us under their feet and we cannot help ourselves? . . . Has Mr. Jefferson declared to the world, that we are inferior to the whites, both in the endowments of our bodies and our minds? (10)

Through his invocation of slavery's history as an ancient social institution, Walker notes the manner in which modern chattel slavery stands as a gross deviation of Western power in its unprecedented animalization of the African race in the self-proclaimed land of liberty. He takes direct aim at Jefferson's charge that orangutans prefer African women to females of their own species, which, in Jefferson's view, proves the African's subhuman, ape-like status in the racial hierarchy. Thus Walker's aim is clear. He stresses that African subjugation at the hands of whites provided the occasion for chattel slavery's ethical rationalizations in racist thought, thereby revealing the circular logic at the heart of the institution's philosophical underpinnings. American slaveholders claimed that the Africans' enslavement was indicative of their nature, thereby absolving themselves of any moral culpability, rather than choosing to see the Africans' enslavement as the very cause of their degraded condition. Walker continues his abolitionist missive against Jefferson, insisting that all African Americans who are able should purchase a copy of Jefferson's *Notes* and see for themselves what the former president had written. Walker believes that it is incumbent upon African Americans themselves to refute the arguments at the heart of the text and that it is unacceptable and ineffective for African Americans to let white sympathizers speak for them. He avers that if African Americans do not themselves refute Jefferson's claims, they will thereby confirm them (15). With his adamant call Walker stresses the necessity for African American discursive self-determination. Since Jefferson declares the intellectual inferiority of blacks, Walker contends that African Americans alone can successfully refute this claim through firm textual rebuttals that would reflect their moral and intellectual equality, their talents and learning, and not least of all their unquestionable humanity.

To Walker's theoretical and textual challenge, and to Jefferson's own response to the ideas of Hume and Kant, we may also apply the phenomenological concept of historicity as it relates to ideological intertextuality and its creation of discursive predecessors and successors. David Carr contends that Husserl's and Heidegger's formulation of historicity affirms that the actions and experiences among people go beyond that of reciprocity; indeed these interactions may also be applied to and signify primary and secondary treatments of a specific "problem." This remains true whether successors employ the predecessors' work as the basis of their own or they begin by dismantling the predecessors' work and starting anew (Carr 112–15). As an abolitionist text, Walker's *Appeal* seeks to repair the philosophical and historical debasement of African humanity contained in Jefferson's *Notes* and stem the text's furtherance of racist thought that began its initial ascendance in Hume's footnote in the mid-eighteenth century. Walker begins again and seeks redress by invoking the history of slavery throughout the ages and underscoring the ways in which chattel slavery is unparalleled in its inhumanity. This same emphasis allows him to recast enslaved African Americans as the progenitors of Western civilization by virtue of their racial and historical connection to ancient Egypt (8). His new beginning calls for moral, historical, and philosophical reconsiderations of Western thought through the person of the enslaved African subject. His *Appeal* establishes the collective historical significance of enslaved Africans and uses this reestablishment of ontological historicity to simultaneously argue for the immediate abolition of slavery while rousing enslaved Africans to initiate their own liberation. In his call for diasporic unity among enslaved Africans throughout the world, Walker admonishes them to remember that he "advanced it therefore, not as a problematical, but as an unshaken and for ever immovable *fact*, that your full glory and happiness, as well as all other coloured people under Heaven, shall never be fully consummated, but with the *entire emancipation of your enslaved brethren all over the world*" (29).

Without a doubt Walker's text was geared toward raising a revolutionary consciousness within each enslaved individual, yet his rhetorical purpose was also the creation of a unified collectivity whose aim was the actualization of Freedom for all enslaved Africans throughout the diaspora. This stirring emphasis on individual and collective liberation represents one of the principal reasons why his *Appeal* is considered one of the earliest textual manifestations of Black nationalist ideology. As the abolitionist movements in England, France, and the United States gained momentum and support in the nineteenth century, Walker was not only calling for chattel slavery's demise on ideological, moral, and legislative grounds; he also demanded that enslaved Africans the world over rise up and claim their Freedom for themselves, with or without the aid of the courts or the court of pubic opinion. Seen in this light, Walker's text is also a successor to Jefferson's *Notes* as it tackles the entrenchment of white supremacy in Western letters through his proposed solution: African diasporic unity. Consequently it may be argued that Walker apprehended enslaved Africans as a separate nation of people, one that shared ancestral ties and whose common goals were emancipation and equality in the slaveholding nations of the West.

This matter of a shared racial heritage among enslaved Africans in the Americas segues into the *Appeal*'s recuperation of a collective ancestral past in ancient Africa, for Walker persuades his readers to recall the ancient African influence on the development of Western civilization by emphasizing Egypt as the originary source of Western culture, whose lasting impact transcended the ages and was reflected in nineteenth-century Western society:

> When we take a retrospective view of the arts and sciences—the wise legislators—the Pyramids, and other magnificent buildings—the turning of the channel of the river Nile, by the sons of Africa or of Ham, among whom learning originated, and was carried thence into Greece, where it was improved upon and refined. Thence among the Romans, and all over the then enlightened parts of the world, and it has been enlightening the dark and benighted minds of men from then, down to this day. I say, when I view retrospectively, the renown of that once mighty people . . . I am indeed cheered. (19–20)

Walker's *Appeal* emphasizes the ancient African's central role in the advancement of Western civilization. Employing comparative historical analyses of various slave systems throughout antiquity, he makes the case that Africans' historical import to and for the West should be a source of pride for all people of African descent. At the same time, he disproves scientific racism's central claim: that Africans lack the capacity to create advanced civilizations and that they exist apart from the tide of Western development. Hinks notes that Walker's assertion is significant for two reasons: it reflects a common strain in nineteenth-century African American abolitionist oratory and writing, and the *Appeal*'s emphasis on enslaved Africans' connection to this advanced ancient civilization supports the idea that they were the originators of Western civilization, not the recipients of it (Hinks 181, 192–93). Additionally, however, the *Appeal*'s inclusion of enslaved Africans in the narrative of ancient Western history presents a nineteenth-century manifestation of what Sartre terms "committed" analytical history, the purpose of which is "to lend a voice to the exploited and oppressed even as it unmasks the bad faith of individuals and societies, holding up a critical mirror" (Flynn 255–56). The *Appeal* issues a clarion call to the oppressed African masses in the Americas. It repudiates the bad faith of Western slaveholding societies in the Americas by elucidating the manner in which the insatiable greed for capitalist accumulation propelled the slave system into its third century of existence. Equally important, however, is that Walker's text incriminates the episteme of scientific racism that justified his people's subjugation. The *Appeal* in itself casts a critical reflection on the democratic, enlightened, Christian slaveholding nation of America so that its citizens could see their nation for what it truly was.

Walker's text also addresses Jefferson's call to his own readers. Jefferson writes that lovers of natural history and philosophy will concede the truth of a racial hierarchy that places whites in a superior position over blacks specifically because this ranking is a part of nature's order (133). Walker responds:

> This very verse, brethren, having emanated from Mr. Jefferson, a much greater philosopher the world never afforded, has in truth injured us more, and has been as great of a barrier to our emancipation as any thing that has ever been advanced against us. . . . I am glad Mr. Jefferson has advanced his positions for your sake; for you will either have to contradict or confirm him. . . . the Americans . . . are waiting for us to prove to them ourselves, that we are MEN, before they will be willing to admit the fact. (27)

Walker insists that Jefferson's furtherance of racist thought was the most significant obstacle to the nineteenth-century abolitionist cause. Scientific racism not only rationalized slavery; it also perpetuated it by conflating African identity and chattel status. Moreover Walker calls for a collective African American discursive response as the only corrective for his people's ontological negation in nineteenth-century racist doctrine; this response would prove the enslaved Africans' humanity and ontological worth.

The resultant conflation of African identity and slave identity that Jefferson justifies and Walker decries was made possible by the related ideological and institutional manifestations of racism that were instantiated during Western chattel slavery's four-century existence. Underscoring the slave trade's late fifteenth-century beginnings is crucial to any discussion of racist discourse, yet it is equally important to note that the hegemonic aspects of anti-African racism during the eighteenth and nineteenth centuries mark a chasm in the development of slavery as a system in Western history: "The Atlantic slave trade and plantation economy in the Americas signify a decisive change in the institution of slavery. The systematic racism associated with its structural development cannot be said to exist in the historical stages that precede, and lead up to this moment" (Erickson 500). African enslavement during modern racialized slavery in the West represents a cultural, socioeconomic, and sociopolitical rupture that began in the late

fifteenth century and continued on, particularly as seventeenth-, eigh-
teenth-, and nineteenth-century legislation like the Slave Codes and
the Fugitive Slave Laws forged impenetrable linkages between the elevation of slaveholder rights and privileges and the continued denigration of enslaved African life to the realm of slaveholder property. The
Founding Fathers' fidelity to the Enlightenment rights of man doctrine
and Lockean property rights served as the principal rationale for their
dual roles as holders of slaves and originators of democracy. Therefore
it bears repeating that

> the rights of man, . . . an organizing principle upon which the nation
> was founded, was inevitably yoked to Africanism. Its history, its ori-
> gin, is permanently allied to another seductive concept: the hierar-
> chy of race. As the sociologist Orlando Patterson has noted, we should
> not be surprised that the Enlightenment could accommodate slavery;
> we should be surprised if it had not. The concept of freedom did not
> emerge in a vacuum. Nothing highlighted freedom—if it did not in fact
> create it—like slavery. (Morrison 38)

The ideal of Freedom could not truly exist without its dialectical coun-
terpart: the material reality of chattel slavery. Enslaved Africans' denigration in bondage made the abstract principle of Freedom both plain
and concrete; thus the very framers of the American revolutionary
ethos were dependent on the exigencies of capitalism and slavery to
theorize their nation's defining concepts of liberty.

This paradox of the American free-market (slave) economy and the
nation's self-conceptualization did not escape Walker and his supporters, hence his *Appeal* was circulated as widely as possible. A dearth of
information on the *Appeal*'s circulation in the North indicates that the
document was not viewed as the incendiary missive that it was in the
South. However, an article in the *Boston Daily Transcript* emphasized
that Walker's text seemed to have imbued African American Bosto-
nians with a sense of purpose and pride. It was the *Appeal*'s circulation
in the southern slaveholding states that caused the greatest threat; it
made its first appearance in Savannah, Georgia, then circulated among
African American preachers and runaways in North Carolina and
South Carolina and among sailors in North Carolina, Georgia, and
Delaware. Its seemingly unstoppable dissemination caused sailors sus-
pected of transporting the pamphlet to be quarantined in Charleston,
Wilmington, and Savannah. The great amount of interaction among
African American preachers and fugitive slaves in North Carolina and
Virginia, many of whom read the *Appeal* to illiterate slaves, has led his-

torians to theorize that Nat Turner's insurrection was the result of the *Appeal*'s ability to incite revolutionary, Christian abolitionist fervor (Hinks 117–67; Dinius 67).

To be sure, while many sections of Walker's *Appeal* may be reflective of contemporary African American abolitionist thought, its theoretical and discursive originality made it the principal textual instrument of African American resistance and liberation in the early nineteenth century. Walker used an arresting constellation of historical, political, and philosophical evidence pertaining to the enslaved African's paradoxical position in the West to undermine America's hypocritical allegiance to its peculiar institution, the source of the country's wealth and power.

Walker's untimely demise did not end the rigorous moral and philosophical engagement among African American abolitionists. Frederick Douglass assumed Walker's role as a "restless disturber of the public peace" (2), for Douglass was a former slave who experienced the daily torments of enslavement. His entire oeuvre—three autobiographies, numerous oratorical addresses, articles, and multiple correspondences—was geared toward the realization of two crucial and related goals: the abolition of slavery and acknowledgment of his people's humanity. With Walker's death, the Lion of Anacostia emerged. Douglass continued the work of his predecessor, and his impassioned oratory and writings came to define the American abolitionist movement during the second half of the nineteenth century.

DOUGLASS'S EPISTEMOLOGICAL RUPTURES

With Douglass' 1854 speech, "The Claims of the Negro Ethnologically Considered," he effectively established himself as Walker's philosophical successor. Douglass builds on the *Appeal*'s major proposition: that enslaved Africans in the Americas are of the same racial family as the ancient Egyptians who laid the cultural and social foundations for modern Western society (Levine, "Road to Africa" 226). In "Claims" Douglass uses the cause of abolition to stress the need for African people's historiographical restoration within the narrative of Western development. Consequently he interpellates the American school ethnologists as ideologues of nineteenth-century polygenetic, racist theories, which still held currency two centuries after their initial inception. George Gliddon's, Samuel Morton's, and Josiah Nott's textual assertions of African inferiority were, in Douglass's eyes, the principal ideological hindrance to the abolitionist cause. By the time Douglass wrote his speech, expositions of scientific racism (like those of the American school ethnologists) had become even more sophisticated in their theorization of biological, physiological, and morphological African racial difference. The American school ethnologists had firmly established racist thought's primacy within the halls of American academe (where Morton presented his findings to the American Philosophical Society in 1843) and among politicians and the public. Their studies in Egyptology were centered on postulations of innate African backwardness on what they had delineated as empirical, historical, and physiological grounds. Echoing Hume's footnote almost verbatim, Morton posited that as early as antiquity, during the dawn of Western civilization, Negroes had been slaves to their Caucasian masters in Egyptian society. This, he asserted, was supported by the fact that he had identified three distinct racial morphological types among the Egyptian skulls his colleague Gliddon had collected: Negro slave skulls, smallest in size; Caucasian master skulls, the largest; and mulatto skulls, of median size. Morton had substantiated these questionable findings through a reiteration of Hume's footnote in which he upheld "the notorious fact that no people other than Caucasians had ever developed a great civilization" (Stanton 70). Morton's *Crania Aegyptiaca* was so well received that South Carolina's governor James Hammond drew from the text in order to strengthen his argument that "the philosophy of subjugation [and chattel slavery] lay in the doctrine of Races" (Stanton 53). In "Claims," Douglass refutes Gliddon's, Morton's, and Nott's findings on historical, linguistic, and cultural grounds while simultaneously detailing the manner in which the American school's false theories of African subhumanity implacably buttressed the chattel slave system. In his systematic refutation of racist thought, Douglass further established his prominence as an abolitionist and philosopher; moreover he mined his personal experiences as another man's chattel to write three separate autobiographies over the course of his life.

Several critics agree that the ratification of the Fugitive Slave Laws in the 1850s led Douglass to imbue his antislavery writings and speeches with intensified moral outrage over the tyranny of chattel slavery that was "*the sin and shame of the American people,*" particularly since those laws no longer "confined [slavery] to the states south of the Mason and Dixon's line" (Douglass, "Lecture on Slavery No. 2" 145–47). What is more, during this time Douglass identified the racist trajectory of Western philosophy as the principal cause of the entrenchment of racialized slavery and the resultant erection of fixed racial hierarchies in American society.[22] His increased preoccupation with the ideological structures of the slave system is borne out in *My Bondage and My Freedom* (1855), published just one year after "Claims." In this second of his autobiographical works, Douglass narrates the effects of his expanding intellect on his evolving self-concept. No longer satisfied with simply narrating the events of his life as the "talking chattel" at abolitionist lectures, he explains how the Garrisonian abolitionists' own racial paternalism[23] relegated him to the circumscribed role of the token slave raconteur:

> Many came, no doubt, from curiosity to hear what a Negro could say in his own cause. I was generally introduced as a *'chattel'*—a *'thing'*—a piece of southern *'property'*—the chairman assuring the audience that *it* could speak. . . . 'Give us the facts,' said Collins, 'we will take care of the philosophy.' It was impossible for me to repeat the same old story month after month and keep my interest in it. . . . I could no longer obey, for now I was reading and thinking. New views of the subject were presented to my mind. It did not entirely satisfy me to *narrate* wrongs; I felt like *denouncing* them. (*My Bondage and My Freedom* 271–72)

It is quite telling that Douglass recounts these events and directly quotes his compatriot's condescending remarks identically in both *My Bondage and My Freedom* and *Life and Times of Frederick Douglass* (1892). That he chose to quote the Garrisonians' presumption of their inherent philosophical predilection (as white Americans) and his perceived inaptitude (as an African American) in both of his last two autobiographies speaks volumes to the far-ranging influence of racist thought, even among those white abolitionists who professed to deprecate it. Douglass's narrative repetition indicates the significance of these developments on both personal and discursive grounds; furthermore it may be argued that his emphasis on the Garrisonians' insistence that they, as whites, were better suited to address the philosophy of slavery is what galvanized him to address the epistemological structures of racist thought from the 1850s on. Given his growing concern with the Fugitive Slave Laws as evidence of Western racism's intensification, it only stands to reason that he would attack the thought system at slavery's core, which was used to divest enslaved Africans of their humanity, historiographical relevance, and ontological worth. Douglass knew that the battle for African American liberation had to be fought on the philosophical terrain of discourse, which he astutely described as a "moral

battle field" ("Claims" 289). His mission to challenge the very epistemological structures that supported racialized slavery in the Americas is
made plain in *My Bondage and My Freedom*, in three separate speeches,
and in a letter to his former owner: "Lecture on Slavery No. 1" (1850),
"Lecture on Slavery No. 2" (1850), "The Claims of the Negro Ethnologically Considered" (1854), and "Letter to Thomas Auld" (1850).

It has been asserted that Douglass's recuperative project (in *My
Bondage and My Freedom* and "Claims") of establishing a historical
connection between enslaved Africans in the Americas and the ancient
Egyptians was misguided in its "tendency to argue for African contributions to the progress of civilization based on an inherently European
hegemonic conception of civilization, which . . . [favored] a lost race
of dynastic Egyptians more akin to Europeans" (Chaney 405). However, this assessment of Douglass's ethnographic and historiographical
intervention is misleading on several counts, as it fails to acknowledge
the breadth of his extensive research. First, following the vindicationist tradition, Douglass uses both ancient and modern Western historical, cultural, and linguistic sources in "Claims" (including Herodotus,
Volney, and Robert Gordon Latham) to effectively disprove Morton's
thesis in *Crania Americana* (1839), which identifies the ancient Egyptians as a branch of the European racial family. Douglass points to texts
written by Vivant Denon and James Prichard, which include citations
by Herodotus, Volney, Barron Larrey, and John Ledyard, to reveal multiple physical characteristics (hair, skin, nose, and lips) and linguistic
similarities between the ancient Egyptians and ancient Copts (dark-
skinned, wooly-haired Ethiopians), thus establishing the ancient Egyptians' racial membership in the larger African racial family. Douglass
also references the work of the philologist Latham to establish linguistic parallels between the Semitic languages of Egypt and Ethiopia and
those of western and southern Africa, all spoken by the ancestors of
enslaved Africans in the Americas (Douglass, "Claims" 301–2). Second,
he furthers his challenge to Morton's argument by identifying several
contradictions and inconsistencies in *Crania Americana*, including
Morton's own description of the Egyptians as one that matches that of
Negroes according to America's infamous "one drop rule": "Complex-
ion brown. The nose is straight, excepting the end, where it is rounded
and wide; the lips are rather thick, and the hair black and curly" (qtd.
in "Claims" 297). Third, to further substantiate his position, Douglass calls Morton's efforts to separate the ancient Egyptians from other
Africans tantamount to declaring Europeans wholly distinct from

European Americans (299). In presenting these arguments, Douglass substantiates his (and Walker's) historiographical propositions on the enslaved Africans' ancestral ties to the ancient Egyptians. An incomplete reading of "Claims," however, may lead readers to infer that Douglass was somehow ignorant of the philosophical debate into which he had entered. Nothing could be further from the truth. Douglass intervened in this debate to discredit the American school ethnologists so as to undermine their epistemological and philosophical primacy in the slaveholding society of America. His efforts and those of other vindicationist abolitionists would, in turn, contribute to the chattel slave system's eventual demise.

Douglass's opening remarks in "Claims" on the role of the American scholar and the question of the Negro's humanity make his intentions quite clear. He impresses upon his audience the vital nature of his talk, explaining that he is "animated by a desire to [address] a matter of living importance—a matter upon which action, as well as thought is required" (289). Foreshadowing Du Bois's signature remark about the twentieth-century problem of the color line, Douglass contends, "The relation subsisting between the white and black people of this country is the vital question of the age. In the solution of this question, the scholars of America will have to take an important and controlling part" (289). Douglass clearly establishes the role of America's intelligentsia in shaping the nation's discourse, policy, and public opinion on slavery, abolition, and equality. To explain his position, he avows that his decision to interject his views is tied to his own Freedom and the Freedom of his people: "I assume at the start, that wherever else I may be required to speak with bated breath, here, at least, I may speak with freedom the thought nearest my heart" (289). Here Douglass raises the issue of Freedom in its triplicate manifestations. The freedom he wishes to employ as a speaker refers to his ontological Freedom as an autonomous individual, that innate state of existence that allows him to express the fullness of his character and his crucial message. Yet he is also speaking of his own physical Freedom, since he had been enslaved little over a decade earlier, and he is also referring to the collective Freedom of his brothers and sisters in bondage.

As Douglass embodies and implicitly refers to Freedom's varied manifestations, he forcefully acknowledges the primary conjectural obstacle to the abolitionist cause: the question of the Negro's humanity. Simply put, is the Negro a human being? Douglass effectively establishes the purpose and theoretical parameters of his talk in the following manner: "I shall aim to discuss the claims of the Negro, general and special, in a manner, though not scientific, still sufficiently clear and definite to enable my hearers to form an intelligent judgment respecting them. The first general claim which may here be set up, respects the manhood of the Negro. This is an elementary claim, simple enough, but not without question. It is fiercely opposed" ("Claims" 289–90). He unmistakably voices his opposition to the construction of the Negro slave's subhumanity, yet he apologizes for his "unscientific" methods. He seemingly does so to shift criticism from his unlettered education. His lack of academic degrees notwithstanding, he uses his impressive skills as an autodidact to discredit the findings of the aforementioned lettered men due to their furtherance of racist thought and their works' influence on slaveholding politicians. Douglass appeals to his audience's collective conscience, reminding them that no thinker should be swayed by contemporary trends in racist thought: "It is the providence of prejudice to be blind; and scientific writers, not less than others, write to please, as well as to instruct, and even unconsciously to themselves, (sometimes) sacrifice what is true to what is popular. Fashion is not confined to dress; but extends to philosophy as well—and it is fashionable now, in our land, to exaggerate the differences between the Negro and the European" (298). This fashion, according to Douglass, includes the suppression of historical truth about enslaved Africans' racial, morphological, and linguistic links to the ancient Egyptians in Gliddon's, Morton's, and Notts's works. Douglass identifies their findings as part of a larger hegemonic imperative when he announces the ethnologists' influence on southern slaveholders. He charges, "The debates in Congress on the Nebraska Bill . . . will show how slaveholders have availed themselves of this doctrine in support of slaveholding. There is no doubt that Messrs. Nott, Glidden, Morton . . . were duly consulted by our slavery propagating statesmen" (295). As an abolitionist and thinker Douglass was compelled to address the symbiotic alliance between pro-slavery advocates and nineteenth-century proponents of racist thought. His pointed explanation of how contemporary congressional debates hinged on the American school's findings reveals the intricate workings of Western hegemonic discourse and praxis.

Nearly one century later Du Bois builds on Douglass's central arguments in his 1946 work, *The World and Africa*. Du Bois revisits Douglass's references to Herodotus, his comparisons between European and American ethnic groups, and his insistence on scientific racism as the necessary ideological prerequisite for U.S. exploitation-based capitalist accumulation:

The Greeks looked upon Egypt as part of Africa not only geographically but culturally, and every fact of history and anthropology proves
that the Egyptians were an African people varying no more from other
African peoples than groups like the Scandinavians vary from other
Europeans. . . . It is especially significant that the science of Egyptology
arose and flourished at the very time that the cotton kingdom reached
its greatest power on the foundation of American Negro slavery. *We may
then without further ado ignore this verdict of history, widespread as it is,
and treat Egyptian history as an integral part of African history.* (99)

Douglass, and later Du Bois, identifies Africa's paradoxical relationship to the West: though Africa was the site of human societies' transition from "primitive" to advanced civilizations, the very race of
people that made this development possible were effectively written
out of the history they had instantiated. The slave system's perpetuity
depended on the continual debasement of the enslaved, so a reinterpretation of Western civilization's origins had to be widely propagated and accepted. This denigration of the African's humanity and
character, Douglass charged, was furthered in the circular logic used
to rationalize African enslavement. In a frequently cited excerpt of
"Claims," Douglass puts forth one of his strongest arguments on the
power of pro-slavery discourse and its negation of the enslaved population's collective worth:

Ignorance and depravity, and the inability to rise from degradation to civilization and respectability, are the most usual allegations
against the oppressed. The evils fostered by slavery and oppression,
are precisely those which slaveholders and oppressors would trans-
fer from their system to the inherent character of their victims. Thus
the very crimes of slavery become slavery's best defense. By making
the enslaved a character fit only for slavery, they excuse themselves for
refusing to make the slave a freeman. A wholesale method of accom-
plishing this result, is to overthrow the instinctive consciousness of the
common brotherhood of man. (295)

Douglass refers to the plantations system's construction of the indolent,
dumb beast of burden just as he implicates that system in forcing the
very circumstances of slaves' perceived subhumanity by enforcing illit-
eracy, working the enslaved to exhaustion or death, and punishing them
for minor infractions. Slaveholders characterized their slaves as incapable of progress even though it was the system itself that produced what
they viewed as evidence thereof. The works of Gliddon, Morton, and
Nott only buttressed this assessment. Douglass's reference to "a charac-

ter fit only for slavery" points to the slaveholders' perceived birthright to count slaves as property or chattel and not as human persons.

For the purposes of this chapter, I will examine the ways in which scientific racism's entrenchment within American society led Douglass to greater existential ruminations in *My Bondage and My Freedom*, in his oratorical addresses, and in his correspondence with his former owner in the 1850s. As he became increasingly frustrated that the rationalization of racial hierarchies led to what he viewed as the insupportable reduction of human beings to property, or things, his introspection and discourse reflect his engagement with this particular ontological problem. The dehumanization and commodification of enslaved Africans, for Douglass like Walker before him, became a defining moral charge waged against the chattel slave system. Since Douglass made direct connections among ideology, praxis, and the material conditions of the enslaved, he was compelled to discredit the very thought system undergirding chattel slavery. It is a matter of course, then, that he would be forced to ponder the existential ramifications of Western society's denial of his and his people's humanity. His reflections could be nothing but existential for he was directly engaging the major philosophical questions of his day, while the thinkers he opposed not only denied his humanity but also dismissed his very capacity to reason. Thus Douglass's struggle was waged on ontological, philosophical, and epistemological grounds. Broadus Butler, Cynthia Willet, Lewis Gordon, and others have recognized this conflation of discursive concerns in Douglass's oeuvre. However, to elucidate this chapter's focus on Douglass's abolitionist works of the 1850s, I will analyze Angela Davis's critique of Sartrean existentialism in "Unfinished Lecture on Liberation II" and offer a phenomenological analysis of narrative structure to underscore the import of his thematic repetition in response to the mid-nineteenth-century intensification of racist thought in the United States.

The epigraph to the Givens Collection's edition of *My Bondage and My Freedom* sets the tone for what proves to be Douglass's burning existential question: How has the system of chattel slavery made it possible for human beings to be reduced to the ignoble status of things and, consequently, property? On the title page Douglass quotes Samuel Taylor Coleridge: "By a principal essential to Christianity, a PERSON is eternally differenced from a THING; so that the idea of a HUMAN BEING necessarily excludes the idea of PROPERTY IN THAT BEING." Here Douglass presents readers with the narrative and ontological framework through which he will recount the events of his life as a slave—the property of another—and as a fugitive and freeman who was able to lay claim to his own body and existence. The pressing nature of enslaved Africans' status as property figured so prominently in his mind that in his preface he reminds his audience of two relevant facts. First and foremost, Douglass clarifies that in recent years (the 1850s) he has refused to narrate the personal events of his life at public speaking engagements so as to avoid charges of self-aggrandizement and self-promotion. Instead he opts to address "the questions of Slavery in light of fundamental principles" and "placed [his] opposition to slavery . . . upon the indestructible and unchangeable laws of human nature, every one of which is perpetually and flagrantly violated by the slave system" (2). The basic principles, the fixed natural laws of humanity to which he refers, are those epigrammatic remarks on the absolute and natural differences between people and property.

Second, Douglass assures readers that his intent in writing a second autobiographical work is not to assume the popular nineteenth-century role of the heroic narrator "but to vindicate a just and beneficent principle, in its application to the whole human family, by letting in the light of truth upon a system" (2). Advocating for Freedom as a manifestation of human existence belonging to all of humanity became Douglass's raison d'être as an activist and philosopher. His implication that Freedom is inextricable from the experience of being human establishes Douglass as a theoretical forebear to Sartre, who declared, "What we call human freedom is impossible to distinguish from the *being* of 'human reality'" (*Being and Nothingness* 60). Ironically Sartre iterates this conceptualization as a free European man, someone who had neither been enslaved nor experienced systemic, racialized oppression. It is this irony that Davis explores in "Unfinished Lecture on Liberation II."

Deftly using the example of Douglass's narration of his enslavement, resistance, and escape, Davis questions the relevance of Sartre's proclamation for the lived reality of enslaved Africans in the Americas. Could the enslaved be said to possess their natural human Freedom in spite of the material conditions of bondage requiring them to risk death in order to actualize Freedom? And since physical death precludes the lived, temporal experience of Freedom, could enslaved Africans truly experience their liberty? Through her example of Douglass's resistance, Davis answers these questions with her postulation that the attainment of Freedom was realized when Douglass challenged the concrete and ideological structures of the master-slave relationship—the bit, the whip, the stocks, and the master-slave dyad of owner and property (Davis 131–32). Certainly Douglass's rejection of the concrete, hegemonic markers of subjugation explains his use of narrative repetition in his autobiographical work, for he highlights his triumph over the slave system's mortal combination of physical and psychological brutality, specifically designed to disconnect him and all slaves from their inherent sense of Freedom. This is why he asks throughout *My Bondage and My Freedom*, "O, why was I born a man, of whom to make a brute" (166). As a thinking person he is aware that his enslavement vivifies the philosophy of racial subjugation designed to obliterate his natural relationship to his own Freedom, seemingly enforcing his transformation into a subhuman brute. This overarching system of racist hegemony notwithstanding, Douglass prevailed and escaped to the North. Despite the reality of their bondage and systematized subjugation, enslaved Africans apprehended their Freedom as inseparable from and intrinsic to their existence as human beings. Like Douglass, they first understood, then visualized, and finally actualized their Freedom. The fact that enslaved Africans constantly reaffirmed their humanity, actualized their resistance, and maintained their adherence to African ancestral and cultural expressions, in spite of the torrent of punishments and legislative measures employed to crush their will, speaks to a collective ontological self-awareness and self-worth. This is precisely the "collective being, the ontological totality" (Robinson 171) of the Black radical tradition. Enslaved Africans' resistance to the physical and psychological oppression borne out in the chattel slave system's adherence to racist epistemes supports the veracity of Douglass's statement in "Lecture on Slavery No. 2" (1850), where he offers a statement on the human character as Freedom personified that is strikingly existentialist and foreshadows one Sartre would make two centuries later. Douglass clarifies, "Such is the truth of man's right to liberty. It existed in the very idea of man's creation. It was *his* even before he comprehended it. *He was created in it, endowed with it, and it can never be taken from him. No laws, no statutes, no compacts, no compromises, no constitutions, can abrogate or destroy it*" (140). Similarly, two centuries later Sartre contends, "Man is free, man is freedom. . . . Of course, freedom as the definition of man does not depend on others" (*Existentialism and Human Emotions* 23, 46). For Douglass, and later Sartre, human freedom exists unequivocally. No physical condition or lived reality, be it fettered bondage or unfettered liberty, can change this immutable fact. Freedom exists with or without its physical or concrete manifestation; it can neither be granted nor taken away for it exists as a potentiality that can always be made actual. This is what Douglass and other enslaved Africans proved through their four centuries of resistance. They knew themselves to be free and they used their agency to actualize their Freedom as fugitives, agitators, and insurrectionists. In this regard a potential ending for this portion of Davis's lecture on Douglass would be that he and other enslaved Africans who resisted chattel slavery's physical and psychological fetters to destroy the master-slave relationship should be understood as proto-existentialists.

Despite Douglass's bold escape, his tireless life work in the cause of Freedom, and his increasingly philosophical writings and lectures in the 1850s, it is Sartre who is readily and commonly identified as a humanistic philosopher concerned with the equality of humankind. This axiomatic tendency of elevation in the case of Sartre and negation in the case of Douglass is due to the fact that

> the role of the Black philosopher . . . has been both formidable and
> paradoxical. It has been formidable, because it always has had to
> be taken into account. It has been paradoxical, because once taken
> into account it has been either co-opted or denied full status and
> recognition. . . . The preponderance of Black American philo-
> sophical inquiry . . . has combined ontological analysis with moral
> prescription—the analysis of what is with the analysis of what ought to
> be. (Butler 1)

Broadus Butler's analysis of Douglass as a philosopher is astute in its evaluation of the epistemological structures that preclude Douglass's (and other African American philosophers') inclusion within the ranks of Western thinkers; in addition Butler rightfully underscores the prevalence of ontological analysis in the works of Douglass and other philosophers of African descent. Nonetheless it may also be argued that the ontological analysis that defined Douglass's mid-nineteenth-century literary and oratorical works became increasingly prominent as he witnessed scientific racism's ascendance within Western thought. This forced him to decry its deployment in the relegation of human beings to the status of property under the chattel slave system.

In *My Bondage and My Freedom* Douglass elucidates this commodification of human beings by recalling a shift in his relationship with his mistress, Sophia Auld, and her son, Tommy. Remarking on the way the system's imputation of unchecked slaveholder power destroyed his mistress's relationship with him, Douglass writes that he, his mistress, and her son

> got on swimmingly together, for a time. I say *for a time*, because the
> fatal poison of irresponsible power, and the natural influence of slavery
> customs, were not long in making a suitable impression on the gentle
> and loving disposition of my excellent mistress. At first, Mrs. Auld
> evidently regarded me simply as a child, like any other child; she had
> not come to regard me as *property*. This latter thought was a thing of
> conventional growth. The first was natural and spontaneous. A noble
> nature, like hers, could not, instantly, be wholly perverted; and it took
> several years to change the natural sweetness of her temper into fretful
> bitterness. (107)

Douglass acknowledges that slaveholders' embrace of abusive power,
sanctioned by the dominant culture, is precisely what distorted his mistress's nature and subsequent treatment toward him. Once it became
possible for her to view him as her property there was no need for her to
treat him as a child or, more specifically, the precocious child to whom
she read Bible verses and provided early reading lessons (108). Sophia
Auld's gradual apprehension of Douglass as property, and Douglass's
own opposition to this necessary feature of slaveholding praxis, is best
clarified through an explication of chattel slavery's ontological nullification that

> denies the slave any status as an Other or a self. The slave is property,
> which means that the (unjust) legal system of slavery regards him as no
> more than a system of relations: a "life estate"; a "fee simple absolute
> estate"; a "fee simple absolute subject to conditions subsequent." These
> are terms in Anglo property law. . . . In none of these relations is there
> a slave's point of view. To state a slave's point of view is to initiate a rup-
> ture in such a system. (Gordon, *Existentia Africana* 47–48)

Gordon's elucidation of the slave as a system of relations, as opposed to
a human being, clarifies the fact that slaveholders perceived their chattel as lacking any ontogenic reality in their own right. Their reasoning was that a life estate, or living property, could possess no inherent
rights: no property, since property could not own property; no family, the common thinking being that slaves' family relations were not
"worth" maintaining; and finally no will other than the slaveholder's.
The fact that Douglass related his experiences in slavery in order to
challenge the system of ideas at its core, from the pre–Civil War years
to Reconstruction and into the 1890s prior to his death, represents the
very conceptual rupture that Gordon describes. It is one that caused
the same reactionary dissuasion that Douglass elicited from the Garrisonians when he announced his intent to launch his own newspaper,

the *North Star* (*My Bondage and My Freedom* 298). It may be argued that the Garrisonians' "carefully crafted discipline of unseeing" (Gordon, *Existentia Africana* 61) led Douglass to establish his positions in "Claims," and both "Lecture on Slavery No. 1" and "Lecture on Slavery No. 2."

On December 1, 1850, Douglass delivered "Lecture on Slavery No. 1" at Corinthians Hall in Rochester, New York. In it he explains

> the legal and social relation of master and slave. A master is one (to speak in the vocabulary of the Southern States) who claims and exercises a right of property in the person of a fellow man. This he does with the force of the law. . . . The law gives the master absolute power over the slave. He may work him, flog him, hire him out, sell him, and, in certain contingencies, *kill* him, with perfect impunity. The slave is a human being, divested of all rights—placed beyond the circle of human brotherhood—cut off from his kind—his name. (135)

Douglass's description of the master-slave legal relation vivifies Gordon's description of the slave as a system of relations. In his portrayal of the master as one empowered by legal statutes to enforce utter subjugation, Douglass lays bare the lived and actual consequences of categorizing human slaves as subhuman property. He also notes that the slaves' condition of bondage is predicated upon their placement outside the human family, which in effect justifies the system's codification of slaves' nonexistent rights.

In contrast to the slave system's reduction of human beings to property, Douglass also emphasizes Freedom as the quintessence of human existence in his letter to Thomas Auld, his former owner. In it he states his reasons for writing on the anniversary of his escape and vividly recalls, "Just ten years ago this beautiful September morning, yon bright sun beheld me a slave—a poor, degraded chattel—trembling at the sound of your voice, lamenting that I was a man, and wishing myself a brute" ("Letter to His Old Master" 324). Douglass makes clear to his former owner that neither slavery's systematic denial of his humanity, nor his owner's own immorality could alienate him from the conscious awareness of his very self. He wishes that he had been born a brute so that he could be less conscious of his bondage. He continues to mine the existential implications of his past enslavement by apprising Auld of his moral justifications for actualizing his emancipation:

> The morality of the act, I dispose as follows: I am myself; you are yourself; we are two distinct persons. What you are, I am. You are a man,

and so am I. . . . I am not by nature bound to you, or you to me. Nature
does not make your existence depend upon me, or mine to depend
upon yours. . . . We are distinct persons, and are each equally provided
with faculties necessary to our individual existence. In leaving you, I
took nothing but what belonged to me. (325)

In this explanation Douglass shatters the fundamental principle at the
heart of the master-slave relation: the precept that slaves have no will
of their own and are merely the living manifestation of their masters'
dominion and will. He argues convincingly for his ontological autonomy and furthers this position, stressing that his flight was no real
crime since he took only that which was naturally his: his body, his
Freedom, and his own existence.

Douglass's autobiographical reflections on the experiential nature of
his existence in slavery and in freedom, as well as his focus on morality
and philosophy, offer a phenomenological glimpse of narrative's power.
Carr's philosophical reflections on history combine narrative theory
and Heideggerian phenomenology to identify "narrative structure [as]
the organizing principle not only of experiences and actions but of the
self who experiences and acts. The broad sense of the 'practical' . . . is
broad enough to finally merge with the moral and ethical. . . . This
broadest sense is concerned . . . with the question of how to live one's
life as a whole, and with questions about the nature of individual human
existence, character, and personal identity" (73). In using his life experiences to advocate for the abolition of slavery, Douglass addresses the
immoral and unethical nature of the slave system while challenging his
readers' sense of fidelity to their slaveholding nation. He challenges his
audience as American citizens, prodding their commitment to a nation
founded on the principles of equality and democracy yet dependent on
a system of naked exploitation for its socioeconomic and geopolitical
power. He also rather poignantly highlights the existential implications
of categorizing enslaved Africans' as property, instead of recognizing
them as the introspective human beings they are.

Carr avows that while autobiographies are commonly perceived as
retrospective reflections, they should also be understood as textual
attempts to render the past more coherent in its connection to the present and the future. Additionally, since authors of autobiographies often
experience extreme religious or political conversions, their introspection seeks to render a "multiplicity of activities and [life] projects" into
a cohesive whole (75). Douglass's autobiographical oeuvre, his oratorical addresses, and his letter to his former owner attest to this unifying

feature of historiographical narrative. His existential and political conversion occurred the moment he realized that his Freedom was his and his alone. This transformation led him to rebel and eventually escape the plantation to begin his life as a publicly recognized abolitionist. His past life as a slave is illuminated through his work as an abolitionist and vice versa. Douglass's past as another man's chattel and his present as a freeman and abolitionist are reconciled through his work as an orator, which allows him to imbue these seemingly contrasting identities with an overarching, integrated narrative purpose: freedom, justice, and equality for enslaved Africans and all Americans. His multivalent projects of autobiographical reflection, oratory, and correspondence in the 1850s projected the image of his slave past so as to render it applicable to the present reality of slavery and a potential future of emancipation and equality that had existed only in his mind's eye. Through these various life projects in the cause of equality, Douglass creates a philosophical synthesis in which his experiences in bondage, his self-education, and his ascendance to statesman are used as living examples to nullify the epistemological structure of scientific racism at the heart of America's racial inequities.

Nearly a century and a half later, Paul Gilroy highlighted Douglass's commitment to challenging the erasure of ancient Africa within the narrative of civilization's development in Western discourse. He also notes that although Douglass does not mention Hegel by name (in his speeches or writings), his relationship with Ottilia Assing, the German translator of *My Bondage and My Freedom*, suggests his exposure to several German philosophers, including Hegel (Gilroy, *Black Atlantic* 60). Hegel's philosophy of historical development in *Lectures on the Philosophy of World History*, which banishes Africa and Africans from the annals of human civilization, would begin its lasting impact on Western discourse in the nineteenth century as chattel slavery in America was entering its final decades. Hegel's analysis of world history is so blatantly anti-African and rife with European chauvinism that he characterizes the chattel slave system as a civilizing measure that instilled in Africans their negligible humanity since "the only significant connection between Negroes and the Europeans has been—and still is—that of slavery" for "the condition in which [Africans] live is capable of no development or culture, and their present existence is the same as it has always been" (183, 190).

It is quite clear that Hegel's anti-African position represents a continuation of Enlightenment racist thought expressed in the writings of

Hume, Kant, and Jefferson. Hegel, however, goes even further than his predecessors. He establishes his theory of world history through the development of the human spirit, but his model of collective human ontological development is tainted in its treatment of the African continent as a civilizational void, since in his view "[Africa] has no history in the truest sense of the word. . . . For it is an unhistorical continent with no movement or development of its own" (190). In Hegel's view Africa was, and will ever remain, apart from the advancing tide of global history and culture. To further this position, and to stress the separateness of Egypt from the remainder of the African continent, Hegel asserts, "Africa consists of three continents, which are entirely separate from one another, and between which there is no contact whatsoever. The first of these is Africa proper. . . . The second is the land to the north of the desert . . . which might be described as European Africa. And the third is the region of the Nile, the only valley land of Africa, which is closely connected with Asia" (173).

In addition to portraying Egypt as an African region isolated and distinct from the remainder of the continent, Hegel continues the hegemonic project of depicting this ancient African civilization as Asiatic and all of northern Africa as European. But this historiographical revision seems to have been insufficient in its treatment of African negation, for he also establishes his claim of African non-Being by stating that Africans are bereft of that which separates human beings from animals—the conscious awareness of their own Being: "The characteristic feature of the Negroes is that their consciousness has not yet reached an awareness of any substantial objectivity, for example of God or the law—in which the will of man could participate and in which he could become aware of his own being" (177). In *Lectures*, a work that is widely considered a peak in Western letters, Hegel has relegated Africans to the status of animals, lacking a moral and spiritual core that would create self-awareness. His theory of African non-Being furthers the dualism of anti-African and Eurocentric discourse by establishing a negative ontological rubric in which African identity, or blackness, has no a priori significance. For Hegel, black African identity becomes merely a reflexive point of white Western self-reference, not an ontogenic reality in its own right.[24] Following the theoretical lead of Hume, Kant, and Jefferson, Hegel's staunch insistence on European cultural, moral, and intellectual superiority and an all-encompassing African inferiority reveals the degree to which eighteenth- and nineteenth-century Western philosophy became defined by a hegemonic imperative to historicize Africans and African enslavement in terms that would further the interdependent discourses of anti-African racism, chattel slavery, and Western capitalism.

Since Douglass was aware of Hegelianism's ideological impact, it is clear that his focus on debunking chattel slavery's philosophical roots may be read as an antihegemonic exercise whose purpose was to discredit the theoretical and practical bases of enslaved African subjugation through the revelation of the Negro's crucial place in Western history. Douglass forges ahead in "Claims," citing historical evidence of the Negro as the creator of Western civilization and recalling Egypt's influence on ancient Greece and Rome. At the same time he also challenges the Hegelian practice (used by the American school ethnologists) of excising Egypt and northern Africa from the African continent:

> The desirableness of isolating the Negro race, and especially of separating them from the various peoples of Northern Africa, is too plain to need a remark. Such isolation would remove stupendous difficulties in the way of getting the Negro in a favorable attitude for the blows of scientific Christendom. Dr. Samuel George Morton may be referred to as a fair sample of American Ethnologists. His . . . *"Crania Americana" . . .* is widely read in this country.—In this great work his contempt for Negroes, is ever conspicuous. I take him as an illustration of what had been alleged as true of his class. The fact that Egypt was one of the earliest abodes of learning and civilization, is as firmly established as are the everlasting hills. . . . smiling serenely on the assaults and the mutations of time, there she stands in overshadowing grandeur, riveting the eye and the mind of the modern world—upon her, in silent and dreamy wonder—Greece and Rome—and through them Europe and America have received their civilization from the ancient Egyptians. This fact is not denied by anybody. But Egypt is in Africa. (296)

Douglass highlights Morton's obvious reasons for attempting to extricate Egypt from the remainder of the African continent, for admitting Egypt's undeniable geographical position and cultural connections to the African continent would destroy the American ethnologists' firm position on innate African inferiority on historiographical, cultural, and practical grounds.

The Africana counterhegemonic tradition of interpellating ancient Egyptian history as proof of both African humanity and the evils of Western slavery did not end with Walker and Douglass. Three decades after Douglass delivered "Claims," in 1883, George Washington Williams published his two-volume work, *History of the Negro Race in*

America, citing the ancient writings of Herodotus and the more modern accounts of Volney as evidence of both the ancient Egyptians' African racial identity and the African contribution to Western civilization. While Williams's work was considered the first significant historical work by an African American author and was widely reviewed, other less celebrated texts, like Edward Augustus Johnson's *A School History of the Negro Race* (1891) and Leila Amos Pendleton's *Narrative of the Negro* (1912), invoked ancient Egypt as the cradle of civilization whose influence spread northward to Greece. These groundbreaking works were used as standard textbooks for Negro schools in North Carolina and Washington, D.C., respectively in the late nineteenth and early twentieth centuries (Bruce 684–88). Clearly Walker and Douglass had inspired a new generation of African American vindicationists to challenge racist thought's ascendance in Western discourse.

Scientific racism's categorical negation of African humanity, historicality, and intellectualism created the perfect conditions for this thought system's ascendance to the rank of an epistemology during the final two centuries of Western chattel slavery's existence. Ironically, by positioning Africans at the bottom of the racial hierarchy, Hume, Kant, Jefferson, Hegel, and the American school ethnologists catalyzed two centuries of theoretical resistance among Africana thinkers and writers premised upon the existential paradox of African non-Being. Just as these white American and European thinkers were proclaiming Africana peoples incapable of thought, Walker, Douglass, and others were at work creating a vindicationist, abolitionist countercanon that discredited their theoretical adversaries' claims. Not only did the works of Hume, Kant, Jefferson, and Hegel force the very intellectual response of which they believed Africana people incapable, but they also inspired a three-centuries-long legacy of epistemological resistance in which Africana thinkers pondered questions of Being and Freedom. It seems clear that Hume, Kant, Jefferson, and Hegel knew that the battleground for cultural and political supremacy would be fought and won on the fields of historical and philosophical discourse. But so too did Walker and Douglass. Through their epistemological critiques of racist thought, Walker and Douglass announced their roles as historical agents and philosophers who countered the Humean logic of scientific racism underpinning the chattel slave system. Their counter-hegemonic abolitionist treatises position Africana people as central to the historiographical, sociopolitical, and cultural spheres from which they were seemingly exiled. Thus Walker and Douglass forcefully challenged aspects of the very Western philosophical tradition that had denied them.

Two early twentieth-century Africana thinkers would continue Walker's and Douglass's recuperative mission by reinvigorating Marxism through the experience of enslaved Africans. W. E. B. Du Bois's and C. L. R. James's preoccupation with the material conditions and lived reality of enslaved Africans recasts this collectivity as workers, the proletariat source of modern Western capitalism who simultaneously acted as liberationist agents to topple Western empire in the Caribbean.

CHAPTER TWO

The African Diasporic Proletariat

We can now say that the Western intellectual tradition operates within an exclusionary paradigm. . . . For the African human, the exclusion was complete—it was both ontological and epistemic erasure. Both these forms of erasure have profoundly shaped contemporary discussions about black thought—the meaning and construction of intellectual traditions.

—Anthony Bogues, *Black Heretics, Black Prophets*

Where the nineteenth-century Africana vindicationists David Walker and Frederick Douglass sought to connect Negro American history to a larger historical discourse that situated ancient Africa as the foundation of Western civilization, two twentieth-century Africana philosophers sought to reconceptualize enslaved Africans in the Americas as workers, an African diasporic proletariat central to the birth of modern Western capitalism and empire. W. E. B. Du Bois's *Black Reconstruction in America, 1860–1880* (1935) and C. L. R. James's *The Black Jacobins: Toussaint L'Ouverture and the San Domingo Revolution* (1938) mark a shift within the disciplines of history and political philosophy as their African diasporic and anticapitalist themes were put forth at a time when Western history was dominated by more parochial studies of the nation-state. Although "transnational perspectives appeared in the work of W. E. B. Du Bois, notably in *Black Reconstruction*, of the West Indian Trotskyite C. L. R. James, and other black activist-scholars . . . they were marginalized by professional academics" who established the discipline's parameters around local histories of the nation-state (Tyrell 1018–20). Despite the peripheral status of *Black Reconstruction* and *The Black Jacobins* in the Western historiographical canon, these texts initiated a discursive transition in early twentieth-century historical discourse as both works "inaugurate [a] shift in focus from the nation-state to a transnational or Pan-African frame of refer-

ence" (Edwards, "Dossier on Black Radicalism" 4). Thus Du Bois and
James must be understood as Black radical thinkers during the post–
World War I era, a time rife with Pan-Africanist, anti-imperialist, and
global Black radical activity in the Francophone, Anglophone, and Hispanophone segments of the African diaspora.[1]

The epistemological import of *Black Reconstruction* and *The Black
Jacobins* lies in their historiographical and theoretical correctives to
Western radical theory's marginalization of Africana peoples within the
interrelated narratives of modern Western capitalist development, industrialization, and Western empire. Because Du Bois and James recontex-
tualize the enslaved and colonized African population of the Americas as
black workers and a black proletariat, respectively, their works are seminal interdisciplinary texts that subvert what Marx termed the "'idealist historiography' and . . . theoretical procedures of the Enlightenment"
(qtd. in R. Williams 18) and Marx's own science of history. In *Black
Reconstruction* and *The Black Jacobins*, Du Bois and James go beyond
creating oppositional sociopolitical theory. Their works actually redefine
Marxian thought by placing enslaved African labor at its center, thereby
redirecting the timeline of historical materialism and reconceptualizing
its lexical framework. The periodization and primary terms of engagement for Western modernity and proletariat mass action, then, become
the four centuries of Western chattel slavery, and enslaved African diasporic proletarians are now historical agents of social revolution. Though
Marxism's anticapitalist critique represents a watershed development in
Western thought, its principal focus on the European proletariat reveals
an ethnic chauvinism that is both highlighted and problematized by Du
Bois and James. *Black Reconstruction* and *The Black Jacobins* break with
both traditional and radical Western historiography in their related theses that define Western chattel slavery as the primary source of modern
capitalist accumulation. Their repositioning of enslaved African labor
as the principal material and socioeconomic foundation of modernity
insists on a counterhegemonic reading of Western history and theory
that reveals Africana peoples as foundational agents in Western societal
progress, no longer subordinate to the Marxian European proletariat.

While Du Bois turned to Marxism after having witnessed the limits
of liberalism in his fight for Negro American equality, and James was
a self-proclaimed "trained Trotskyite" when he wrote *The Black Jacobins*,[2] both were moved by the historical, ideological, and sociopolitical
forces of their day. Their dual identification as socialists and black radical thinkers seemingly compelled them to problematize and expand

Western radical theory's scope by foregrounding the monumental event of African racial slavery in the West. In contrast to Marxian thought, their texts emphasize that the capitalist accumulation of chattel slavery should not be deemed subordinate to that of seventeenth-century European mill production, for James's reinterpretation of Marxist theory "[places] colonialism and plantation slavery both at the rosy dawn of the accumulation process and central to nineteenth-century economic developments. . . . In standard Marxist historical narrative, the birth of capitalist production originated during the late 1700s with the emergence of mills production and the production of textiles. Plantation slavery was subsidiary to this, and slave labor an anomaly" (Bogues 79). Quite rightly Bogues highlights the manner in which *The Black Jacobins* challenges the Marxian chronology of capitalist accumulation by elucidating Western chattel slavery's relationship to the unprecedented growth of Western plantation economies. However, this equation was first proffered in Du Bois's *Black Reconstruction*,[3] where Du Bois links American capitalist accumulation to the Industrial Revolution and to an enslaved African diasporic proletariat and its corollary in the exploited colonial workforces of Asia (5, 15, 210–13, 583–87, 728).

As African diasporic subjects who matured in the wake of chattel slavery's demise, Du Bois and James demonstrate that Western slavery ushered in the modern capitalist system. As black radical thinkers, they were further compelled to challenge anti-African and white supremacist ideologies in Western discourse, as these not only perpetuated Africana inequality in the years immediately following Emancipation, but their legacy of racism continued well into the twentieth century and dictated the sociopolitical and cultural zeitgeist of these thinkers' time. Their preoccupation with the nineteenth century, the "century of resistance," as John Henrik Clarke averred (47), became the sociopolitical and phenomenological foundation of their Black radical thought:

> [Their] era began with the ending of slavery. They were, it might be said, the children of the slaves. The phenomenology of slavery formed and informed them. And in the vortex of its ending, more particularly in the wake of the social forces that compelled new and different situatings of Blacks and others destined to serve as labor forces, these theorists discovered their shared social and intellectual location. The twentieth century was for the most part their biographical station, but merely one site in the zone of their interrogation. (Robinson 177)

One site in Du Bois's and James's field of inquiry was thereby informed by the phenomenology of slavery and its dialectical counterpoint: Africana resistance. Phenomenology's focus on the analysis, description, and meaning of Being (Schrader 33–34; Kocklemans 664–66) renders it germane to explorations of human existence, especially those centered on the exigencies of enslavement and resistance. It seems a matter of course that as twentieth-century thinkers Du Bois and James would utilize the Marxian map of historical materialism to explore the phenomenological dimensions of enslavement and oppression (for enslaved and free Africans) to enrich their histories of American Reconstruction and the San Domingo Revolution, respectively.

The legacy of scientific racism and the prevalence of twentieth-century social Darwinist thought as framing hegemonic discourses, their centrality to chattel slavery and second-wave imperialism, as well as their sociopolitical and quotidian manifestations in twentieth-century Western culture, represent the other "zone of interrogation" informing Du Bois's and James's scholarship. As they wrote and published *Black Reconstruction* and *The Black Jacobins*, both thinkers played pivotal roles in the early twentieth-century Pan-African movement, which was founded on the related ideological and political precepts of anti-imperialism and African diasporic unity. Through their scholarship and activism the African diaspora is realized in both theory and praxis. This conflation of philosophical and sociopolitical discursive aims is realized in *Black Reconstruction* and *The Black Jacobins*, as both texts explore the material and psychological effects of Western hegemony on the African diasporic workers at their center. This thematic focus, in addition to Du Bois's and James's revision of Marxian thought, is what established these works as inaugural texts of Black radical and Black Atlantic studies.[4]

Cedric Robinson, Paul Gilroy, and Anthony Bogues generally agree that Du Bois's and James's primary contribution as radical theorists is their reinvigoration of Marxism, which foregrounds the Africana historical experience of enslavement, exploitation, resistance, and revolution. Robinson's *Black Marxism* situates *Black Reconstruction* and *The Black Jacobins* as literary encapsulations of the Black radical tradition, citing the authors' principal inspiration as the four-centuries-long praxis of Africana agency and resistance during and after the chattel slavery era (184). Using Pierre Bourdieu's definition of *heresy* to explain Du Bois's and James's Black radical critique of Marxism, Bogues categorizes *Black Reconstruction* and *The Black Jacobins* as heretical discourses for two reasons: the works proclaim the humanity and agency of enslaved Africans in the Americas while simultaneously challenging established Western doxa that declare the authors' (and all African peoples') ontological negation and epistemological irrelevance (70–71). Both Robinson and Bogues make extremely insightful arguments about Du Bois's and James's reconceptualization of Marxist historiography; however, it must also be noted that Du Bois's discussion of American capitalist oligarchy prefigures the Marxist theorist Antonio Gramsci's conceptualization of hegemony. In addition few critics have thoroughly examined the manner in which Du Bois and James use the ostensibly Marxist analytical structures of *Black Reconstruction* and *The Black Jacobins* as starting points for psychological and existential examinations of Being and Freedom among the enslaved African diasporic proletariat of the Americas. They explore Being and Freedom by revealing how the enslaved Africans' material conditions in bondage catalyzed an existential awareness of their innate human agency and Freedom, particularly in the figures of Du Bois's free Negro and James's Haitian freedom fighters.[5] This existential focus substantiates Broadus Butler's assertion that the aim of Black philosophers has been to actualize the principle of justice, a process that entails ontological analysis (1–2). Du Bois and James fulfill this philosophical task while also highlighting the theoretical import of African diasporic mass action and revolution for Western socioeconomic growth and progress.

To fully appreciate the import of Du Bois's and James's material and existential analyses, it is necessary to understand that *Black Reconstruction* and *The Black Jacobins* enumerate the details of enslaved Africans' highly exploitative material conditions—conditions that Du Bois and James consistently define as the necessary by-products of Western ruling-class hegemony. Both texts then dovetail into interrogations of existential issues that strictly Marxist analyses would necessarily obviate. This distinct combination of Black radicalism, Marxist historiography, and existential probing distinguishes their works as groundbreaking interdisciplinary texts that display converging philosophical concerns and perform interrelated discursive functions. First, *Black Reconstruction* and *The Black Jacobins* refute canonical claims of African ahistoricality and circumscribed historical relevance in traditional and radical Western histories. Second, both works stand as quintessential theoretical encapsulations of what Robinson has termed the Black radical tradition, a tradition that seeks to restore "collective ontological totality" to Africana peoples (168–71). Third, in these works the treatment of Being and Freedom among enslaved Africans in the Americas predates later existential exegeses in European thought after World War II.

To begin, we must first consider the enormity of Du Bois's epistemo-logical challenge to Marxist thought and American historiography in *Black Reconstruction*, for its earlier publication makes it the preeminent twentieth-century Black radical and Black Atlantic text. Moreover in 1971 James himself remarked on the tremendous impact the work had on his own philosophical evolution ("Lectures" 84–98). *Black Reconstruction* presents a history of American Reconstruction that high-lights Marxism's Eurocentricity by delineating chattel slavery's links to Western capitalism, industrialization, and empire. In so doing Du Bois outlines a pre-Gramscian description of ruling-class hegemony as the overarching power structure that made nineteenth-century West-ern industrialism and empire a matter of course. Du Bois opens with this declaration: "Easily the most dramatic episode in American his-tory was the sudden move to free four million black slaves in an effort to stop a great civil war, to end forty years of bitter controversy, and to appease the moral sense of civilization" (*Black Reconstruction* 3). He then skillfully decenters European proletariat labor as the primary source of capitalist accumulation by showing that the enormous prof-its of chattel slavery fed the North's and the West's burgeoning steel, railway, and manufacturing economies. He provides a detailed analy-sis of how the nineteenth-century American sociopolitical and cultural landscape became defined by social Darwinist thought and the codi-fication of racism. The hegemonic imperative of white supremacy and Negro enslavement and disenfranchisement is reflected in his indict-ment against the American historical profession as the institutional agent of Western domination. *Black Reconstruction*'s final chapter, "The Propaganda of History," lambastes American historians for perpetuat-ing the fallacy of Negro American culpability in the failure of Recon-struction, thereby highlighting their failure to adhere to their own principles of scientific objectivity. Du Bois closes *Black Reconstruction* by urging readers to consider Western chattel slavery and Emancipa-tion as two epochal moments in the human drama that is the making of Western civilization.

Du Bois himself attempts to redress the chauvinism of Western canonical historiography by highlighting chattel slavery, Emancipa-tion, and Black Reconstruction's significance for the making of the modern American nation. This is his theoretical reinvention, his his-torical revelation.

DU BOISIAN REVELATION

Du Bois announces his theoretical intent in the title of *Black Recon-struction*. By renaming American Reconstruction, he foregrounds African American humanity and agency during one of the most con-tentious and blatantly anti-African periods in modern Western history. Who, before Du Bois, had ever referred to American Reconstruction as a specifically *Black* historical and sociopolitical event? The preface, "To the Reader," reflects this innovation and Du Bois's position on con-temporary theories of African inferiority, while providing a revealing self-reflexive commentary on his Western reading public. He charges, "It would only be fair to the reader to say frankly in advance that the attitude of any person towards this story will be distinctly influenced by his theories of the Negro race. . . . In fine, I am going to tell this story as though Negroes were ordinary human beings, realizing that this attitude will from the first seriously curtail my audience" (n.p.). He thus challenges both the late nineteenth-century scientific racism of the Reconstruction era and contemporary twentieth-century social Darwinist theories of African lowliness with his declaration of African humanity and implying its necessary by-product: agency.

The first chapter, "The Black Worker," establishes Du Bois's radical historiographical method, as he inserts enslaved and free Africans into the lexicon and timeline of historical materialism. The African slave is now the black worker, and with this new appellation he commits the unprecedented act of reenvisioning Western history and radical theory by defining chattel slavery as a system of labor that irrevocably shaped the modern world. Robinson explains, "Slavery was the specific histori-cal institution through which the Black *worker* had been introduced into the world system. However it was not as *slaves* that one could come to an understanding of the significance that these Black men, women and children had for American development. It was as *labor*" (199). This renaming of enslaved Africans as Black workers forces a reconsidera-tion of Black labor's significance and its pivotal role in capitalist accu-mulation for colonial and antebellum America and, as Du Bois argues, for the entire Western world. In the pages immediately following, Du Bois compels the reader to apprehend the enormous import of enslaved African labor for three interconnected developments in Western his-tory: modern industrialization, global capitalism, and Western empire:

> The giant forces of water and of steam were harnessed to do the world's
> work, and the black workers of America bent at the bottom of a grow-

ing pyramid of commerce and industry; and not only could they not be spared, if this new economic organization was to expand, but rather they became the cause of new political demands and alignments, of new dreams of power and visions of empire. . . . Black labor became the foundation stone not only of the Southern social structure, but of Northern manufacture and commerce, of the English factory system, of European commerce. (5)

Du Bois's vivid depiction of exploited Black labor fueling the global capitalist machine makes immediately clear the necessity of enslaved labor for the West's capitalist imperative and for what he later terms "industrial empire." By emphasizing the socioeconomic causality between industrialization and capitalist empire building, he further connects the South's consolidation of agricultural and political power to its calculated disenfranchisement of Negro Americans. This combination of agricultural and industrial ruling-class dominance gave birth to what he terms America's capitalist dictatorship—an economic totalitarianism that, through its disenfranchisement of Negro Americans, effectively set the stage for Western empire's global degradation of *all* colored laborers: "The black voter struggled and appealed, but it was in vain. And the United States, reinforced by the increased political power of the South based on disfranchisement of black voters, took its place to reinforce the capitalistic dictatorship of the United States, which became the most powerful in the world, and which backed the new industrial imperialism and degraded colored labor the world over" (630).

Du Bois links chattel slavery, its late nineteenth-century demise, and the degradation of black labor to the rise of European colonial empires and their exploited labor forces in Africa and Asia. He contextualizes this shift from Western chattel slavery to exploited African and Asian colonial labor by stressing social Darwinism as the accepted ideological rationale for Western exploitation: "Within the very echo of that philanthropy which had abolished the slave trade, was beginning a new industrial slavery of black, brown, and yellow workers in Africa and Asia. Arising from this . . . came the change in attitude towards these darker peoples. . . . They were inferiors. These inferiors were to be governed for their own good. They were to be raised out of sloth and laziness by being compelled to work" (632). Here Du Bois establishes a new chronology of Western modernity, a chronology whose origin lies in chattel slavery, colonialism, and their philosophical foundations in eighteenth- and nineteenth-century scientific racism. Modernity, according to Du Bois, should not be solely understood as the transition from agrarian feudalism to industrial production, as Marx avers (Cox 210–18). Instead modernity must be seen as the epochal culmination of the interrelated sociopolitical and economic forces of chattel slavery and colonialism that gave rise to exploited global labor forces of color in Africa and Asia as well as America, a modernity made possible and acceptable through the influence and legacy of racist thought and praxis. The resultant global outcomes are capitalist dominance, Western imperial expansion, and colonial exploitation. Thus Du Bois's theoretical innovation and his insertion of enslaved African labor within historical materialism's primary terms of engagement—labor, industrialization, capitalism, and modernization—constitute a global, historiographical critique of Western slavery and Marxist thought that centralizes Western hegemony, chattel slavery, and African and Asian colonial exploitation. No longer may "the peculiar institution" be viewed as a historical aberration. Instead it must be understood as a socioeconomic institution integral to the development of Western industry, capitalism, and empire, one that was historically buttressed by the hegemonic legitimization of racist thought.

THE BLACK WORKER'S RESISTANCE

Du Bois introduces chattel slavery's import to global capitalist development in the opening pages of *Black Reconstruction*. He also points to the slave system's impact on Negro American cultural production and charges that this most oppressive and exploitative of labor systems instilled within Negroes a distinct cosmological and philosophical ethos that led to the only true form of American art—the African American oral tradition: "Of all human development, ancient and modern, not the least singular and significant is the philosophy of life and action which slavery bred in the souls of black folk. . . . The subtle folk-lore of Africa, with whimsy and parable, veiled wish and wisdom; and above all fell the anointing chrism of slave music, the only gift of pure art in America. . . . Nothing else of art or religion did the slave South give to the world, except Negro song and story" (14).

Du Bois's assessment of African American orature is extremely revealing for two reasons. First, he locates the oral tradition within a historical continuum of cultural production that represents a watershed moment in Western history, which in turn led to a collective Negro American worldview and apprehension of Negro agency. Second, by identifying slave music as the only indigenous American art form, he highlights the significance of Negro American cultural productions for American culture as a whole. He continues this discussion of African American orature's historical significance by citing Douglass's famous 1852 speech, "What Is the Fourth of July to Me?," as the pinnacle of Negro American oral expression (14). That Du Bois credits African American orature for engendering a "philosophy of life and action" among Negro Americans is extremely significant, for this ethos and agency is precisely what compelled slave populations to rebel against the slave system prior to and during the Civil War, specifically during what he terms "the general strike."

In the fourth chapter, "The General Strike," Du Bois continues to situate chattel slavery and Reconstruction within a global historical context by renaming the cessation of slave labor during the Civil War a general strike. He holds that this strike predates the Russian proletariat's general strike: "Among Negroes, and particularly in the South, there was being put into force one of the most extraordinary experiments of Marxism that the world, before the Russian revolution, had seen" (358). Thus Du Bois shifts the timeline of Marx's proletariat revolution. Further stressing Negro American historicity and agency, he cites the emancipated slaves' determination to end their oppression by crippling the plantation system, despite the abuse they encountered from northern regiments:

> [Black workers] were mistreated by the soldiers; ridiculed; driven away, and yet they came. They increased with every campaign, and as a final gesture, they marched with Sherman from Atlanta to the sea. . . . This was not merely the desire to stop work. It was a strike on a wide basis against the conditions of work. It was a general strike that involved directly in the end perhaps a half million people. They wanted to stop the economy of the plantation system, and to do that they left the plantations. (67)

Prior to *Black Reconstruction*, the cessation of slave labor had never been historicized as a mass action, a systematic effort to shut down the southern plantation economy, because enslaved Africans were perceived neither as workers nor as historical agents. Through Du Bois's insightful periodization, however, the reader is given to understand the general strike's larger historical import for Western history in general and radical history in particular. Du Bois's black worker becomes one segment of a larger African diasporic proletariat that resisted capitalist oppression when it shut down the southern plantation system. His contemporary, James, remarked on this aspect of *Black Reconstruction*'s theoretical innovation:

> When did the idea of the general strike come into industry? . . . It came
> in 1905 in Russia. . . . Du Bois knew that . . . but he said there was a
> general strike that took place in 1862 in the United States by the slaves!
> That's what his chapter on the general strike means. He knew that in
> 1905 that was the historical development and it began there, but he says
> there was one *before* that. There was one by the slaves in the planta-
> tions. And *that* is the writing of history. ("Lectures on the Black Jaco-
> bins" 93)

That James emphasizes Du Bois's historic and historical feat in *Black Reconstruction* indicates his awareness that Du Bois was engaged in the making of history and the rewriting of Western history, a revision that underscored the Africana historical experience of resistance as that which altered the course of modern history itself.

Chapter 14, "The Counter-revolution of Property," introduces the necessary precondition to labor exploitation: ruling-class dominance. Du Bois explains how nineteenth-century American capitalists, both northern industrialists and southern slaveholders, were able to main-tain the unconscious submission and complicity of both black and white laboring classes:

> The guidance and dictatorship of capital for the object of private profit
> were not to be questioned or overthrown; but it must maintain its
> ascendancy by controlling the public opinion of the laboring class.
> This was accomplished . . . by the power to give and withhold employ-
> ment . . . the power to influence public opinion through the prestige of
> wealth, news, and literature, and the power to dominate legislatures,
> courts, and offices of administration. (605)

Du Bois's description of an overarching, insidious ruling-class dom-inance that infiltrates all facets (and classes) of society, culture, and politics bespeaks a pre-Gramscian model of hegemony. Terry Eagle-ton delineates Gramscian hegemony through a model of sociocultural, political, and institutional diffusion that echoes Du Bois's description of ruling-class authority. Insisting that the very success of hegemony lies in its imperceptibility, its inconspicuous merging with the fabric of daily life, Eagleton avows:

> The concept of hegemony thus belongs with the question: How is the
> working class to take power in a social formation where the dominant
> power is subtly, pervasively diffused throughout habitual daily prac-

tices, intimately interwoven with "culture" itself, inscribed in the very
texture of our experiences from nursery school to funeral parlor? How
do we combat a power which has become the "common sense" of the
whole social order, rather than one which is widely perceived as alien
and oppressive? (*Ideology* 114)

As Du Bois and Eagleton show, the hegemonic becomes the everyday
logic of society. This insidious ruling-class dominance is precisely what
Du Bois was challenging in *Black Reconstruction*, although, unlike his
European radical counterparts, he confronted a ruling class that was
not only exploitative but also anti-African and white supremacist. This
particular triumvirate of oppressive forces led him to explain how the
hegemonic aspects of anti-African racism and white supremacy were
manipulated by the southern planter class and the intellectual elite
to ensure chattel slavery's survival, maintain the slaveholders' socioeconomic and political power, and solidify enslaved black workers as
Negroes, separate and utterly apart from humanity. Du Bois goes on
to explain how nineteenth-century thinkers proliferated and disseminated discourses of scientific racism to maintain chattel slavery and
rationalize its legality:

> In order to maintain its income without sacrifice or exertion, the South
> fell back on a doctrine of racial differences which it asserted made higher
> intelligence and increased efficiency impossible for Negro labor.... [The
> planter's] subservient religious leaders reverted to the "Curse of Canaan";
> his pseudo-scientists gathered and supplemented all available doc-
> trines of race inferiority; his scattered schools and pedantic periodicals
> repeated these legends, until for the average planter born after 1840 it
> was impossible not to believe that all valid laws in psychology, economics
> and politics stopped with the Negro race. (38–39)

This perceived cessation of reason in the face of Negro American existence epitomizes the unholy alliance between the southern planter class
and prominent ideologues of nineteenth-century racist thought like the
American school ethnologists, as the previous chapter details. Douglass had vigorously refuted their specious claims, and almost a century
later Du Bois was still struggling against their epistemological legacy.

DU BOIS'S THEORETICAL RESOLVE

Social Darwinist theories of African racial inferiority and ahistoricality were firmly in place by the 1934 publication of *Black Reconstruction*;

consequently Du Bois's scholarship was dismissed and his engagement with Marxist theory, which underscored Africana agency, was considered untenable. It is no wonder, then, that the *American Historical Review* willfully ignored *Black Reconstruction* when it was first published (Tyrell 1018–19). That Du Bois was marginalized by the American historical profession should come as no surprise, for it simply reveals the degree to which his work threatened the putative veracity of canonical histories. His expansion of Marxist terminology and theory and his labeling of chattel slavery as the cornerstone of capitalism may be viewed as "historically and socially *constituting*" language that is indicative of "the *changing practical consciousness of human beings*, in which both the evolutionary and the historical processes can be given full weight" (R. Williams 43). These historical processes are Western chattel slavery and enslaved African toil as black American labor. The changing consciousness is Du Bois's reading audience's newfound awareness of Western slavery's global economic impact. Through his theorization the reader may fully appreciate these historical developments as global socioeconomic and political events that challenge Western theory's focus on Europe and the European proletariat as the progenitors of modern revolution.

Du Bois's radical historiography represents a decisive shift in his application of Marxist theory. As *Black Reconstruction* shows, he recognized Marxism's import for identifying class struggle as the key to ending ruling-class domination, yet *Black Reconstruction* also reveals Marxism's limitations in accommodating a ruling class that is both white supremacist and anti-African. Consequently it should come as no surprise that Du Bois uses *Black Reconstruction* to critique Marxist theory, for he held that Marxism had to be adapted in order to fully address the issues of Negro oppression: "Marxian philosophy is a true diagnosis of the situation in Europe in the middle of the 19th century. . . . But it must be modified in the United States of America and especially so far as the Negro group is concerned" (Du Bois qtd. in Bogues 77).

As *Black Reconstruction* shows and as Du Bois himself reiterated, even Marxism—a radical philosophy created to end ruling-class oppression—is incapable of addressing the enslavement and oppression of a proletariat that is not European but African. This fundamental shortcoming further substantiates the totalizing oppression of enslaved Africans in the West, for if a radical philosophy like Marxism cannot acknowledge chattel slavery as the foundation of Western capitalist development, how can its tenets even attempt to address the subjugation and liberation of Africana peoples? This was one of Du Bois's implicit theses in *Black Reconstruction*: the hegemonic expression of African negation in Western discourse, be it traditional or radical, precludes Western theoretical formulations from fully acknowledging the Negro's crucial role in Western development. Traditional and radical Western theories subordinate the presence, significance, and contribution of black workers to the inception of European proletariat resistance;[6] therefore Du Bois's project of renaming the slave the black worker is actually a project of reconceptualizing history:

> In the changing of the names of things, [Du Bois] sought to provide the basis for a new conceptualization of their relationship. . . . The institution of American slave labor could not be effectively conceptualized as a thing in and of itself. Rather, it was a particular historical development for world capitalism which expropriated the labor of African workers as primitive accumulation. American slavery was a *subsystem* of world capitalism. (Robinson 199–200)

Robinson deftly highlights Du Bois's terminological revision as that which radically alters the reader's understanding of the undeniable yet commonly overlooked link between Western slavery and modern capitalism. Through *Black Reconstruction*'s catholic analysis, chattel slavery may no longer be viewed as an archaic American institution; rather it must be understood as a four-hundred-year-old socioeconomic institution that created the wealth and prosperity of the entire Western world. In this way Du Bois's theoretical revision in *Black Reconstruction* places him in the same category of political philosopher as Marx. Just as Marx's science of history subverts earlier Enlightenment discourses of objectivist or rational historiography by proposing the dialectic of ruling-class oppression and proletariat resistance, Du Bois's Black radicalism further complicates Western radical theory by introducing the variables of *white supremacist* ruling-class oppression and *Black* proletariat resistance.

Many critics contend that *Black Reconstruction* surpasses prosaic history and enters the realm of political theory; I would also argue that *Black Reconstruction* quite forcefully asserts that the discipline of history is not and should not be deemed discrete from Western hegemonic discourse. In its final chapter, "The Propaganda of History," Du Bois comments at length on the extent to which the American historical profession has been instrumental in the institutionalization of anti-African racism, as most Western historians held fast to the tenets of Negro American inferiority, white southern loyalty, and ruling-class dominance. Du Bois remarks:

I write then in a field devastated by passion and belief. . . . Three-
fourths of the testimony against the Negro in Reconstruction is on the
unsupported evidence of men who hated and despised Negroes and
regarded it as loyalty to blood, patriotism to country, and filial trib-
ute to the fathers to lie, steal or kill in order to discredit these black
folk. . . . This chapter . . . becomes of sheer necessity an arraignment
of American historians and an indictment of their ideals. . . . It simply
shows that with sufficient general agreement and determination among
the dominant classes, the truth of history may be utterly distorted and
contradicted and changed to any convenient fairy tale that the masters
of men wish. (725–26)

Du Bois charges that history was and may continue to be manipulated
and dictated by biased Western historians committed to perpetuating
myths of Black culpability for the "failure" of Reconstruction, and his
indictment that the ruling classes document history offers a searing critique of Western discourse in general and the historical profession in
particular.

THE BLACK WORKER'S EXISTENTIAL REALITY

As previously noted, both Du Bois's and James's works were directly
influenced by the phenomenology of slavery. Du Bois seemingly uses
Black Reconstruction's critique of Western historiography and radical
theory to expand the text's theoretical focus with an examination of
black workers' phenomenology, their subjective awareness of their own
Being. The result is marked existential probing that occurs throughout the text. To initiate this discussion, "The Black Worker"—a chapter seemingly focused on a discussion of citizenship, voting rights, and
labor exploitation—introduces a phenomenological reading with the
"dangerous" anomaly that was the free Negro, an individual whose very
existence threatened the survival of Western slavery, white supremacy,
and Western capitalism. Du Bois explains, "As slavery grew to a system
and the Cotton Kingdom began to expand into imperial white domination, a free Negro was a contradiction, a threat and a menace. . . . As an
educated property holder, a successful mechanic or even professional
man, he more than threatened slavery. He contradicted and under-
mined it. He must not be. He must be suppressed, enslaved, colonized"
(7). The attainment of physical Freedom for certain Negro Americans
was antithetical to the realization of Western capitalism; nineteenth-
century American slaveholders understood that maintaining ruling-

class dominance was contingent upon the unequivocal subjugation of the majority of Negro Americans. This subjugation, by necessity, had to include Negro Americans' submission to white southerners, or, as they named themselves, "masters." Free Negroes were, in some cases, exempt from this submission, thereby necessitating their ontological erasure by southern whites: "[They] must not be. [They] must be suppressed, enslaved, colonized." The white southern insistence that Free Negros' erasure be contingent upon their subjugation is extremely revealing, for according to this position free Negroes' ontological nullification could be instantiated only through their capitulation to the material conditions of white supremacist rule. Du Bois links the free Negroes' ontological erasure to the material oppression of enslavement and colonization, seemingly establishing a causal link between their material conditions and their individual subjectivity, thereby providing a phenomenological analysis: "He must not be. He must be suppressed, enslaved, colonized."

Free Negroes thus represent a significant existential threat to white supremacist hegemony. That even a small number of free Negroes were perceived as endangering the southern plantocracy speaks to the level of insecurity among the slaveholding class. Free Negroes notwithstanding, in the wake of the Haitian Revolution southern slave owners also feared insurrection among the enslaved. Du Bois goes on to offer a comparative diasporic analysis of slave revolts in the United States with those in the West Indies, giving special attention to the admission of poor whites into the ruling class's hegemonic order:

> The [U.S.] system of slavery demanded a special police force and such a force as made possible and unusually effective by the presence of poor whites. This explains the difference between the slave revolts in the West Indies, and the lack of effective revolt in the Southern United States. . . . There were actually more white people to police the slaves than there were slaves. . . . The result was that the system was held stable and intact by the poor white. Even with the late ruin of Haiti before their eyes, the planters, stirred as they were, were nevertheless able to stamp out slave revolt. The dozen revolts of the eighteenth century had dwindled to the plot of Gabriel in 1800, Vesey in 1822, of Nat Turner in 1831 and crews of the *Amistad* and *Creole* in 1839 and 1841. Gradually the whole white South became an armed and commissioned camp to keep Negroes in slavery and to kill the black rebel. (12)

With this comparison Du Bois effectively identifies the nineteenth-century African diaspora as a site of revolutionary action; enslaved

Africans in the United States and the West Indies are not only workers but also members of an enslaved African diasporic proletariat ready to engage in violent conflict for their Freedom despite the entrenchment of hegemonic power and its constellation of lethal punishments.

Du Bois continues to probe the phenomenological dimensions of Negro Freedom by critiquing the paradoxical nature of Enlightenment discourse through the figure of the fugitive slave. Echoing Douglass and citing the incomprehensibility of reducing human beings to property, Du Bois affirms the enslaved African's right to be deemed, first and foremost, a human being:

> It is simply said that under any condition of life, the reduction of a human being to real estate was a crime against humanity of such enormity that its existence must be immediately ended. . . . But now, first, must be demanded that ordinary human freedom and recognition of essential manhood which slavery blasphemously denied. This philosophy of freedom was a logical continuation of the freedom philosophy of the eighteenth century which insisted that Freedom was not an End but an indispensable means to the beginning of human progress. (20)

Du Bois's contention that Western progress was halted because of chattel slavery's perpetuation into the late nineteenth century is driven home throughout *Black Reconstruction*. Like Walker and Douglass before him, Du Bois cites Enlightenment doctrine to point out the inherent hypocrisy of chattel slavery's four-century reign. He uses the language of the Enlightenment to portray slaves who dare to escape as those asserting their humanity in a system that consistently denies it. For Du Bois the fugitive slave is "the piece of intelligent humanity who could say: I have been owned like an ox. I stole my own body and now I am hunted by law and lash to be made an ox again. By no conception of justice could such logic be answered" (20). With this stunning metaphor he illuminates the fundamental existential drive behind enslaved Africans' impetus to escape: the drive to resist enslavement, the need to reassert their humanity, and the necessity to physically actualize their free will. As a form of physical resistance, escape becomes a means of existential actualization. Escape represents a way of actualizing Freedom just as the embrace of suicide, or "the jubilee," did for other enslaved Africans (Gilroy, *Black Atlantic* 66–69). The actualization of Freedom, be it physical resistance or subjective awareness, becomes antithetical to the subjugation and dehumanization inherent in the capitalist exploitation of the chattel slave system. In this vein the Black radical tradition of resistance lies in enslaved Africans' desire to reaffirm their personhood through the actualization of Freedom. The long-standing tradition of Black radical resistance is a crucial element in reclaiming a collective sense of Being that the oppressor willfully tries to destroy, for it

> cast[s] doubt on the extent to which capitalism penetrated and re-formed social life and on its ability to create entirely new categories of human experience stripped bare of the historical consciousness embedded in culture. . . . The Black radical tradition had defined . . . the continuing development of a collective consciousness informed by the historical struggles for liberation and motivated by the shared sense of obligation to preserve the collective being, the ontological totality. (Robinson 170–71)

In their understanding that the condition of Freedom exists inherently and that the will to resist oppression actualizes this Freedom, enslaved Africans struggled to reclaim "the collective being, the ontological totality" that chattel slavery attempted to annihilate. Fighting this annihilation thus becomes a revolutionary act regardless of the outcome, irrespective of the number of fallen enemies (Robinson 168).

Du Bois's critique of Marxism is particularly amplified by the way race is imbricated upon the related ideations of labor and alienation, for the traditional Marxist definition of worker alienation highlights that "wage labor is perceived as alienation. . . . The question that Du Bois raises was what would happen when labor was embodied in both body and person—in other words, when labor was combined with the property of a person. . . . The slave was a slave—he or she was property in its totality" (Bogues 83). What occurs when labor and property are embodied in the worker? To this Du Bois seemingly answers that a form of alienation arises which surpasses that of the Marxian proletariat. The Black worker's particular alienation is characterized by a shattered consciousness, a particular self-degradation and self-alienation that is born of the chattel slave system, its attendant discourses of anti-African racism, and the ideological and quotidian manifestations of racism that, combined, sought to reduce the Black worker to a subhuman. This existential alienation is epitomized by the internalization of Western racism, a brand of psychological enslavement that Du Bois has termed the Negro inferiority complex. He discusses the Black worker's inferiority complex in a description of the material conditions that attended it:

> There was in 1863 a real meaning to slavery different from that we may apply to the laborer today. It was in part psychological, the enforced

personal feeling of inferiority, the calling of another Master; the stand-
ing of hat in hand. It was the helplessness. It was the defenselessness of
family life. It was the submergence below the arbitrary will of any sort
of individual. It was without a doubt worse in these vital respects than
that which exists today in Europe or America. (9)

Du Bois's focus on the forced inferiority complex, evinced by the calling of one's owner "master," reflects one of the most degrading elements
of the black worker's plight. It is not enough that these enslaved laborers
were deemed less than human, but daily and hourly they were forced
to interpellate their assigned inferiority when they addressed the archi-
tect of their subjection as "master." As Du Bois so pointedly notes, chattel slave culture was predicated upon the domination of the enslaved
by all members of the slaveholding class: man, woman, and child. One
example of this was the common practice of white children, some from
the moment of their birth, owning adult slaves just as they would own
a dog, a cat, or a farm animal.

Du Bois's examination of chattel slavery's phenomenological dimensions reaches its peak in chapter 9, "The Price of Disaster." Again he uses
a description of southern social conditions to segue into their existential implications for Negro Americans. To explain the intractability of
white southerners toward the de jure enfranchisement of newly emancipated slaves, he states, "It was the American Blindspot that made the
experience all the more difficult, and to the South incomprehensible.
For several generations the South had been taught to look upon the
Negro as a thing apart. He was different from other human beings. The
system of slave labor, under which he was employed, was radically different from all other systems of labor" (370).

In charging the chattel slave system responsible for the southern
apprehension of enslaved Africans as "things apart," Du Bois elucidates
how the symbiotic ideologies of anti-African racism and white ruling-
class hegemony caused the Black worker's totalizing alienation. This
conflation of societal ideology and social practice led to insurmountable feelings of inadequacy and despair: "The result of this had to be
unfortunate for the Negro. He was a caged human being, driven into a
curious mental provincialism. An inferiority complex dominated him.
He did not believe himself a man like other men. . . . Large numbers
sank into apathy and fatalism! There was no chance for the Black man;
there was no use in striving: ambition was not for Negroes" (701). So
successful were white supremacist doxa in their instantiation of Negro
degradation that Negro Americans had internalized this racism and

believed themselves incapable of any achievement whatsoever. Plausible as this hypothesis seems, it contradicts Du Bois's earlier exhortation of African American orature as representative of American cultural and artistic production and the catalyst for Africana agency and resistance in the text's first chapter.

In *Black Reconstruction*'s penultimate chapter, aptly titled "Back towards Slavery," Du Bois furthers his analysis of southern plantation culture's hegemonic dimensions by detailing its adherence to racial and caste hierarchy. Intrinsic to this hierarchy was the complete disenfranchisement of newly emancipated Negro Americans because

> caste has been revived in a modern civilized land. . . . First, it was presented and defended as "race" separation, but it was never mere race separation. It was always domination of blacks by white officials. . . . Besides this a determined psychology of caste was built up. In every possible way it was impressed and advertised that the white race was superior and the Negro an inferior race. This inferiority must be publicly acknowledged and submitted to. Titles of courtesy were denied colored men and women. Certain signs of servility and usages amounting to public and personal insult were insisted upon. (694–95)

Through his clear description of "archaic and barbaric" southern governmental policies that manifested the vaster workings of white supremacist, Western hegemony, Du Bois illustrates how the continued oppression of disenfranchised Negro Americans was justified by and reflected in racist public policy and societal conventions that reinforced notions of African racial subordination For example, what he terms "signs of servility . . . amounting to pubic and personal insult" may be found in the common, and still extant, racist practice of perpetually infantilizing adult and elderly African American women and men by calling them "girls" or "boys."

DU BOIS VERSUS EMPIRE

Delineating how Western slavery created the hegemony of global capitalism and its resultant racial, socioeconomic, and political hierarchies is only one aspect of *Black Reconstruction*'s theoretical intervention, for in the first chapter Du Bois makes one of his boldest and most radical statements that, once again, places Marxism's Eurocentricity in high relief. He uses syllogistic reasoning to reveal linkages among the Freedom of humankind, the emancipation of labor, and the Freedom of the enslaved and colonized by conjecturing, "The emancipation of man is the emancipation of labor and the emancipation of labor is the freeing of that basic majority of workers who are yellow, brown, and black" (16). Du Bois's radicalism thus surpasses that of most Marxists. His call for Freedom is a call for greater class *and* race consciousness. His declaration extracts the historical event of proletariat revolution from the European continent and places it into its colonial dominions, where native labor is exploited for purely imperial gain. His anti-imperialist stance is contextualized in his 1940 autobiography, *Dusk of Dawn*, where he names the predominant forces of hegemonic ideology and their impact on his own work and on that of his peers:

> My thoughts, the thoughts of Washington, Trotter, and others, were the expression of social forces more than of our own minds. These forces or ideologies embraced more than our reasoned acts. . . . The total result was the history of our day. That history may be epitomized in one word—Empire; the domination of white Europe over black Africa and yellow Asia, through political power built on the economic control of labor, income, and ideas. (96)

For Du Bois, Western empire is neither a distant abstraction nor a passing phase. Rather it is the twentieth-century manifestation of capitalism born of four centuries of chattel slavery, its ideological constructs of hegemonic discourse and empire building in colonial territories, and the Western hegemonic imperative to create and maintain wealth through the continued exploitation of the Black and colored laboring classes.

Du Bois uses his anticapitalist, anti-imperialist globalism to situate the plight of emancipated Negro Americans within the same historical context as other postrevolutionary peasants. He details the Black workers' Reconstruction-era quest for land rights as similar to the struggle of feudal European peasants: "The German and English and French serf, the Italian and Russian serf, were, on emancipation given definite rights in the land. Only the American Negro slave was emancipated without such rights and in the end this spelled for him the continuation of slavery" (*Black Reconstruction* 611). In *The Souls of Black Folk* he recounts this "continuation of slavery" with great alacrity in descriptions of the southern debt-peonage and sharecropping systems, which, in combination, sank newly emancipated Negro Americans into an inescapable mire of poverty and dependency, thereby continuing their de facto state of slavery (309–19).

Black Reconstruction concludes in the same manner that it begins: by placing the plight of enslaved Africans in the context of the global drama that is Western history. Du Bois contends that the catastrophe of Reconstruction surpasses that of Greek tragedy and is therefore equivalent to seminal developments in Western history:

> The most magnificent drama in the last thousand years of human history is the transportation of ten million human beings out of the dark beauty of their mother continent into the new-found Eldorado of the West. They descended into Hell; and in the third century they arose from the dead, in the finest effort to achieve democracy for the working millions which this world had ever seen. It was a tragedy that beggared the Greek; it was an upheaval of humanity like the Reformation and the French Revolution. (727)

With this ending Du Bois completes his project of highlighting the historical significance of the European slave trade and chattel slavery. He powerfully situates these events as watershed developments in Western civilization, culture, and politics, just as he demonstrates their centrality to capitalism and imperialism. In this way Du Bois creates not only a theory of history; he creates history itself through a new system of radical knowledge production. No one before him had written of the epochal historical and philosophical import of the enslaved African in and to the West. But after Du Bois, the Trinidadian scholar C. L. R. James would seek to problematize Marxism once again, this time using the San Domingo Revolution and its leader, Toussaint L'Ouverture, to signify the enslaved and colonized African's apprehension of Freedom as the occasion for liberationist existential actualization.

JAMESIAN ENLIGHTENMENT

According to the preface of *The Black Jacobins*, the San Domingo Revolution was the manifestation of the ethical and political ideals of eighteenth-century Enlightenment thought. For James, the Black Jacobins' was an African proletariat revolution that saw enslaved and colonized subjects actualizing Enlightenment principles of Freedom, thereby becoming agents of radical historical and sociopolitical change. James opens the text with his proclamation of the San Domingo Revolution as a historical anomaly: "The revolt is the only successful slave revolt in history, and the odds it had to overcome is evidence of the magnitude of the interests that were involved. The transformation of slaves, trembling in hundreds before a single white man, into a people able to organize themselves and defeat the most powerful European nations of their day, is one of the great epics of revolutionary struggle and achievement" (ix). With his emphasis on the Haitian Revolution as a triumphant slave revolt, James deftly reminds the reader that the enslaved women, men, and children of San Domingo were transformed into a revolutionary army that, against all odds, defeated the most advanced European militias of the eighteenth century. The improbability of the Haitians' victory over the imperial might of the West and its eradication of African racial slavery in Haiti should place James's text in Western studies of revolution and modernity, yet as Bogues so astutely avers, "This revolution, called 'unthinkable' . . . has been neglected in studies of revolution. But the nature of the event encouraged James to tell a tale that shifted the main historical axis of the 'Age of Revolution,' narrating a different tale about the rise of modernity" (79). James repositions the Age of Revolution along a historical axis that recounts the rise of proletariat mass action as an African diasporic phenomenon. Moreover, in naming this revolution "one of the great epics of revolutionary struggle," he inserts the Africana struggle for liberation into the genealogy of both traditional and radical Western historiography, thereby furthering the counterhegemonic discourse at the heart of his and Du Bois's radical Western letters. It was James's and Du Bois's aim to stretch Marxism's contextual limitations by introducing enslaved Africans into Western historiographical and political theory as laborers whose toil irrevocably shaped the modern world.

James remarks on the global historical vision of Du Bois's *Black Reconstruction*, "He had opened out the historical perspective in a manner I didn't know. . . . He was always driven by the need of expanding and making clear to black people in what way they were involved in world history. . . . Du Bois taught me to think in those terms. . . . Who was thinking in terms of the Black worker in 1865? Who was thinking about the Black worker in 1935?" ("Lecture on the Black Jacobins" 85–86, 91). James's comment in part reveals his criticism of Marxist theory. In asking who was concerned about the Black worker's plight, he suggests that no one except Du Bois was, not even progressive Western radical theorists. Only Du Bois was preoccupied with the ramifications of chattel slavery as a system of capitalist labor, and now James was duly concerned.

James's reinvigoration of Marxist historiography continues in the first chapter of *The Black Jacobins*, where a genealogy of African resistance to chattel slavery is established as early as the Middle Passage and continues with slave resistance on the plantations. His emphasis that enslaved Africans courted death to attain Freedom reveals the degree to which oblivion was a fate preferable to a life of bondage. Enslaved Africans "undertook vast hunger strikes; undid their chains and hurled themselves on the crew in futile attempts at insurrection. . . . Some took the opportunity to jump overboard, uttering cries of triumph as they cleared the vessel and disappeared below the surface" (9). James further explores slave resistance through a psychological analysis of the dialectics of oppression, revealing the oppressors' need to dehumanize the enslaved and the slaves' refusal to capitulate. He writes, "The difficulty was that though one could trap them like animals, transport them in pens, work them alongside an ass or a horse and beat both with the same stick, stable and starve them, they remained . . . quite invincibly human beings; with the intelligence and resentments of human beings" (11–12). Despite the slaveholders' systematic efforts to set enslaved Africans apart from humanity, the enslaved Africans of San Domingo continually reasserted their humanity and agency. James also explains the disregard for slaves' well-being as necessary for the very survival of the slaveholding class. "To cow them into the necessary docility and acceptance necessitated a calculated brutality and terrorism, and it is this that explains the unusual spectacle of property-owners apparently careless of preserving their property: they had first to ensure their own safety" (12). Interestingly this passage echoes *Black Reconstruction*'s description of the American South as an "armed camp" to contain the Black rebel.

Another means slaveholders used to ensure their safety was maintaining the plantation's paradoxical character as the simultaneous womb of capitalism and tomb of the enslaved by working laborers to death: "The life in San Domingo killed them off fast. The planters deliberately worked them to death rather than wait for children to grow up" (14). As James so vividly recounts, slaveholders found it more expedient to work their slaves to death, as it was more economical to replace deceased slaves with newly enslaved Africans than maintain the slaves' survival. Given this fact of capitalist exploitation, it is not surprising that scores of slaves committed suicide to end their misery and, according to James, to bring malice upon their owners: "Suicide was a common habit, and such was their disregard for life that they often killed themselves . . . to spite their owner. Life was hard and death, they believed, meant not only release but a return to Africa" (15). The slaves' willful resistance against the slaveholders is a struggle against their socioeconomic status as property. Slave suicide therefore becomes an act of protest against the dehumanization of capitalist exploitation, a physical annihilation that is at once liberation from the corporeality of chattel slavery and a spiritual return to the motherland.

James's statement on slave suicide as an act of resistance recalls Du Bois's statement in *Black Reconstruction* that the fugitive slave, or the escaped Black worker, "steals his own body." For the enslaved proletariat in *The Black Jacobins*, suicide becomes the ultimate act of stealing one's body, for one steals one's very self from the clutches of slaveholders, paradoxically, through the act of suicide. These accounts of slave insurrection, fugitive activity, and suicide in *The Black Jacobins* and *Black Reconstruction* cannot be thoroughly explained by Western radical theory. Marxism, as Du Bois and James have shown, cannot fully explicate the array of issues related to African oppression under chattel slavery. Western radical theory was developed to explain the dialectics of capitalist oppression and proletariat resistance in a strictly European context, without the complicating elements of racialized slavery and its attendant discourses of racist thought. Slave insurrection, fugitive action, and suicide reflect the manner in which chattel slavery's material conditions catalyzed a particular existential awareness with which the enslaved grasped their inherent Freedom. In enslaved Africans' refusal to capitulate they assert their human right to actualize Freedom and exist as autonomous beings free from the master-slave dyad. Thus flight, rebellion, and suicide become acts of self-determination that highlight both individual and collective quests for ontological recuperation.

TOUSSAINT L'OUVERTURE: ENLIGHTENMENT LEADER

James's critique of Western historiography continues in his naming of Toussaint L'Ouverture, a former slave and the leader of the San Domingo Revolution, as one of the greatest historical figures of the Enlightenment. James "believes, and is confident the narrative will prove, that between 1789 and 1815, with the single exception of Bonaparte himself, no single figure appeared on the historical scene more greatly gifted than this Negro, a slave until he was 45" (x). Placing L'Ouverture in the same category as Bonaparte initiates a revision of Western historiography that foregrounds the importance of Africana resistance in San Domingo to the developing ideological and ethical inheritance of the West. James forces readers to radically alter their understanding of Western history by acknowledging how the material realities of slavery and colonialism compelled enslaved Africans to transform the Enlightenment theorization of Freedom into the actualization of Freedom.

L'Ouverture's stature as a formidable Enlightenment leader is furthered in James's analysis of his letter to the Directory, an impassioned yet measured missive warning against the French government's plan to reinstate slavery in San Domingo. In this letter, which James denotes as a milestone in L'Ouverture's career, L'Ouverture promises that he and his fellow freedom fighters would die a thousand deaths before submitting to enslavement: "We have known how to face dangers to obtain our liberty, we shall know how to brave death to maintain it" (*Black Jacobins* 196, 197). According to James, the determination to maintain Freedom was born of L'Ouverture's identity as a slave. Having experienced his life as chattel enabled him to grasp the true meaning of Freedom in a way that his European and American counterparts, who could only hypothesize Freedom, never could. His was a keen perception unencumbered by the equivocation and exception of bourgeois idealism. His awareness of Freedom was as immediate and concrete as the scorching sugar cane plantations on which he had toiled:

> That was why in the hour of danger Toussaint, uninstructed as he was, could find the language and accent of Diderot, Rousseau, and Raynal, of Mirabeau, Robespierre. . . . And in one respect he excelled them all. For even these masters of the spoken and written word, owing to the class complications of their society, too often had to pause, to hesitate, to qualify. Toussaint could defend the freedom of the blacks without reservation, and this gave his declaration a strength and a single-mindedness rare in the great documents of the time. (198)

L'Ouverture's cognizance of the "social death" of slavery sparked an existential awareness of Freedom as a process of actualization. For L'Ouverture Freedom was not an abstraction to be qualified but a reality to be attained and, if necessary, attained through death. James advances his comparison between L'Ouverture's philosophical formulation of Freedom and those of privileged eighteenth- and nineteenth-century Western thinkers by stressing the singularly historic achievement of L'Ouverture's letter to the Directory:

> Pericles on Democracy, Paine on the Rights of Man, the Declaration of Independence, the Communist Manifesto, these are some of the political documents which, whatever the wisdom or weaknesses of their analysis, have moved men and will always move

them. . . . Toussaint was a slave, not six years out of slavery . . . dictating his thoughts . . . written and rewritten by his secretaries until their devotion and his will had hammered them into adequate shape. . . . He accomplished what he did because, superbly gifted, he incarnated the determination of his people never to be slaves again. (197–98)

James again contrasts L'Ouverture's democratic vision to those of his privileged Western counterparts, yet he argues that L'Ouverture's letter should be regarded as one of the greatest political documents of the age since a man who had risen from the utter degradation of chattel slavery had crafted it. Under the chattel slave system L'Ouverture, like Douglass, was meant to internalize his ascribed degradation and dehumanization. He was meant neither to embody the promise of Freedom nor to write a philosophically inspired treatise challenging the veracity and universality of the eighteenth-century Rights of Man doctrine. With this critique James contextualizes L'Ouverture's letter as a concrete historic and discursive meditation on Freedom written by one who personified its very essence. What is more, L'Ouverture's letter also defines Freedom as an inevitability for the enslaved masses of San Domingo, as they had lived under chattel slavery and refused to do so again.

James's treatment of L'Ouverture and the San Domingo Revolution during the Age of Revolution stands in stark contrast to Homi Bhabha's reading of *The Black Jacobins* in *The Location of Culture* (1994). While James clearly establishes a genealogy of Africana resistance to chattel slavery in San Domingo and emphasizes the import of slavery's ties to Enlightenment discourses, Bhabha's reading of *The Black Jacobins* focuses rather myopically on his assertion that the event of the San Domingo Revolution mimics the French Revolution, thereby shifting the spatiality of modernity. In the concluding chapter of *The Location of Culture*, Bhabha situates his postcolonial conceptualization of modernity along a critical continuum informed by the works of Jürgen Habermas, Jean-François Lyotard, Claude Lefort, and Michel Foucault. Though his critique of Foucault's Eurocentrism is accurate, Bhabha employs a somewhat circumscribed reading of *The Black Jacobins* to revise Foucault's "spatial sign of modernity":

Foucault traces "the ontology of the present" to the exemplary event of the French Revolution and it is there that he stages his sign of modernity. . . . What if the "distance" that constitutes the meaning of the Revolution . . . spans the temporal difference of the colonial space?

> What if we heard the "moral disposition of mankind" uttered by Toussaint L'Ouverture for whom, as C. L. R. James so vividly recalls, the signs of modernity, "liberty, equality, fraternity . . . what the French Revolution signified, was perpetually on his lips, in his correspondence, in his private conversations." (243–44)

Bhabha proposes that L'Ouverture's internalization of the moral disposition of man represents a valid signifier of modernity, yet this interpretation fails to address James's dialectic of Western subjugation and Africana resistance, which is fundamental to his thesis in *The Black Jacobins* and its explicit critique of Marxism. The seminal nature of James's analysis of enslaved African labor in San Domingo lies in his insistence that enslaved Africans represent a modern proletariat and that their self-identification as an exploited laboring class led to their resistance and revolution. James holds that the enslaved Africans of San Domingo "worked on the land, and, like revolutionary peasants everywhere, they aimed at the extermination of their oppressors. But working and living together in gangs of hundreds on the huge sugar factories . . . they were closer to a modern proletariat than any group of workers in existence at the time, and the rising was, therefore a thoroughly prepared and organized mass movement" (*The Black Jacobins* 85–86). Bhabha's failure to thoroughly consider the material conditions of chattel slavery and imperialism and therefore the dialectic of racial oppression and Africana resistance in L'Ouverture's preoccupation with liberty, equality, and fraternity relegates the leader of the first successful slave revolt in history to the limited role of a colonial "mimic"—to borrow one of Bhabha's terms—as opposed to a leader in the African diasporic struggle for liberation. This oversight also leads to a reductive analysis of James's achievement in *The Black Jacobins*. Without properly contextualizing Western slavery and its attendant discourses of racist thought, Bhabha occludes the manner in which James's work stands as a greater challenge to traditional and radical Western theory.

Even more troubling is that Bhabha makes no mention of *The Black Jacobins*' genealogy of Afro-Caribbean resistance in San Domingo prior to the Haitian and French revolutions. James cites the seventeenth-century attempts at insurrection under the Maroon chief Mackandal, occurring an entire century before the French and Haitian revolutions, as evidence of an autochthonous penchant for resistance. James holds that Mackandal's vision of Freedom included driving European imperialists out of San Domingo:

Mackandal was an orator, in the opinion of a white contemporary, equal in eloquence to the European orators of the day. . . . Not only did his band raid and pillage plantations far and wide, but he himself ranged from plantation to plantation to make converts, stimulate his followers, and perfect his great plan for the destruction of white civilization in San Domingo. . . . The Mackandal rebellion never reached fruition and it was the only hint of an organized attempt at revolt during the hundred years preceding the French Revolution. (20–21)

Like L'Ouverture's comparability to eighteenth-century European thinkers, Mackandal is compared to his late seventeenth-century European counterparts, who were well schooled in the arts of rhetoric and persuasion. Only this freedom fighter used his wit to incite rebellion among enslaved Africans in a French colony and, ironically, advanced principles of liberty, equality, and fraternity among the enslaved masses in a French colonial dominion *an entire century before* these principles had become the cornerstone of Enlightenment thought in Europe and the United States.

THE BLACK PROLETARIAT'S REVOLUTIONARY AGENCY

James contextualizes the Haitian freedom fighters of *The Black Jacobins* by citing Africana historicality and agency and renaming chattel slavery as the socioeconomic font of modern capitalism. Yet his first chapter is titled "The Property," seemingly to denote the commodified status of Africans under chattel slavery. "The Property" stands in contrast to Du Bois's first chapter, "The Black Worker," yet the realism of "The Property" links the enslaved Africans' quest for liberation to the ideological, socioeconomic, and political imperatives of chattel slavery. In this way James foregrounds the dialectical and symbiotic pairing of a white European ruling class and an enslaved black African proletariat integral to chattel slavery's unique system of capitalist exploitation, imperial domination, and racial oppression. He writes, "The black Jacobins of San Domingo were to make history which would alter the fate of millions of men and shift the economic currents of three continents. The slave-trade and slavery were woven tight into the economics of the eighteenth century. Three forces, the proprietors of San Domingo, the French bourgeoisie and the British bourgeoisie, throve on the devastation of a continent and on the brutal exploitation of millions" (25–26). James demonstrates how the socioeconomic dynamics among these mutually dependent groups led to a radical Africana uprising that changed the course of Western history. This multifaceted analysis of eighteenth-century imperialism represents the primary zone of James's historiographical interrogation, for he compels the reader to comprehend both chattel slavery and Africana resistance not only as the socioeconomic and ideological foundation of Western modernity but as a dialectical phenomenon that irrevocably changed the course of Western history itself. In their historic battle to end slavery and gain sovereignty and independence from France, Haitian freedom fighters single-handedly triumphed over "one of the [most profitable] foundations of the modern world—[African] racial slavery" (Bogues 220n26).

In the fourth chapter, "The San Domingo Masses Begin," James charges that chattel slavery led enslaved Africans to become the epitome of revolutionary peasants for they effectively organized to triumph over nearly impossible odds, defeating both French colonial rule and the chattel slave system: "They were closer to a modern proletariat than any group of workers in existence at the time, and the rising was, therefore, a thoroughly prepared and organized mass movement" (*The Black Jacobins* 86). Like Du Bois, James reconceptualizes enslaved Africans as workers, aptly naming them the first modern proletariat of the eighteenth century, an organized collectivity whose principal desire was Freedom and, in the enslaved San Domingans' case, self-governance. That James characterizes the slave revolt as a planned mass movement speaks to his own theoretical mission to illuminate Africana resistance to chattel slavery as central to studies of Western revolution. At the same time, this reconceptualization of enslaved Africans as a modern proletariat offers a revision of Marxism and its attendant socioeconomic and political classifications: "In the end [*The Black Jacobins*] was organically linked to revolutionary political practice. The telling of the . . . only successful black slave revolt in modernity rewrote Marxist categories of labor, as well as the nature of the political economy of early capitalism and of radical historiography. As a consequence, James pushed Marxist theory in new directions" (Bogues 74–75).

Like Du Bois before him, James redefines Marxian thought so that alienated European mill and factory workers no longer stand as the definitive symbol of Western modernity; instead an enslaved African diasporic proletariat represents the rise of the modern era. What is more, by titling this chapter "The San Domingo Masses Begin," James connotes a collective ontological rebirth in liberation, suggesting that the enslaved African masses were awakened as a social class through their collective quest to actualize Freedom.

The epigraph to "The San Domingo Masses Begin" is an African Vodun chant:

> Eh! Eh! Bomba! Heu! Heu!
> Canga, bafio te!
> Canga, moune de le!
> Canga, do ki la!
> Canga, do ki la!
> Canga, li! (85)

This transcription announces James's emphasis on locating African culture as the cornerstone of the enslaved Africans' revolutionary ethos. Where *Black Reconstruction* presents a more implicit connection between African American orature and African American resistance, *The Black Jacobins* provides an explicit account of how African cosmology—in the form of Haitian Vodun and its oral tradition—became the primary conduit for revolutionary action in San Domingo. James explains that the San Domingo proletariat

> [was] organizing for revolution. Voodoo was the medium of conspiracy. In spite of all prohibitions, the slaves traveled miles to sing and dance and practise the rites and talk; and now, since the [French] revolution, to hear the political news and make their plans. Boukman, a Papaloi or High Priest . . . was the leader. . . . By the end of July 1791 the blacks in and around Le Cap were ready and waiting. The plan was conceived on a massive scale and they aimed at exterminating the whites and taking the colony for themselves. (86)

That the masses of San Domingo began their revolution by practicing the rites of an African cosmological system to subvert Western chattel slavery and empire is extremely significant. The enslaved Africans of Boukman's incipient revolution in 1791 utilized their native cultural, spiritual, and cosmological system to end their oppression. With these purposeful actions, they called on their ancestors; they embodied the strength of a unified collectivity to assert their agential liberationist impulse and ensure their own emancipation.

JAMES'S RADICAL METHODOLOGY

Interestingly James came to this Africana-centered view of history through his study of Western radical theory. He credits his exposure to Marxism and his contact with other British colonial subjects from the African diaspora during his residence in England for making his now classic study *The Black Jacobins* possible ("Lectures" 67–71):

> So I hope you understand now that this book is not an accident. It didn't just fall from a tree. It is the result of a whole series of circumstances by which I thoroughly master, as I did in those days, Marxism. I had come from the Caribbean with a certain understanding of Western civilization. I had read the history of the Marxist movement, and I had written four hundred pages on the Marxist movement, from its beginning in 1864 to what was taking place in 1936. I was a highly trained Marxist and that is the person who wrote *The Black Jacobins*. (71)

Although James acknowledges his Western radical sensibility as the determinant factor behind his Marxist analysis of the Haitian Revolution, it may be said that his interdisciplinary approach surpasses traditional Marxist historiography since his study includes an innovative interpretation of chattel slavery and Western empire's links to the French and Haitian revolutions. The second chapter of *The Black Jacobins*, "The Owners," cites the work of the French historian Jean Juarès on the connection between the French bourgeoisie's burgeoning prosperity, which was garnered from the profits of slavery, and their subsequent awakening as an oppressed class under French monarchical rule: "'Sad irony of human history,' comments Juares. 'The fortunes created at Bordeaux, at Nantes, by the slave-trade, gave to the bourgeoisie that pride which needed liberty and contributed to human emancipation'" (47). The French bourgeoisie's pride, James argues, was engendered by the nation's imperialist endeavors, which necessitated the brutalization of enslaved Africans in San Domingo. James supports this point by describing the French people's expectation that the profits gleaned from chattel slavery and colonialism were as abundant as they were inexhaustible:

> How could anyone seriously fear for such a wonderful colony? Slavery seemed eternal and the profits mounted. Never before, and perhaps never since, has the world seen anything proportionately so dazzling as the last years of pre-revolutionary San Domingo. Between 1783 and 1789 production nearly doubled. Between 1764 and 1771 the average importation of slaves varied between ten and fifteen thousand. In 1786 it was 27,000, and from 1787 onwards the colony was taking more than 40,000 slaves a year. (55)

In this passage James plainly shows that the capitalist accumulation of chattel slavery provided the economic foundation for the French Revolution.

He goes on to demonstrate how the French bourgeoisie's resistance in turn reignited revolutionary fervor among an already recalcitrant enslaved African population in San Domingo, an entire century after the failed seventeenth-century attempts of Mackandal: "The enormous increase of slaves was filling the colony with native Africans, more resentful, more intractable, more ready for rebellion than the creole Negro. Of the half-a-million slaves in the colony in 1789, more than two-thirds had been born in Africa" (55–56). These enslaved Africans were the San Domingo masses, the same masses who, under the leadership of Boukman, had heard the stories of the French Revolution and were ready to seize the colony for themselves: "They had heard of the revolution and had construed it in their own image: the white slaves in France had risen, and killed their masters, and were now enjoying the fruits of the earth" (81).

In *The Black Jacobins*, James's narrative arc places the San Domingo masses in a genealogy that foregrounds the historical legacy of Africana resistance to chattel slavery in Haiti, beginning during the Middle Passage, continuing in Mackandal's seventeenth-century plot to overthrow European rule, achieving near success with Boukman's 1791 rebellion, and reaching its apotheosis under the leadership of Toussaint. Thus it is imperative to understand that "the French Revolution became the permissive context for the Haitian Revolution, not *the* cause of the revolution" (Bogues 81–82). This relates directly to Bhabha's (mis)reading of Toussaint, the Haitian Revolution, and the temporality of modernity. There was no mimicry involved in this New World revolution, only the reemergence of an extant Black radical ethos that gained even greater force with the contemporary example of the French Revolution.

James explores the links between French modernity and chattel slavery in San Domingo by identifying San Domingo's colonial representation in the French National Assembly as the principal impetus behind debates on Freedom and liberty as the natural rights of man (Patterson and Kelley 30): "In less than five minutes the great Liberal orator had placed the case of the Friends of the Negro squarely before the whole of France in unforgettable words. The San Domingo representatives realised at last what they had done: they had tied the fortune of San Domingo to the assembly of a people in revolution and thenceforth the history of liberty in France and of slave emancipation in San Domingo is one and indivisible" (*The Black Jacobins* 60–61). James's insistence that the discourses of Freedom and slavery in eighteenth-century San Domingo and France were interdependent and mutually informed evinces the degree to which *The Black Jacobins* must be critiqued as a radical intervention into Western historiography and political theory. Traditional Western theory mistakenly names the Haitian Revolution as an extension of the French Revolution, and radical Western theory is remiss in its omission of the African diasporic proletariat struggle. While James uses Marxism as the theoretical framework for *The Black Jacobins*, he does so to question Marxism's Eurocentric definition of capitalist development and to address Marxism's blind spot toward enslaved African proletariat labor and its absence in the annals of early capitalist development. Robinson explains:

> From Marx and Engels, [James] had taken the concept of a revolutionary class and the economic foundations for its historical emergence. But the slaves of Haiti were not a Marxian proletariat. . . . Moreover James seemed willing to challenge Marx and Engels on the very grounds they had laid for the sociological and political significance of early capitalism. . . . While the European proletariat had been formed by the ideas of the bourgeoisie . . . in Haiti and presumably elsewhere Africans had constructed their own revolutionary culture. (275)

The enslaved African proletariat of Haiti succeeded in subverting the French imperialist (and white supremacist) ruling class from the bottom up. I would argue that this struggle also represents resistance against the devaluation of African labor under the system of chattel slavery. This point is illustrated in the account of an unnamed Haitian freedom fighter who was labeled an anarchist in French history. When asked why he burned the vast plantations of San Domingo to the ground, he responded, "We have a right to burn what we cultivate because a man has a right to dispose of his own labour" (James, *The Black Jacobins* 361). In this act of defiance one may see how the Haitian proletariat, despite its enslavement and exploitation, perceived themselves as workers and historical agents possessing the inalienable right to destroy labor from which they received neither sustenance nor profit. With his emphatic self-identification as a laborer, this freedom fighter embodies and articulates the very aspects of his humanity that the chattel slave system sought to destroy. He burned plantations to be free; thus the struggle for Freedom in Haiti, and elsewhere in the African diaspora, becomes an existential battle for an autonomous liberated existence.

BLACK LIBERATION AS EXISTENTIAL ACTUALIZATION

It seems a matter of course that *The Black Jacobins* would include analyses of black subjectivity since James, like Du Bois, was informed by the phenomenology of slavery. Indeed *The Black Jacobins* and *Black Reconstruction* had to be conceptualized as historical studies that addressed theoretical, political, and philosophical concerns, for the plight of enslaved Africans under four hundred years of chattel slavery problematizes the strictly class-based dialectics of oppression and resistance elucidated by Marxism. James and Du Bois were compelled to see beyond Marxism and employ more layered examinations of African racial slavery because theories of inherent racial difference in discourses of scientific racism were the principal rationale for African enslavement in the West. Thus in *The Black Jacobins* and *Black Reconstruction*, the symbiosis of anti-African racism and white European and American hegemony is thoroughly emphasized. Integral to this critique are explorations of Being and Freedom. Consequently I do not completely agree that "Du Bois was more successful than James in writing about the social mind of the slaves" (Bogues 85). It is true that James does not devote a great deal of his study to examining the Haitian freedom fighters' collective psychology. However, his analysis of the anonymous freedom fighter's conceptualization of his labor's worth and the freedom fighters' collective actualization of Freedom, though comparatively brief, offer great insight into the existential dimensions of the Haitian people's struggle.

Nowhere is James's existential analysis of Freedom more explicit than in *The Black Jacobins*'s final chapter, "The War of Independence." For the formerly enslaved Africans of San Domingo who had tasted Freedom and refused to capitulate to reenslavement, death was the only alternative to Freedom. They embraced death for the cause of liberation, remaining revolutionaries to the end. When they battled to seize the San Domingo capital, Le Cap, from the French military, several freedom fighters were captured and put to death. James narrates these events with great attention to the philosophical import of their liberationist quest: "When Chevalier, a black chief, hesitated at the sight of the scaffold, his wife shamed him. 'You do not know how sweet it is to die for liberty!' And refusing to allow herself to be hanged by the executioner, she took the rope and hanged herself. To her daughters going to execution with her, another woman gave courage. 'Be glad you will not be the mothers of slaves'" (361–62). The wife's declaration that dying for the cause of Freedom is a fate to be relished reveals the depth of her desire for liberation. In James's deft portrayal she becomes a martyr for the greater cause of Freedom who would rather die by her own hand than by that of a colonial executioner. And for the mother who comforts her children, begging them to understand the honor of death as preferable to the degradation of slavery, the choice is the same: liberty or death.

In this final chapter James includes a telling analysis of the French military's response to the bravery of the Haitian revolutionaries. Rather than admire their indefatigable courage, the French soldiers instead chose to rationalize the Haitians' bravery by adhering to and articulating the tenets of scientific racism. The freedom fighters had more than proven their humanity by exercising their free will and choosing death over a life of enforced bondage, yet the French were unwilling to recognize their human dignity. They saw the freedom fighters as subhuman and rationalized their bravery as the by-product of an aberrant African physicality insensible to pain: "The French, powerless before this fortitude, saw in it not the strength of revolution but some peculiarity special to blacks. The muscles of a Negro, they said, contracted with so much force as to make him insensible to pain. They enslaved the Negro, they said, because he was not a man, and when he behaved like a man they called him a monster" (362).

James's assessment of the intractability of racist thought among these French officers is unmistakable. Their belief in inherent African raciological and physiological difference prevented them from acknowledging the freedom fighters' humanity. When faced with the Haitians' unquestionable bravery, the French remained unmoved. Convinced of their own racial superiority, they were able to see the freedom fighters only as subhuman monsters immune to physical pain. In their estimation the San Domingo revolutionaries were creatures apart from humanity. They could never admire the freedom fighters for who they were in fact: a people whose fortitude reflected the true spirit of the West's Enlightenment principles of Freedom.

Interestingly James's narration of the Haitian freedom fighters' resolve to actualize Freedom in their embrace of death prefigures Gramsci's designation of Freedom in *Selections from the Prison Notebooks*. In "Progress and Becoming," Gramsci outlines the significance and practical application of philosophy in society. Seemingly echoing James's conceptualization of Freedom as the existential manifestation of free will, Gramsci contends, "The measure of freedom enters into the concept of man. . . . But the existence of objective conditions, of possibilities or of freedom is not yet enough: it is necessary to 'know' them, and how to use them. And to want to use them" (360). Not only does Gramsci make the distinction between understanding Freedom and knowing Freedom, but he also highlights the importance of using these "objective conditions" to make Freedom actual. James foreshadows Gramsci's distinction between understanding Freedom and knowing Freedom by revealing how French Enlightenment thinkers like Rousseau and Robespierre used discursive means to create a proscribed understanding of Freedom, while the Haitian freedom fighters embraced revolution to instantiate the lived reality of Freedom. Here we may apprehend how James, like Du Bois, uses the historical instance of African diasporic revolution to reveal that the theory and practice of Freedom may become one and the same. Moreover Gramsci, like James, places emphasis on the individual's ability to transform the world through the knowledge of Freedom: "Man is to be conceived as an historical bloc of purely individual and subjective elements. . . . To transform the external world . . . is to potentiate oneself and to develop oneself" (360). As the embodiment of historical forces that actualized Freedom and charted the course of Western modernity, the Haitian freedom fighters changed the course of world history through their unwavering pursuit of liberation from chattel slavery and French colonial rule.

In *The Black Jacobins*' final chapter James, like Du Bois, addresses the formidable influence of Western canonical history, only James is decidedly more optimistic in his prediction of how the San Domingo Revolution will be viewed in perpetuity:

> What happened in San Domingo . . . is one of those pages in history which every schoolboy should learn, and most certainly will learn, some day. The national struggle against Bonaparte in Spain, the burning of Moscow by the Russians that fills the histories of the period, were anticipated and excelled by the blacks and Mulattoes of the island of San Domingo. The records are there. For self-sacrifice and heroism, the men, women and children who drove out the French stand second to no fighters for independence in any place or time. And the reason was simple. They had seen at last that without independence they could not maintain their liberty, and liberty was far more concrete for former slaves than the elusive forms of political democracy in France. (356–57)

James's insistence on the historical import of the San Domingo Revolution is quite telling. He believes in its future study because of its relevance to Western history; moreover he defines its import through the Haitian freedom fighters' awareness of Freedom as it was catalyzed by the material conditions of their enslavement. As James shows, the enslaved women, men, and children of San Domingo could better grasp the significance of liberty than those members of the French bourgeoisie who could only glimpse Freedom's import in the realm of theoretical abstraction. Unfortunately, however, James's optimism was just that, for in most cases the Haitian Revolution is not taught in the context of radical Western historical developments alongside the Russian Revolution. Its instruction is relegated to courses in Africana, Caribbean, and ethnic studies, even though *all* students of Western and global history would benefit from the Haitian Revolution's many lessons.

In *Black Reconstruction* and *The Black Jacobins*, we find the work of two philosophers who sought to contextualize the rise of eighteenth- and nineteenth-century modernity through the related historical events of chattel slavery, modern global capitalism, and empire. Du Bois's and James's shared radical sensibility gave birth to historic revisions of traditional and radical Western theory by casting their Eurocentricity in high relief. The enslaved African diasporic proletariat of *Black Reconstruction* and *The Black Jacobins* introduced an even more problematic dialectic of capitalist oppression: white southern and European ruling classes and an enslaved African proletariat. However, this African diasporic proletariat created a culture of resistance that Du Bois and James duly recognized as the catalyst of modern Western capitalism and empire. After World War II a French colonial subject would take their counterhegemonic project one step further by naming the colonized subject's liberated consciousness the pinnacle of existential actualization and the vital component in the creation of a new and just world for all.

CHAPTER THREE

Frantz Fanon

Existentialist, Dialectician, and Revolutionary

Any theory that fails to address the existential phenomenological dimension
of racism suffers from a failure to address the situational dimension,
what Fanon called l'éxperience vécue ("lived experience") of race.

—Lewis Gordon, "Existential Dynamics of Theorizing Black Invisibility"

Unlike Du Bois's signification of Douglass's orature in *Black Reconstruction* and James's references to *Black Reconstruction*'s historiographical innovation in "Lectures on the Black Jacobins," Frantz
Fanon's *Black Skin, White Masks* invokes neither Du Bois nor James by
name. Fanon's interdisciplinary study does, however, recall Du Bois's
and James's larger theoretical project of centralizing the Africana subject's pivotal role in watershed moments of Western historical and ideological developments. As a psychiatrist and political philosopher, Fanon
is concerned with the psychology, material conditions, and ontological
reality of the colonized subject; thus in *Black Skin, White Masks* he rein-
terprets psychoanalysis, historical materialism, and existentialism to
thoroughly scrutinize the colonial subject's lived experience of racism.
Though it is generally held that existentialism and historical materialism are opposing philosophies, and existentialism is generally viewed
as "a 'philosophy of crisis'" (Schrader 2), this perception should not
occlude its more practical and implicitly material preoccupation with
the realities of the human condition. Indeed existentialism's influence
"derives from the fact that it has concerned itself with human existence
in its cultural and historical context. . . . Existential philosophers have
deliberately and self-consciously addressed themselves to the human
situation as they themselves have been involved in it" (3). That exis-

tentialism is firmly grounded in historical and cultural contexts and its theorists' experiences of these social fields reveals its potential for a more radical interrogation and application of its two principal themes, Being and Freedom. These themes have been integral to the Africana historical experience of Western chattel slavery and empire, just as they are integral to Africana scholars' counterhegemonic discursive mission. In *Existentia Africana*, Lewis Gordon writes:

> The . . . ontological question was examined by many philosophers and social critics of African descent in the nineteenth century, including such well-known and diverse figures as Martin Delany, Maria Stewart, Anna Julia Cooper, and (early) Du Bois. It was not until the late 1940's, however, that a self-avowed existential examination of these issues emerged, ironically through the work of a European philosopher—namely, Jean-Paul Sartre. (8–9)

Due to their people's history of enslavement, oppression, and marginalization in the West, Africana thinkers engaged with the existentialist issues of Being and Freedom in the late nineteenth and early twentieth centuries well before their European counterparts. As Gordon points out, it is quite ironic that more than a century after these philosophical questions were raised by African people—those directly affected by the material conditions of chattel slavery, racial oppression, and their attendant phenomenological effects—Sartre would categorize these same concerns under the philosophical rubric of existentialism.

In the 1950s Fanon and Sartre applied the ontological and phenomenological aspects of existential philosophy to historical materialism, forging a multidisciplinary discourse against the capitalist and hegemonic exigencies of Western empire. They expanded existentialism's philosophical base to incorporate the complicating elements of anti-Arab and anti-African racism on colonial identity formation during the French-Algerian War. The subsequent decolonization of Algeria, which served as the revolutionary template for the remainder of the colonized Third World, provided Fanon and Sartre with a contemporary example of Marxian materialism in the context of empire—one that readily accommodated the sociopolitical aspects of existentialist thought with respect to global decolonization (Le Sueur 227–30, 241–49). While it is generally held that Fanon's radicalism was born of his commitment to the Algerian decolonization struggle, the seeds of his radicalism lay in the 1952 publication of his first book, *Black Skin, White Masks* (Martin 392). In it a distinctly Fanonian theoretical method is established.

Fanon not only breaks with the Negritude philosophy of his mentor, Aimé Césaire; he also combines elements of psychoanalysis, Hegelian dialectics, historical materialism, and existentialism, effectively establishing a theoretical foundation that would become the basis of his later political writings.[1] In the same way that Du Bois's *Black Reconstruction* and James's *The Black Jacobins* rewrote Marxian historiography by centralizing the enslaved African's role in the birth of modern capitalism and empire, Fanon's *Black Skin, White Masks* (1952) expands existential philosophy's focus on Being and Freedom to foreground the historical reality of anti-African racism and European colonialism, thereby revealing existentialism's potential use as a discursive critique against empire.

FANON'S RADICAL METHODOLOGY

A trained psychiatrist when he wrote *Black Skin, White Masks*, Fanon ostensibly employs psychoanalytic methods to probe the colonized subject's "abnormal" psyche. His methodology combines what he terms ontogeny, phylogeny, and sociogeny—an innovative therapeutic process that analyzes the individual colonial subject, the collective colonized subject class, and the larger colonial society as dysfunctional outgrowths of European empire (11). He uses this method of analyzing the colonized and the colonizer to theorize on Being and Freedom within what he terms the Manichaean colonial world, a world where the colonizer represents the embodiment of universal good and the colonized that of pure evil. In Fanon's critique of Manichaeism as representative of the colonial conflict's magnitude,[2] we may readily apprehend the historical and ideological legacy of sixteenth-century Western empire's burgeoning discourses of racial difference, predicated upon the dualism of an inherently superior European identity (white, good) and an essentially inferior Africana identity (black, evil). Yet Fanon's white-black binary is further complicated by three centuries of philosophical and political developments, for his Manichaean colonial world is delineated through an anti-imperialist and pro-liberation discourse that revises elements of Hegelian dialectics, Marxist materialism, Heideggerian phenomenology, and Sartrean existentialism[3] by positing the colonial subject's quest for Freedom.

Fanon utilizes this theoretical pastiche to elucidate the totalizing oppression of Western hegemony and empire and its impact on several related fields of the colonial subject's lived experience: the psychological, the material, the dialectical, and the existential. Therefore, as someone committed to "analyzing and destroying" the "psychoexistential complex" resulting from the "juxtaposition of the black and white races" (*Black Skin, White Masks* 12), Fanon must reveal breadth and depth of these complexes. Thus he applies, and thereby revises, key principles from these divergent schools of Western thought in his analysis of the colonial subject in particular and the ideological structures of European colonialism in general. In doing so he not only reveals the (individual) psychological and (social) institutional effects of imperial hegemony; he also illuminates their firm hold on the colonized subject's psyche in its manifestation as an insidious inferiority complex.

The ideological structures of colonialism, indeed colonialism's very survival demands the complete eradication of native culture, history, citizenship, and language and the replacement of these with European systems of culture, history, citizenship, and language. This supplanting of native culture is accomplished by the reconditioning of native populations. On this point Fanon states, "Insofar as [the native] conceives of European culture as a means of stripping himself of his race, he becomes alienated. . . . It is a question of a victim of a system based on the exploitation of a given race by another, on the contempt in which a given branch of humanity is held by a form of civilization that pretends to superiority" (224). The natives must be convinced of their essential inferiority in order for them to submit to foreign rule, thereby ensuring the colonial project's survival. The colonial world creates and perpetuates this collective complex among colonized subjects; thus European cultural imperialism and internalized inferiority become the dualistically defining characteristics of the lived experience of the colonized subject class. Fanon further expostulates, "The feeling of inferiority of the colonized is correlative to the European's feeling of superiority" (93). Although Fanon depicts the colonial world as a nearly impenetrable systemic fortress of Western hegemony, his diagnosis is not fatal. He posits the potential for native Freedom and in so doing reveals the colonial subject's necessary quest for existential actualization— human potential fulfilled by risking death in a violent confrontation for human recognition and, most important, Freedom. He reveals the liberated consciousness of the colonial subject and the resultant liberated society as the quintessential site of existential actualization. Thus with the theoretical mélange of psychoanalysis, dialectics, materialism, and existentialism of *Black Skin, White Masks* Fanon accomplishes two unprecedented and related discursive feats: Being and Freedom reach their apotheosis within the historical and political context of Africana liberation, and, somewhat paradoxically, European-centered schools of thought are revised to posit the colonial subject's liberated consciousness as the quintessential site of existential actualization.

The imagistic title of *Black Skin, White Masks* announces Fanon's discursive mission: to reveal the existential crisis at the heart of the black or colonized subject's lived experience under the inherently racist workings of empire. The title announces the multidisciplinary approach he uses to probe the colonized subject's crisis of self-identification, as the binary formulation of Black skins and white masks describes several theoretical dichotomies: psychoanalytical, in the employment of a mask to obscure true identity; dialectical, in the play of opposing racial identities and symbolically Manichaean forces; and ontological, in the subsuming of black identity with the mask of white identity. Negroes are black, but, according to Fanon, the stultifying effects of colonialism's white mask prevent them from existing by and for themselves; they must exist by and for white civilization, for as Fanon states in his introduction, "White civilization and European culture have forced an existential deviation on the Negro" (14).

This existential deviation is manifested in colonized subjects' forced denial of their own native identity. Wearing a white mask negates native black identity and all that it represents: racial and ethnic particularity, racial self-identification, and native history and culture. A colonial subject himself Fanon understood colonialism as the historical, ideological, and material deviation that breeds what he terms psychological "disalienation" in colonized subjects. So even though he begins by declaring that *Black Skin, White Masks* is a psychological study, he simultaneously insists that the colonized subject's inferiority complex is the direct result of extenuating social and economic forces created by the material realities of colonialism. In his introduction he plainly states, "The analysis that I am undertaking is psychological. In spite of this it is apparent to me that the effective disalienation of the black man entails an immediate recognition of social and economic realities. If there is an inferiority complex, it is the outcome of a double process: — primarily, economic; subsequently, the internalization—or, better, the epidermalization—of this inferiority" (10–11). The social and economic realities of colonialism that necessitate native poverty and degradation and imperial wealth and privilege, according to Fanon, also contribute to the inferiority complex of the colonized subject class, for a causal link is established between the material conditions of colonial oppression and the native's identity as a black-skinned colonized subject. Fanon's colonial disalienation, or self-alienation, is the internalization of native inferiority. This condition makes the colonized subjects' plight ineluctable, for as long as they are black they will remain degraded in the eyes of the European colonizer and justifiably oppressed. The colonized are seemingly locked into a cycle of oppression, a lived reality that catalyzes the psychological complex of self-alienation. In revealing how colonial oppression creates and maintains psychological complexes, Fanon illuminates the ways in which a detailed study of colonialism imbricates two critical approaches that are generally perceived as fundamentally opposed: historical materialism and psychoanalysis. On the juxtaposition of these contrasting sciences in *Black Skin, White Masks*, Anne McClintock notes:

> The audacity of [Fanon's] insight is that it allows one to ask whether the psychodynamics of colonial power and anti-colonial subversion can be interpreted by deploying . . . the same concept and techniques used to interpret the psychodynamics of the unconscious. . . . In *Black Skin, White Masks* . . . he insists that racial alienation . . . not only is an "individual question" but also involves what Fanon calls a "socio-diagnostic." Reducing Fanon to a purely formal psychoanalysis, or a purely structural Marxism, risks foreclosing precisely those suggestive tensions that animate . . . the most subversive elements in his work. (94)

It is these suggestive tensions between Marxism and psychoanalysis that establish critical commonalities, which in turn forge unexpected linkages between these seemingly divergent approaches. In *Black Skin, White Masks*, Fanon demonstrates how the (individual) colonized subject's abnormal psychological state is the result of an aberrant (social) material reality: that of a dominated, subjugated, and degraded colonized existence. The colonized subject's awareness of Being is therefore distilled from the oppressive material conditions of Western domination that shape the individual's psyche and ontology. For this reason his statement bears repeating: "If there is an inferiority complex, it is the outcome of a double process:—primarily economic; subsequently—, the internalization—or, better, the epidermalization—of this inferiority."

CONTEXTUALIZING FANON

Before examining Fanon's explorations of Being and Freedom in *Black Skin, White Masks*, it is necessary to situate him according to his motivations: professional, stemming from his chosen field of psychiatry;

social, originating in his identification as a colonial subject; and intellectual, arising from his intense study of Western philosophy.⁴ During his psychiatric residency in France at Saint Alban Hospital in 1952, Fanon studied under a professor who exposed him to sociotherapy, a branch of psychiatry stressing the indivisibility of patients from their specific social environments and societal orientations. Sociotherapy offers a diagnostic method that places equal weight on individuals and their social orientation, which moved Fanon to probe the individual psyche and apply his findings to an examination of the societal factors involved in individuals' psychological complexes.

Fanon applied sociotherapy to the individual colonized subject, to the social setting of the French colonial Antilles, and to the wider colonial world.⁵ Concomitant to his professional forays into sociotherapy, he was exposed to a significant amount of existentialist literature that was popular in France in the 1950s. He studied the works of Heidegger and Sartre, among other philosophers, whose exegeses on phenomenology and ontology complemented his earlier undergraduate education in the principal authors of Western radical theory: Marx, Lenin, and Trotsky (Gendzier 19–21). His methodology in *Black Skin, White Masks* was born of his application of sociotherapeutic analysis to his examination of the colonial situation for he uses colonized subjects as psychiatric patients, just as he analyzes their larger sociopolitical context as subjects of European empire, influenced by its ideological and political discourses of racism.

While some consider Fanon's theoretical amalgam idiosyncratic,⁶ the philosopher George Schrader comments on the rather seamless conceptual progression from Freudian psychoanalysis to Heideggerian phenomenology. Schrader contends that Freud's study of the unconscious motives behind human behavior offers a conceptual bridge to Heidegger's theory of ontology: "It is quite easy to make the transition from Freud's psychoanalytic theory of human behavior to Heidegger's fundamental ontology. We need only expand our analysis in order to grasp the basic principles of his ontology. . . . Heidegger's thesis is that ontological concerns are operative in all . . . (empirically manifest) human activity. If Heidegger is correct . . . ontology is relevant to the most commonplace features of our experience" (37). One such prosaic feature of human experience would be desire; according to Freud, human behavior is the cumulative manifestation of unconscious desires, desires that then shape the understanding of Being. Just as Freudian psychoanalysis suggests that the unconscious dictates our experience of

Being through the (un)conscious manifestation of our desires, choices, and actions, Heideggerian phenomenology posits Being as the center of our lived experience, a lived experience that cannot be divorced from the world in which we live. Lewis Hinchman and Sandra Hinchman remark that in *Being and Time* "Heidegger builds on Husserl's central argument that subject and object, human awareness and the environing world, are indissolubly linked. One cannot even in principle treat the ego as something detached from its surrounding. . . . The phenomenologist must open himself up to the rich totality of experience" (189). Somewhat paradoxically Heidegger's "rich totality of experience" includes a deliberate consideration of the individual's lived reality; thus Heidegger revises phenomenology by positing a somewhat materialist premise: individuals, and their sense of Being, are inextricably bound to the subjective experience of their social world. Indeed *Being and Time* "begins with the phenomenological study of everyday life. Heidegger . . . transformed phenomenology . . . into a method through which to carry on a more radical inquiry into ontology, the study of what it is *to be*" (189). Given that Heidegger's work offers a radical intervention into the study of Being, it is no surprise that Fanon—himself the embodiment of historical, ideological, and geopolitical forces—would be drawn to Heidegger's thesis that individual ontology is the dichotomous reflection of individuals and their societal milieus.

Fanon's professional vocation as a psychiatrist and his social orientation as an intellectual seemingly allowed him to build on this connection between the psychoanalytic and the existential, yet he accomplished something that neither Freud nor Heidegger were capable of due to their exclusive focus on the European subject. Fanon applied Freudian psychoanalytic theories of consciousness and Heidegger's phenomenological theories of Being to a dialectical *and* material analysis of the colonial world.[7] As Fanon himself states of his incorporation of divergent methods to his examination of colonialism in *Black Skin, White Masks*, "Although I had more or less concentrated on the psychic alienation of the black man, I could not remain silent about certain things which, however psychological they may be, produce consequences that extend into the domains of other sciences" (48). Clearly the extreme forces of hegemonic domination intrinsic to and necessary for the survival of empire compelled him to use the colonial condition as a starting point in his inquiries into these sciences and philosophies.

Irene Gendzier avers that Fanon's political stance was the direct result of his engagement with Western thinkers: "Out of the amalgam of men and ideas that affected Fanon, there were other historic figures, notably Marx, Freud, and Hegel, whose presence is to be discerned in his works. It was through the inner debate he engaged with these men, a debate molded by events in which he found himself, that Fanon eventually evolved an intellectual and political position of his own" (21).

Although Gendzier is correct in identifying Fanon's "inner dialogue" with these Western thinkers, her position that he acquired his theoretical and political vision through them reveals an unfortunate Western bias. Fanon formulated his exposition on the profound and stultifying effects of racism as ideology and praxis on the colonized psyche specifically because his lived reality as a colonial subject had already exemplified many of the themes and problems addressed in the works of Marx, Freud, and Hegel, whom he had studied and subsequently critiqued. His critical dialogue with these thinkers is made clear in several of the chapter titles and subtitles of *Black Skin, White Masks*: "The Negro and Psychopathology," "The Negro and Hegel," and "The Negro and Recognition." So too are his revisions and innovations to the European subjective and social realities at their core. Fanon's debate with these Western theorists raises several questions about the epistemic, ideological, and institutional aspects of anti-African racism that are foregrounded in his critique of the Manichaean colonial world—a world whose dualistic black-evil, white-good binary quite conveniently lends itself to another interpretive juxtaposition of Freudian psychoanalysis and Marxian materialism. In a psychoanalytic reading, the savagely "evil" black native may symbolize the wildly undisciplined id, and the "good" white colonizer the tempered, controlling superego. A materialist reading of the Manichaean colonial world's black-white binary reveals the dialectics of empire: the white European ruling colonial class oppresses the black native or colonized class until resistance, which is immanent, occurs.

Nevertheless the self-reflexive format of the autobiographical sections in chapter 5, "The Fact of Blackness," suggests that Gendzier is quite right in her contention that for Fanon, "to write was a form of action; it was in its origins self-centered and reflexive. But by its very nature it was also a method of communicating . . . in its conception, a process that engaged the conscience and consciousness of its author" (4). Fanon opens the text by asking, "Why write this book?" (*Black Skin, White Masks* 7), and subsequent pages reveal that he wrote to delineate the psychological effects of the hegemonic, historical, and sociopolitical forces of anti-African racism and Western domination. He announces psychoanalysis as his primary method in *Black Skin, White Masks,* declaring, "Before beginning the case, I have to say certain things. The analysis that I am undertaking is psychological" (10). Although this is true, Diana Fuss quite rightly insists:

> Psychoanalysis' interest in the problem of identification provides Fanon with a vocabulary and an intellectual framework in which to diagnose and to treat not only the psychological disorders produced in individuals by the violence of colonial domination but also the neurotic structure of colonialism itself. At the same time, Fanon's investigation of alterity within the historical and political frame of colonialism suggests that identification is neither a historically universal concept nor a politically innocent one. A by-product of modernity, the psychoanalytic theory of identification takes shape within the larger cultural context of colonial expansion and imperial crisis. ("Interior Colonies" 20)

Indeed Fanon's application of psychoanalytic principles to the colonial problem allows him to establish the colonial subject's individual identity formation as indiscrete from the ideological, political, and material history of European imperialism and colonial domination. He declares emphatically that colonized subjects' self-identification is informed by their awareness of the specific power relationship of domination and oppression.

While Fuss is correct in asserting that psychoanalysis provides Fanon with the lexical and critical framework for his examination of the colonized individual and the larger colonial society, I would argue further that Fanon uses psychoanalysis in the colonial setting as a theoretical springboard to leap into a more nuanced reading of unexpected thematic linkages among psychoanalysis, dialectics, materialism, and existentialism—all of which he teases out through an analysis of colonized subjects' lived experience. On his employment of psychoanalysis and his acute awareness of the need for dialectical engagement in the colonial setting, Fanon explains, "When I began this book, having completed my medical studies, I thought of presenting it as my thesis. But dialectic required the constant adoption of positions. Although I had more or less concentrated on the psychic alienation of the black man, I could not remain silent about certain things which, however psychological they may be, produce consequences that extend into the domain of other sciences" (*Black Skin, White Masks* 48). Despite the book's psychoanalytic subject matter and Fanon's related need to meet his professional training requirement, he reveals his deep engagement

with Hegelian and Marxist discourse by holding fast to the require-
ments of dialectic. He explicitly states that he could not write *Black
Skin, White Masks* as a purely psychological study because he saw the
colonized subject's psychological alienation as stemming from the historical roots of European hegemony and colonial rule. For Fanon, the
crisis of empire provided the ideal sociopolitical and ideological field
within which to apprehend the colonized subject's internalization of
hegemonic ideals and practices, as many of the book's other chapter
titles demonstrate: "The Woman of Color and the White Man," The
Man of Color and the White Woman," "The So-Called Dependency
Complex of Colonized People," and "The Fact of Blackness."

IMPERIAL LANGUAGE IMPOSITION

Fanon's engagement with the historical forces of colonization and
decolonization seemingly compels him to identify the layered aspects
of colonial oppression—material, psychological, and existential—and
their imbrication upon the colonized subject's psyche. To illustrate this
layering, he begins his first chapter with perhaps the most definitive
manifestation of imperial hegemony in the colonies: the imposition of
European language and its impact on native self-identification. "The
Negro and Language" elucidates the manner in which the colonized
subject's individual ontology and self-identification is problematized
by the linguistic and cultural imperatives of empire. Fanon contends
that there is "a basic importance to the phenomenon of language. That
is why I find it necessary to begin with this subject, which should provide us with one of the elements in the colored man's comprehension
of *the other*. For it is implicit that to speak is to exist absolutely for the
other" (17).

Fanon's theorization that imperial linguistic dominance is fundamental to the colonized subject's apprehension of Being (and the colonizer as other) positions language as an expression of both culture
and existence. That the native language is forcibly suppressed under
colonialism is highly significant, for language defines cultural identity.[8] Fanon goes even further to suggest that the adoption of an imperial language has existential implications,[9] as the colonizer's language
forces the colonized subject to "exist absolutely" for the colonizer, the
other.

This position on linguistic communication as the occasion for "existing absolutely for the other" reflects Fanon's dialogue with Sartre's

Being and Nothingness and Heidegger's *Being and Time*. Sartre theorizes extensively on the other, positing, "The appearance of the Other in my experience is manifested by the presence of organized forms such as gestures and expressions, acts and conducts" (307). These gestures and acts include the exchange of language, and in the colonial setting language becomes representative of forced foreign domination. It follows, then, that the foreign language becomes primary, the native language secondary, and the field of language itself, as it pertains to identity formation, a distorted inversion of the natural order. In this regard Fanon's exposition on identity formation in the colonial world is similar to Heidegger's interpretation of language in *Being and Time*: "Language for Heidegger is not a mere instrument of communication. . . . It is the very dimension in which human life moves, that which brings the world to be in the first place. Only where there is language is the 'world,' in the distinctively human sense" (Eagleton, *Literary Theory* 55).

Colonized subjects live in a foreign language and culture that, as the verbal expression of empire, can only denigrate and debase them. This debasement of native culture contributes to colonized subjects' inferiority complex. They are forced to adopt the colonizer's language to be deemed conditionally and marginally human by the foreign colonial administration that now rules their land. Fanon avers:

> The problem that we confront in this chapter is this: The Negro of the Antilles will be proportionally whiter—that is, he will come closer to being a real human being—in direct ratio to his mastery of the French language. I am not unaware that this is one of man's attitudes face to face with Being. . . . Every colonized people—in other words, every people in whose soul an inferiority complex has been created by the death and burial of its local cultural originality—finds itself face to face with the language of the civilizing nation; that is, with the culture of the mother country. The colonized is elevated above his jungle status in proportion to his adoption of the mother country's cultural standards. He becomes whiter as he renounces his blackness. (18)

Here Fanon uses the imposition of European imperial language to establish a causal chain in the colonized subject's psychological and ontological disalienation. First, he proclaims that the edicts of empire, necessitating the subordination of native language and culture to those of France (Europe), force an inferiority complex. Then he contests that the very cause of the colonized subject's inferiority complex—the forced acquisition of European imperial language—forces another dichotomy: marginal social acceptance by the colonizer. The inferiority complex, or white mask of language, is set firmly in place because the colonized become forcibly indoctrinated into a foreign system of knowledge through the ideological state apparatuses of educational, cultural, and social institutions. Because of the proselytizing effects of cultural imperialism, the colonized will then believe that their native culture is primitive, barbaric, and inherently inferior.

In his assessment of Fanon's radical liberationist stance, Messay Kebede argues:

> Colonial discourse and rule have so dehumanized and degraded colonized peoples that they have to go through the whole process of relearning to be human. The tag of primitiveness affixed on them, the contempt for and complete destruction of their cultural legacy, their forced assimilation into the European culture . . . all have resulted in the inculcation, deep into the soul of each colonized person, of a devastating inferiority complex. (540)

Consequently colonized subjects may understand their individual subjectivity only through the distorted prism of racist European acculturation, an understanding that necessarily problematizes their apprehension of Being. The natives don the mask of whiteness—of white civilization, language, and culture—and are effectively self-alienated from their own native identity. Stuart Hall contends that the self-alienation resulting from the internalization of colonial racism is in fact the internalization of the self-as-other since

> racism . . . operates by constructing impassable symbolic boundaries between racially constituted categories, and its typically binary system of representation constantly marks and attempts to fix and neutralize the difference between belonging and otherness. . . . As Fanon constantly reminded us, the epistemic violence is both outside and inside. . . . That is why it is a question, not only of "black skin" but of Black Skin, White Masks—the internalizing of the self-as-other. (445)

Fanon illustrates this internalizing of the self as other through the example of an Antillean schoolchild who is taught that his ancestors are not enslaved Africans, forcibly transported to the Antilles, but the French colonizers who oppressed them: "The black schoolboy in the Antilles who in his lessons is forever talking about 'our ancestors, the Gauls,' identifies himself with the explorer, the bringer of civilization, the white man who carries truth to savages—an all white truth" (Black Skin, White Masks 147). In the Antillean classroom the epistemic violence of colonialism is carried out ideologically through the imposition of European culture, language, and education and historically in the privileging of European history over native history and culture.

Echoing Fanon, Ngũgĩ wa Thiong'o concurs that in the colonial world "literary education was now determined by the dominant language while also reinforcing that dominance. Orature (oral literature) . . . stopped. . . . Thus language and literature were taking us further and further from ourselves to other selves, from our world to other worlds" (12). This removal from the self is only intensified by an educational system in which the tenets of racist thought, expressed in the writings of the Enlightenment ideologues Hume, Jefferson, and Hegel, are inculcated in the colonized subject. The writings of these three proponents of anti-African racism stand at the center of Western discourse and define the ideological, hegemonic mission of empire:

> It was worse when the colonial child was exposed to images of his
> world as mirrored in the written languages of his colonizer. Where his
> own native languages were associated in his impressionable mind with
> low status, humiliation, corporal punishment . . . or downright stupid-
> ity, non-intelligibility and barbarism, this was reinforced by the world
> he met in the works of . . . some of the giants of western intellectual
> and political establishment, such as Hume . . . Thomas Jefferson . . . or
> Hegel. . . . Hegel's statement that there was nothing harmonious with
> humanity to be found in the African character is representative of the
> racist images of Africans and Africa such a colonial child was bound to
> encounter in the literature of the colonial language. The results could
> be disastrous. (18)

That Ngũgĩ announces the presence of these eighteenth- and nineteenth-century philosophers in the twentieth-century colonial classroom reminds us that scientific racism's legacy continues to endure and that the influence and impact of the ideological state apparatus are far-reaching, still affecting and colonizing the youngest of Africana minds. Canonical racism's epistemological and psychological impact on colonized subjects, indeed on all African diasporic subjects, becomes yet another manifestation of empire and hegemony as Africana people are indoctrinated into racist discourses that diminish their existence and worth and justify their oppression. Though Fanon's example of imperial education—Antillean schoolchildren who are taught about their ancestors the Gauls—rings with sarcasm, this moment of colonial inculcation further reveals his engagement with Western radical theory and its emphasis on the institutionalization of colonial oppression. His example also underscores colonialism's epistemological violence, a violence perpetuated by the ideological state apparatus of the French-Antillean educational system.

Though Fanon does not name the school system as a contemporary example of Lenin's ideological state apparatus, the indoctrination of Antillean schoolchildren shows how imperialist ideology establishes and maintains empire through the denial of the African ancestral presence and the elision of African contributions to Antillean culture. For Lenin, ideological state apparatuses function "massively and productively by ideology, but they also function secondarily *by repression* (including physical repression), while functioning secondarily by ideology" (Althusser 145). But it "is the educational apparatus [that is] in fact the dominant ideological State Apparatus" (154).

Fanon's example also suggests that each succeeding generation of Antilleans becomes unconsciously complicit in its own oppression; furthermore the language in which these lessons are taught is the colonizer's language, the official imperial language of the Antilles: French. In this regard Paul Nursey-Bray credits Fanon's seemingly prophetic ideological and political vision: "Fanon anticipates a number of contemporary positions in his recognition that a liberated consciousness is not an automatic response to social change. . . . There must, in addition, be a process by which the ideological forms are directly confronted and overturned, a basic revision of 'the idea that the colonized holds of himself'" (135). To overturn the ideological structures of colonialism, these structures must first be identified. Fanon identifies the French-Antillean educational system as an ideological structure and, in doing so, establishes the need for its complete restructuring if the natives are to attempt mental decolonization. Part and parcel of this potential psychic liberation is the issue of language.

If language is the plane on which humans experience a uniquely human existence, as both Fanon and Heidegger agree, then language dictates one's apprehension of Being. For Fanon, colonial subjects experience a complete and utter disunity of Being with the internalization of not only a foreign language but also the imperial language of an oppressively racist value system. He emphasizes the resultant ontological dissonance in his description of a French colonial subject who relocates to France as one who experiences "definitive . . . absolute mutation" (*Black Skin, White Masks* 19). He asks of this relocated colonized subject, "What is the origin of this personality change? What is the source of this new way of being? . . . The fact that the newly returned Negro adopts a language different from that of the group into which he was born is evidence of a dislocation, a separation" (25). The resultant disalienation, as Fanon has termed it, the forced apprehension of the self as the evil other in the Manichaean colonial world, feeds and perpetuates the inherently racist doctrines of European colonial rule. His critique of Manichaeism effectively connotes the extreme power dynamics of colonial rule—as evinced by the episteme of racism intrinsic to the colonial educational system—wherein the colonizer is positioned as the epitome of all that is good and the colonized native is viewed as the quintessence of evil. This symbolic duality cum material duality is emblematic on two related levels.

First, Fanon's implicit aim in *Black Skin, White Masks* is to unearth and explain the colonized subjects' collective psychological complex by exposing its roots in their material reality, discursive engagement, and existential circumstances. Second, his explanation of the ideological and historical structures supporting colonialism posits an extreme hegemonic dynamic that justifies and rationalizes the irrationality (or neurotic structure) of the racist, colonial impulse itself. For it must be remembered that "racism is an ideology that justifies economic exploitation, oppression, and the domination of one country by another, of one race by another. The cruder the form of exploitation, the cruder the accompanying ideology" (Nursey-Bray 136). Fanon's examples of imperial language acquisition and colonial classroom lessons illustrate the crudeness of racism as a violent ideological practice. As Sartre explains, racism must "become a practice: it is not contemplation awakening the significations engraved on things; it is *in itself* self-justifying violence. . . . The activity of racism is a *praxis* dominated by a 'theory' ('biological,' 'social' or empirical racism, it does not matter which) aiming . . . to use every possible means to increase the 'sub-humanity' of the natives" (*Critique* 720–21).

Much like Fanon's definition of racism as both ideology and praxis, Sartre's denotation of racism is highly instructive in its insistence on the epistemic and physical violence of racism in the creation of empire, both of which reveal empire's hegemonic nature. And, quite rightly, Sartre invokes those discourses of racism as predicated on "biological," "social," and "empirical" grounds. With these statements Sartre substantiates the intertextuality of racist discourse found in the writings of Hume, Kant, Jefferson, and Hegel since their works are predicated on "biological," "social," and "empirical" theories of African racial difference.

To illustrate Fanon's and Sartre's similar conceptualizations of racism as ideology, praxis, and self-justifying violence I will revisit Fanon's

Antillean schoolchild being taught the spurious tenets of European cultural and racial superiority. Picture a full classroom of Antillean schoolchildren repeating the teacher's historically fictive litany, "Our ancestors, the Gauls . . ." Ideology is at work, its epistemic and psychological violence obliterating the native history and culture of the Antilles. Now picture a lone child raising her hand in protest, telling her teacher (in perfect French) that her great-grandmother, a former slave, told her that all of her ancestors came from Africa and that the Creole they were forbidden to speak in school was a mixture of their native African language(s) and their acquired French. Now hear the exclamations of shock and surprise around the classroom as the teacher's face screws violently into a frown. The teacher steadies her angry voice and tells the student that her great-grandmother is sadly mistaken. The young girl replies that her great-grandmother is never wrong, prompting the teacher to pull a ruler from her desk drawer. She calls the troublemaking student to the front of the class, telling her to hold out her right hand. Crack! The ruler smacks the girl's small palm. Where are your ancestors from? France, the class answers. The physical violence of corporal punishment ensures that the epistemic violence of colonial ideology and praxis will henceforth go unchallenged.[10] Quite tellingly, a thorough investigation into how the voicing of Martinican Creole would seemingly subvert French imperial culture is conspicuously absent from Fanon's study.

Using the ideological state apparatus of the educational system, Fanon depicts the systemic and hegemonic nature of European imperialism and colonialism. The forced domination of an entire people is justified by institutions that perpetuate the myth of not only native inferiority but an aberrant native evil, an evil that must be contained, controlled, and conditioned by imperial domination. Fanon's Manichaean metaphor allows for a highly symbolic allegory for the philosophy of racism behind colonial domination, while underscoring the debilitating inferiority complex of the colonized class. It bears repeating that under this Manichaean system, native history and culture are reified as the quintessence of evil, of primitivism and backwardness, and since a people's collective self-perception and self-identification are inextricably linked to the colonizer's imperial denigration of that native culture, the natives' collective self-esteem is effectively decimated. On the centrality of racism in Fanon's Manichaean construct Nursey-Bray explains:

> Fanon's discussion of the Manichaean character of the settler/native
> relations . . . is seeking to capture the character of the colonial world at

that precise historical moment when the ideology of racism is para-
mount. . . . An understanding of the Manichaeism of the value structure of the colonial world remains of importance. The ideology of
racism has to be confronted because it imprisons the native within a
value system that construes their identity in negative terms of inadequacy and impotence. (137)

Nursey-Bray is quite right to characterize the colonized subject's self-
identification as "inadequate and impotent"; however, I would argue
further that the native's self-perception of powerlessness goes far
beyond feelings of negative self-worth. It must be remembered that colonized subjects suffer from an inferiority complex predicated on the
colonizer's institutionalization of their professed, and extensively theorized, subhumanity. So although Nursey-Bray's assessment of imperial
and colonial racism's ideological intractability is accurate, the Manichaean poles represented by white and black are not only good and
evil but also being human and being perceived as apart from humanity.
The natives' apprehension of being apart is epitomized in their desire
to become white.

On this craving for racial transubstantiation, Fanon observes, "It is in
fact customary in Martinique to dream of a form of salvation that consists of magically turning white" (Black Skin, White Masks 44). The fact
that some natives desire to become white speaks to the depth of their
self-alienation. The natives no longer wish to be perceived as subhuman
and remain apart; they wish to exist in the world of fully recognized
humanity, the world of whiteness. Being for the native therefore means
being white. Antillean natives' internalization of the anti-African racism at the heart of the colonial project should not be surprising, given
the harsh material realities of colonialism, as Fanon's examples demonstrate. Under these circumstances it would be surprising if the colonized subject maintained an unchanged, precolonial self-perception.

The natives, as both Fanon and Sartre emphasize, are made to feel
subhuman; what is more they are forced to become completely dependent on the colonizer due to the institutionalized racism that reaches
every corner of their social existence. According to V. Y. Mudimbe's
assessment of native inferiority and dependence,[11] "The alienation of
colonialism entails both the objective fact of total dependence (economic, political, cultural and religious) and the subjective process of self-
victimization of the dominated. The colonized internalizes the racial
stereotypes imposed upon him, particularly in his attitudes towards
technology, culture, and language" (175). Mudimbe's analysis of colo-

nial alienation as a dual process of dependence and self-victimization is incisive. However, I would also characterize this dual process, this transformation of the native into a dependent and victimized colonized subject as one that entails an erasure of Being. Through the erasure of native culture and history, mentally colonized natives become a collective tabula rasa on which the colonizer inscribes the hegemonic cultural, ideological, and symbolic edicts of the European imperial order. The colonized subjects' forced dependence ensures that the edicts of empire will go unchallenged, for if colonized subjects internalize racist European conceptualizations of themselves, then they believe in their own inferiority and in the Europeans' right to dominate. Fanon writes that if the native "is overwhelmed to such a degree by the wish to be white, it is because he lives in a society that makes his inferiority complex possible, in a society that derives its stability from the perpetuation of this complex, in a society that proclaims the superiority of one race; to the identical degree to which that society creates difficulties for him, he will find himself thrust into a neurotic situation" (*Black Skin, White Masks* 100). Hence colonial rule remains intact and the colonized remain subjugated and self-alienated. For Fanon, the black-white polarity is palpable within the colonial subject's psyche, where it is also evinced in the domain of sociosexual desire. In chapters 2 and 3, "The Woman of Color and the White Man" and "The Man of Color and the White Woman," Fanon uses the field of sexual relationships to explore the dynamics of interracial desire in the colonial world.

THE DUALITY OF COLONIAL DESIRE

Some critics have identified both a gender bias and a homophobic strain in Fanon's analysis of heterosexual relationships in the colonial world, specifically citing the following chapters: "The Woman of Color and the White Man," "The Man of Color and the White Woman," and "The Negro and Psychopathology" (Bergner 75–79, 80–85; Fuss, "Interior Colonies" 30–35). While aspects of their arguments are well-founded, it is my contention that Fanon's interpretation of Mayotte Capécia's autobiography, *Je suis Martiniquais,* reflects a gendered reading of colonialism and proto-nationalism that, in some ways, anticipates Tom Nairn's interpretation of the modern nation as the two-faced Janus. McClintock's reading of Nairn's Janus-like nation urges us to consider:

> For Nairn, the nation takes shape as a contradictory figure of time: one
> face gazing back into the primordial mists of the past, the other into an

infinite future. . . . What is less often noticed, however, is that the temporal anomaly within nationalism . . . is typically resolved by figuring the contradiction in the representation of *time* as a natural division of *gender.* Women are represented as the atavistic and authentic body of national tradition. . . . Men, by contrast, represent the progressive agent of national modernity. (91–92)

The Janus-faced nation, then, is one in which women symbolize the nation's traditional past. Where the female for Nairn represents the culturally pristine elements of the independent nation, the female for Fanon represents the anachronistic and oppressed aspects of a still colonized nation. In Fanon's interpretation of Capécia's autobiography, woman as nation is pushed even further back in time. Woman, in this case Mayotte Capécia, comes to represent a colonial past that predates the return of native sovereignty and independence from European rule, a colonial past that is rife with the gender-specific subjugation of colonized female natives under the racist, patriarchal edicts of empire.

In Fanon's excerpt of *Je suis Martiniquais,* Capécia couples with her white French paramour in order to ascend the colonial racial hierarchy, despite knowing that her partner, steeped in the tenets of European racial superiority, will never truly consider her his equal: "I should have liked to be married, but to a white man. But a woman of color is never altogether respectable in a white man's eyes. Even when he loves her. I knew that" (qtd. in Fanon *Black Skin, White Masks* 42). In Gwen Bergner's estimation, Capécia's desire to marry a white man represents "her aspirations to privilege her socio-sexual behavior [as it is] influenced by the economic and sexual politics of a racist, patriarchal society" (83).

Bergner's argument is partially correct, yet she does not address Capécia's plainly stated desire for a white European physiognomy or her heartfelt pride in her European ancestry. Capécia provides a chronological genealogy of her family's racial relations and subsequent couplings with Europeans in Martinique, revealing a self-alienation that is made evident in her emphatic aesthetic preference for light or white skin and white family relations: "So my mother, then, was a mixture? I should have guessed it when I looked at her light color. I found her prettier than ever, and cleverer, and more refined. If she had married a white man, do you suppose I should have been completely white? . . . And life might not have been so hard for me? . . . I made up my mind that I could never love anyone but a white man, a blue-eyed blonde, a Frenchman" (qtd. in Fanon 46–47). Here we see the degree to which Capécia subscribes to the enforced ideological and cultural standard of Manichaeism. It seems that for her "white and black represent the two poles of a world, two poles in perpetual conflict: a genuinely Manichean concept of the world" (44–45). Though Bergner charges that Capécia only "sometimes—but not always—lapses into valorizing whiteness" and that Fanon "sees women's economic and sexual choices as emanating from some psychic dimension of the erotic that is disconnected from material reality," ("Who Is That Masked Woman?" 83) it appears that Fanon takes issue with Capécia's emphatic privileging of white racial identity rather than the frequency with which she does so.

The mental colonization that has given rise to Capécia's self-alienation is born of her awareness of colonial society's proscriptions against native black identity and that she may gain access to Being— both social and ontological—through her marriage to a Frenchman. The white mask of her desired relationship with a Frenchman may properly obscure her self-negated identity as a woman of color, and despite the stares of condescension she receives (Fanon, *Black Skin, White Masks* 43), she will have access to the wealth and privilege she had always desired. Not only has she internalized the colonizing other as her self, but her totalizing embrace of whiteness and all that it signifies is evidence that her coveted assumption of white racial identity lies at the root of her inferiority complex.

Fanon's critique of Capécia locates her desire within the sphere of a European imperial tradition that necessitates colonial exploitation and is perpetuated through consensual, and nonconsensual, relations with colonized females who bear racially mixed progeny. Based on Capécia's description of her interracial mother and white maternal grandmother, her ancestors represent the female as the embodiment of a national past, which locates the Janus-faced national project within the realm of white colonial domination and native self-alienation. The female no longer symbolizes a bygone era of cultural purity but the very history of colonialism itself. It is a history that is firmly grounded in French imperialist male exploitation of colonized women. Capécia's biological, social, and symbolic aspirations to whiteness represent a longing for a national past that is forever tied to the sociopolitical exigencies of empire. This is particularly evident in her desire to marry a white man, despite the racism that would prevent him from viewing her as his equal. Fanon follows his excoriation of Capécia's autobiography with another reading of native self-conceptualization in René Maran's novel, *Un homme pareil aux autres*. I will analyze how Fanon highlights the vexed issue of Being through the Antillean protagonist

Jean Veneuse's correspondence with his friend, a Frenchman named
Coulanges.

Fanon excerpts sections of Maran's novel to recount what Veneuse
considers an impossible situation: his wish to marry a white French
woman. Veneuse asks his friend Coulanges for advice, and both Coulanges's advice and the tone of his admonitions are quite revealing. He
demands that Veneuse abandon all foolish thoughts of belonging to the
Negro race since he has, for all intents and purposes, become a Frenchman through the veritable transmutation of his white mask into an
invisible white skin. Since Veneuse has lived in France from the age of
four, Coulanges even goes so far as to question Veneuse's awareness of
his own racial identity. He admonishes him to remember:

> You are really one of us. Perhaps you are not altogether aware of the
> fact. In that case, accept that you are a Frenchman from Bordeaux. Get
> that into your thick head. You know nothing of your compatriots of
> the Antilles. . . . In fact you are like us—you are "us." Your thoughts are
> ours. You behave as we behave. . . . You think of yourself . . . as a Negro?
> Utterly mistaken! You merely look like one. As for everything else, you
> think as a European. Since European men love only European women,
> you can hardly marry anyone but a woman of the country where you
> have always lived, a woman of our good old France, your real and only
> country. (qtd. in Fanon 68)

Aside from insulting Veneuse's intelligence, Coulanges assumes that
he lacks any awareness of himself as physiognomically distinct from a
Caucasian French person. The fact that Veneuse, despite years of French
acculturation and assimilation, still questions the feasibility of his mar-
rying a white French woman indicates a self-identification that is still
connected to his racial and cultural identification as a French Antillean subject of African descent. Coulanges's harsh words seem unnerv-
ing; however, in Fanon's critique they reveal how identity formation is
the exclusive right of the European imperialist. Fanon explains, "The
white man agrees to give his sister to the black—but on one condition:
You have nothing in common with real Negroes. You are not black,
you are 'extremely brown'" (69). Both Coulanges's challenge to the colonized Veneuse and Fanon's response to the same substantiate Fuss's
assertion that in *Black Skin, White Masks* "Fanon proposes that in the
system of power-knowledge that upholds colonialism, it is the white
man who lays claim to the category of the Other, the white man who
monopolizes otherness to secure an illusion of unfettered access to
subjectivity. . . . Colonialism works in part by policing the boundar-

ies of cultural intelligibility, legislating and regulating which identities attain full cultural signification and which do not" ("Interior Colonies" 21). Coulanges, as a white man, polices the boundaries of racial identity by asserting his right to name, or in this case not name, Veneuse as the black native, the colonized Other. Coulanges condescendingly extends whiteness and human subjectivity to the Antillean Veneuse because Veneuse's white mask has become indistinguishable from his "extremely brown skin." Veneuse is no longer a Negro because he has completely adapted—culturally, linguistically, and socially—to French life and has become, for all intents and purposes, a Frenchman and a stranger to the life and culture of his native Antilles. This acculturation compels Coulanges to grant Veneuse full signification as a Frenchman, no longer a colonized subject but a successful human experiment in colonial transubstantiation: the native becomes the colonizer's doppelganger because the colonizer has deigned to deem him so.

While Fanon's readings of Capécia and Maran offer insight into the colonial subject's self-alienation, he forges ahead to explore material and ontological manifestations of racism and their impact on the colonized subjects' lived experience. He begins this inquiry with an analysis of Sartre's *Anti-Semite and Jew* to denote the loaded meaning of overdetermination.

This overdetermination, defined first by Sartre and later revised by Fanon, is best explained by Fanon's excerpt of Sartre's *Anti-Semite and Jew*: "They [the Jews] have allowed themselves to be poisoned by the stereotypes that others have of them, and they live in fear that their acts will correspond to this stereotype. . . . We may say that their conduct is perpetually overdetermined from the inside" (qtd. in Fanon *Black Skin, White Masks* 115). Fanon continues to differentiate between the Jew's and the black's overdetermination, stressing that in most cases Jews have white skin that may obfuscate their Jewish identity, but for blacks, there is no chance of being seen as anything other than black. Using himself as an example, he writes, "In my case everything takes on a *new* guise. I am overdetermined from without. I am a slave . . . of my own appearance" (116). His choice of the word *slave* is particularly arresting. No longer shackled by the bonds of chattel slavery, the black subjects' colonial society and indeed their own colonized minds are now the enslavers.

Fanon insists that blacks' overdetermination is as permanent as their black skin. The reality of this overdetermination and epidermalization is best captured in chapter 5, "The Fact of Blackness" in the English edi-

tion (1967) and "The Lived Experience of the Black" in the direct translation from the French edition (1952). Despite the different denotative
and connotative meanings in these titles, both reveal the manner in
which Fanon uses *Black Skin, White Masks* to interrogate phenomenology and ontology as branches of philosophy centered on "the investigation of appearances" (Hinchman and Hinchman 187). Where the
English edition situates blackness itself as the subject of a phenomenological inquiry, the French edition positions the black subject as the
ontological subject under consideration, and the subject's blackness
becomes the de facto phenomenon of lived experience. In both cases
blackness and the lived experience of being black therefore represent
the ineluctable aspect of existential facticity in the colonial world.

HAILING AND HEGEL: RACIST INTERPELLATION
AND HEGELIAN DISCOURSE

In a chapter that the critic Ian Baucom has called "perhaps the most
influential chapter of [the] text" (15), Fanon proceeds to define "the
fact of blackness"/"the lived experience of the black" through lengthy
autobiographical encounters of his own racial objectification by the
interpellation of whites. He jars the reader's senses with the opening
exclamation: "Dirty nigger" or simply "Look a Negro!" (*Black Skin,
White Masks* 109). He recounts his experiences of racist interpellation,
seemingly positioning himself as the colonial neurotic by delving in to
his own damaged psyche.

Lewis Gordon explains that Fanon "goes to a deeper level of inte-
riority: his own experience as *lived*. He finds, in his autobiographical
moment, a set of theses converging. The chapter 'The Lived Experience of the Black' begins with a little white boy's use of language—of
publicity—to enmesh Fanon in the realm of pure exteriority, the realm
of epidermal schema. There, Fanon's existence is a two-dimensional
objectification" (*Existentia Africana* 33). This two-dimensional objectification indicates an ontological shattering whereby Fanon's very
humanity is called into question. Fanon proceeds to describe a cleaving
of racially stereotyped selves that the white boy's hailing has elicited:

> In the train it was no longer a question of being aware of my body in
> the third person but in a triple person. . . . I was responsible at the same
> time for my body, for my race, for my ancestors. I subjected myself to
> an objective examination, I discovered my blackness, my ethnic char-
> acteristics; and I was battered down by tom-toms, cannibalism, intel-

lectual deficiency, fetishism, racial defects, slave-ships, and above all
else, above all: "Sho good eatin." (*Black Skin, White Masks* 112)

Fanon's ontological triplication illustrates how the black colonized subject becomes a representation for his physicality, race, and forebears
while recalling internalized stereotypes of blackness that hail from the
African continent ("cannibalism and fetishism") to the American South
("Sho good eatin"). These stereotypes imply that black colonized subjects
and African diasporic subjects are one and the same in their experiences
of anti-African racism. African diasporic subjects cannot exist autono-
mously; their ontology is ever problematized by the presence of whites:
"In the *Weltanschauung* of a colonized people there is an impurity, a flaw
that outlaws any ontological explanation. . . . Ontology . . . does not per-
mit us to understand the being of the black man. For not only must the
black man be black; he must be black in relation to the white man" (*Black
Skin, White Masks* 109–10). The black subject's apprehension of Being is
problematized by the ineluctable presence of the white—individual, society, and colonial society. Ontology for the black subject is not an a priori
reality; instead it is a reality permanently compromised and defined by
the inescapable duality with whiteness and all that it represents: white
supremacy, anti-African racism, and racist stereotypes.

Fanon explores this lived binary in autobiographical encounters, and
his reactions bespeak the anger, shock, and trauma befitting one who
is experiencing a form of existential dread. In C. L. R. James's assessment of Heideggerian dread, he contends that in Heidegger's estimation "man is not afraid of anything in particular or of any person in
particular. He says the mere fact that you are living, you are going to be
dead and you do not know what exactly is going to happen to you, he
says that makes in your existence the necessity of some kind of dread
as to what is going to happen to you in your future" (*Wilson Harris*
9). In James's interpretation, Heideggerian dread is the feeling of fore-
boding of the known, death's inevitability, and of the unknown, the
exact moment of death. For Fanon, this dread occurs at the moment of
racist interpellation—"Dirty nigger!"— when the Manichaean colonial
world's epistemic violence has the potential to become physical. Fanon
captures the hailing's recurring nature through repetition; he repeats
the hailing four separate times throughout the chapter, an act of exposition that reflects its frequent occurrence in the colonial world.

The existential themes of Being and Freedom in Fanon's dialectical (and dreadful) colonial world seem to necessitate that due consid-

eration be given to the originator of the modern dialectical process, Hegel. For Fanon, the quest for Freedom is crystallized in his interpretation of the Hegelian dialectic of recognition and struggle in *Phenomenology of Mind*. The Hegelian dialectic of individual consciousness and recognition is laid bare in Fanon's somewhat paradoxical section in chapter seven, "The Negro and Hegel," a title that raises several red flags. Hegel's only position on the Negro is one of complete derision. His *Lectures on the Philosophy of World History* speciously establishes the Negro as neither contributing to civilization nor possessing human consciousness. Moreover *Black Skin, White Masks* does not address the African's historical and ontological erasure in Hegelian discourse. Failing to address and refute the logic of Hegel's anti-African bias makes Fanon's usage of Hegel's dialectic of consciousness and recognition from *Phenomenology of the Mind* somewhat ironic.[12] Hegel's dialectic of human recognition and violent struggle encapsulates perfectly the lot of Africana peoples' four-centuries-long fight for humanity and Freedom under Western chattel slavery and colonialism. The very race that Hegel deemed subhuman is the same race whose long history of oppression and resistance is mirrored in his own seminal dialectic. The irony is considerable.

Given Hegel's virulent anti-African position, Fanon's attraction to Hegelian discourse seems grounded in its animation of history as the preeminent social field that determines human experience, since history and culture make human beings who and what they are: "For Hegel, man is first and foremost a being who functions within the context of history and culture. . . . He viewed human becoming as dominated by world history" (Schrader 13–14). As the colonial encounter was a consequence of Western hegemonic history and European cultural and racial imperialism, we must also consider another European colonial subject's views on the Hegelian dialectic. Amilcar Cabral reminds us, "There was constant resistance to [European colonial] force. If the colonial force was acting in one direction, there was always our force which acted in the opposite direction" (33). Using a dialectical framework, Cabral vividly illustrates the ineluctable nature of colonial oppression and native resistance. Thus it seems that these exigent aspects of Hegel's dialectic are what moved Fanon to reinterpret Hegelian dialectics within the colonial setting.

Fanon utilizes Hegel's dialectical logic in *Black Skin, White Masks* to address several related aspects of the colonial encounter. He proposes that the colonial subject's inferiority complex has been created by the history, politics, and culture of European empire and colonialism. He also posits the colonial subject's self-alienation as the direct result of an oppressive environment stemming from the history and culture of European domination. It is no wonder that this aspect of Hegelian discourse held allure for Fanon, as it probes the connection between human alienation and world history in its recognition that "the particular form of alienation experienced by an individual depends upon his situation in world history and cannot be overcome save as historical-cultural processes follow out of the logic of their development" (Schrader 14). For Fanon, it seems that Hegel established the ideal conceptual framework with which to comprehend colonized subjects' self-alienation as a product of global historical, cultural, and political forces.

HUMAN RECOGNITION AND LIBERATION

Fanon adapts Hegelian dialectics to the modern colonial predicament. Alienation becomes the colonial subject's disalienation, a state of self-hatred created by the history and culture of European empire, and a state of (internalized) oppression that can be overcome only through the historical process of decolonization. This process of radical historical and societal change may be catalyzed through the antithesis of the colonial inferiority complex: a liberated consciousness that catalyzes the colonial subject's quest for Freedom. This Freedom may be attained through a confrontation, indeed a demand for human recognition from the colonizer. Fanon distills key points from Hegel's *Phenomenology of the Mind* to interpret the problematic of human recognition for the colonized by the colonizer. In Fanon's estimation, Hegel stresses, "Man is human only to the extent to which he tries to impose his existence on another man in order to be recognized by him. As long as he has not been effectively recognized by the other, that other will remain the theme of his actions. It is on that other being, on recognition by that other being that his own human worth and reality depend. It is that other being in whom the meaning of his life is condensed" (*Black Skin, White Masks* 216–17). In the colonial setting, Fanon asserts, the colonizer will remain the principal catalyst of the colonized subjects' actions until the colonizer recognizes natives as human; furthermore the meaning of the natives' lives is located in the colonizer's willful denial of their humanity. Unless the colonizer recognizes and acknowledges the natives' humanity a violent confrontation will ensue: "It is solely by risking life that freedom is obtained; only thus is it tried and proved that the essential nature of self-consciousness is not *bare exis-tence*" (Hegel qtd. in *Black Skin, White Masks* 218).

Quite paradoxically Hegel's *Phenomenology of the Mind* makes a rather strong case *against* the epistemological and ontological erasure of Africans inherent in Western discourse, for risking one's life for the attainment of Freedom is and has been the nexus of Africana resistance to slavery, colonialism, and oppression. Fanon extrapolates on Hegel's initial proposition:

> Human reality in-itself-for-itself can be achieved only through con-flict and through the risk that conflict implies. This risk means that I go beyond life towards a supreme good that is the transformation of subjective certainty of my own worth into a universally valid objective truth. . . . He who is reluctant to recognize me opposes me. In a savage struggle, I am willing to accept convulsions of death, invincible disso-lution, but also the possibility of the impossible. (218)

For Fanon, the risk of death concretizes the essence of human exis-tence: the need for human recognition and the quest for Freedom. His insistence that "he who is reluctant to recognize me opposes me" repre-sents the throwing down of the revolutionary gauntlet; that he accepts death as a possible outcome in a struggle for Freedom reveals *Black Skin, White Masks* as the originary text of Fanonian radicalism, a radi-calism that is generally considered to have developed out of his later political and discursive involvement with the French-Algerian War:

> Several of Fanon's interpreters suggest that he became aware of the necessity for violence as a result of his Algerian experience. This does not seem to be the case. For as early as his first book . . . published in 1952, Fanon had unmistakably arrived at this conclusion by way of Hegel. In a section of that book devoted to "The Negro and Hegel," Fanon used the plight of the Negro to elaborate a theory of the condi-tions under which the Negro could liberate himself . . . [concluding] that Freedom . . . can only be established by a dialectical progression in which the subjected individual imposes himself on the other in a vio-lent demand for acceptance. (Martin 392)

In the colonial world this violent demand for recognition reaches its climax in decolonization struggles. Colonized subjects are not recog-nized as human beings worthy of exercising their right to sovereignty; therefore they are forced, by the nature of this dialectic, to demand recognition from their oppressors, and they court death to obtain it. For Fanon, violence and the risk of death mean that the native's life is transformed into the corporeal manifestation of Freedom's "universal objective truth." This transubstantiation allows the colonized to unmistakably represent what is at stake: "Violence expresses this disincarnate, ethereal freedom. It is how freedom exists less as an attribute than as the very subject exacting recognition through the risking of life. The rehabilitating value of violence lies in the equation that the colonized are ready to risk the only and most precious thing they have, namely, their life, for their dignity and equality" (Kebede 550).

Kebede supports Fanon's position that resistance to colonial oppression moves Freedom out of the realm of abstraction and into the inequitable world of human existence, that the injustices of colonial oppression can be eradicated through a physical struggle for Freedom that evinces the formerly colonized subject's newly liberated consciousness. This newly liberated native consciousness is intrinsic to and dependent upon the newly created, progressive social order since "there can be no radical transformation of identity without an entire struggle to radically transform the social order. And no radical transformation of the social structure is possible (nor would it have a purpose) without the transformation of identity—the self-creation of a new kind of human being. It is this self-creation and renewal that is the aim of all effort" (Birt 211). These new humans are those who have initiated their self-re-creation by decolonizing their minds, by disposing of internalized racism through the recognition of their own intrinsic value, and by daring to restructure their formerly oppressive society into one that is egalitarian and just.

Clearly Fanon's call for native Freedom in *Black Skin, White Masks* reflects his ongoing dialogue with Marxist theory and its preoccupation with societal transformation. Yet his radicalism surpasses that of Marx because, rather than characterizing violence as the "midwife of history" (qtd. in Kebede 554), Fanon postulates that an actual historical subject is born of native resistance to colonialism's material, ideological, and hegemonic structures; a newly autonomous individual whose humanity is reconstituted.

The transformative violence used to actualize Freedom in *Black Skin, White Masks* reaches a crescendo in Fanon's later work *The Wretched of the Earth*, where he warns, "Decolonization, which sets out to change the order of the world . . . is a historical process: that is to say that it cannot be understood . . . except in the exact measure that we can discern the movements which give it historical form and content. . . . Decolonization is the veritable creation of new men" (36). And also: "Independence is not a word which can be used as an exorcism, but an indispensable condition for the existence of men and women who are truly liberated, in other words who are truly masters of all the material means which make possible the radical transformation of society" (310). The colonial subject's existential self-actualization, born of life-and-death confrontations for Freedom, leads to a radical societal transformation in which the liberated masses control their sovereignty and the economic and political means of survival.

With *Black Skin, White Masks*, Fanon achieves a critical tour de force and establishes the raison d'être for his philosophical thought. His professional training in psychoanalysis and his critical dialogues with Hegel, Marx, and Freud, among others, allowed him to elucidate areas of theoretical convergence among varied schools of Western thought. Similar to Walker and Du Bois, Fanon uses the Black subject's existence to problematize contemporary Western thought; like Du Bois and James, he uses the African diasporic subject as a point of inquiry in this critical experiment, which makes his achievement in *Black Skin, White Masks* unprecedented. For black subjects were never fully considered in the initial conceptualization of psychoanalysis, historical materialism, or dialectics. Fanon analyzes black colonial subjects' psychology and ontology; he probes their lived experience, illuminating a nexus of psychological, dialectical, material, and existential concerns that define their day-to-day reality. It is a reality that reveals the black colonial subject as the living embodiment of Western discourse's inherent paradoxes. For once again the Africana subject, categorized as subhuman by some of the most respected Western thinkers, wages battles for Being and Freedom that are reflected in Hegelian, Marxist, and existential thought. In revising these critical approaches, Fanon creates a unique hermeneutics, indeed a new system of knowledge, against empire that surpasses the radicalism of both Marx and Sartre, for he positions the attainment of Freedom in the colonial world as the apotheosis of existential actualization. This totality of Being begets a new race of humans capable of creating a world free of oppression, exploitation, and hegemonic domination. Idealistic, yes, but Fanon locates this idealism in the complete eradication of empire, a seemingly impossible feat that, if achieved, would necessitate that Freedom be realized by all.

CHAPTER FOUR

Brathwaite's Nation Language Theory

Sound and Rememory in the Americas

It was the time for sitting on porches. . . . It was time to hear things and talk.
These sitters had been tongueless, earless, eyeless conveniences all day long.
Mules and other brutes had occupied their skins. But now, the sun and the
bossman were gone, so the skins felt powerful and human. They became lords
of sounds and lesser things. They passed entire nations through their mouths.

—Zora Neale Hurston, *Their Eyes Were Watching God*

Where David Walker, Frederick Douglass, W. E. B. Du Bois, C. L. R.
James, and Frantz Fanon redirect Western historiography's narrative
axis by casting enslaved and colonized Africans as historical agents central to the genesis of Western civilization, modernity, and colonial liberation, the Bajan poet and critic Kamau Brathwaite holds these agents
to be the source of an Africana cultural discourse of resistance born in
the Americas. Like his predecessors, Brathwaite credits African orature
for creating a culture of resistance against chattel slavery in the Americas. However, his theoretical intervention in "History of the Voice"[1]
breaks from his predecessors' with his polemic nation language theory.
He renames the African oral tradition in the Americas *nation language*,
an African-based linguistic and cultural system in which Africana orature and music are central in the creation of a counterhegemonic New
World discourse. Similar to his antecedents' reinvigorations of Western
historiography and political philosophy, Brathwaite's theory of nation
language initiates a disruption of Western thought through its expressions of Being and Freedom. The radical nature of nation language
theory, however, is that it identifies the words, songs, *and* music of the
African oral tradition as a diasporic cultural system that has irrevoca-

bly altered the sound and diction of (imperial) English as it is spoken by Caribbean subjects of African, European, and Asian descent. Thus Brathwaite takes on the first aspect of African negation in Western discourse: the dehumanization of the African, the creation of Negro slaves, and the resultant devaluation of their cultural productions.

NATION LANGUAGE'S THEORETICAL RUPTURE

Nation language theory centers on enslaved Africans' cultural developments after the rupture of the Middle Passage, after the deracination from their native land, and upon their dispossession in the Americas, where they were forced to adapt. It is a theory of Africana discourse that privileges the voice in its communication of sound, words, and music from both African and Western cultural sources; consequently nation language theory is a fully encompassing diasporic critique of Africana cultural productions in the New World that acknowledges the paradoxical and ineluctable presence of Western cultural inheritances and influences. Brathwaite's nation language theory and his related conceptualization of tidalectics subvert Western theory in several radical ways.

First, Brathwaite's theory of nation language challenges the primacy of Western letters by implicitly questioning the ideological dyad at its foundation: the perceived superiority of European cultural productions and hierarchical status of the written word. Brathwaite designates an African-based New World vernacular nation language, a complete linguistic system with its own cultural, cosmological, and metaphysical logic. "History of the Voice" announces the discursive import of orality in the genesis of Africana diasporic culture; nation language theory thereby divests the written word of its hierarchical status and highlights Africana words, songs, and music (particularly the blues and jazz) in the establishment of an African diasporic creative protest tradition.

Second, nation language inverts the historical paradigm of imperial language imposition and Africana cultural subordination in the New World. The notion of a purely European-centered imperial linguistic discourse is refuted by Brathwaite's and other critics' historical documentation that supports nation language's impact on New World colloquial English. Paradoxically the submerged language of a dispossessed and enslaved African proletariat resurfaced to become and remain the dominant spoken language in the Anglophone Caribbean. Thus we may consider nation language a linguistic and epistemic revolution born of Western slavery, a sound revolution that has shattered the English pentameter and effectively dethroned the Queen's English as the lingua franca of the Anglophone Caribbean.

Third, nation language theory defies reductionist critical analyses through Brathwaite's interpellation of Western history and theory. He places nation language within a larger historical genealogy that names the fourteenth- and fifteenth-century European national languages and literatures movement begun by Dante as nation language's theoretical forerunner. Equally concerned with American and English colloquial influences, Brathwaite pointedly names the American T. S. Eliot and the Englishman John Arlott as two principal inspirations behind Caribbean writers' use of nation language in their literary texts ("Voice," 267–71, 286n34).

Fourth, by locating the nation simultaneously within language and the African diaspora (Hitchcock 64–66, 68–71), Brathwaite confounds the notion of the nation-state while simultaneously prefiguring Benedict Anderson's formulation of a primordial national orature that voices, defines, and perpetuates the imagined community that is the nation.

Fifth, Brathwaite's related conceptualization of tidalectics raises the specter of Hegel once more, if only to highlight the irony of the dialectician's persistent presence in the Africana counterhegemonic project. *Tidalectics* is clearly a play on *dialectics*, as Brathwaite himself notes (Mackey, *Paracritical Hinge* 9–10), yet in his clever assonant revision lies a penetrating reimagining of European-centered dialectics into an Africana theoretical model that envisions the tide, the water, and the Middle Passage—all of which figure so prominently in his historical, critical, and poetic works (*Islands*, *Middle Passages*, *Ancestors*, and *Arrivants*). With his invocation of the tide, Brathwaite reimagines dialectics in a manner that valorizes the historical experience of Western chattel slavery as the occasion for nation language's birth. Like Fanon, Brathwaite wrestles with Hegel, imperial language imposition, and cultural imperialism. Indeed the present absence of Martinican Creole in Fanon's evocative first chapter begs the question, At what incalculable cost have Africana people lost their native tongue(s)? Brathwaite's theory of nation language answers Fanon plaintively: The native tongue was never lost—only submerged and modified. Listen, speak, sing, and remember.

NEW WORLD LANGUAGE

To fully appreciate the import of Brathwaite's theoretical (re)vision, we must first examine his project of renaming. Just as Du Bois and James rename enslaved Africans black workers and a black proletariat, respectively, thereby acknowledging enslaved Africans' as revolutionary historical agents, Brathwaite's renaming of nation language fulfills a similar discursive mission: to assign full historical and cultural relevance to enslaved Africans' linguistic and musical expression in the Americas. Thus the orature of the enslaved should be deemed language, not dialect, for a people's language encompasses a discrete culture, cosmology, and ethical heritage that dialect (with its pejorative connotations) never could. Ngũgĩ wa Thiong'o further elucidates the connectedness between a people's language and culture in terms that signify a larger cultural inheritance and a collective cosmology:

> Culture embodies those moral, ethical and aesthetic values, the set of spiritual eyeglasses through which [people] come to view themselves and their place in the universe. Values are the basis of a people's identity, their sense of particularity as members of the human race. All this is carried by language. Language as culture is the collective memory bank of a people's experience in history. Culture is almost indistinguishable from the language that makes possible its genesis, growth, banking, articulation and indeed its transmission from one generation to the next. (14–15)

Language is therefore indivisible from culture, history, and cosmology; its invention and voicing become the threshold to a people's worldview. Brathwaite makes this connection clear in his description of nation language, with its "more ritual forms like *kumina*, like *shango*, the religious forms . . . which . . . begin to disclose the complexity that is possible with nation language" ("Voice" 272). Africana religions like kumina and shango are voiced in a language that defines and carries cultural meaning. Thus Brathwaite renames Anglophone Afro-Caribbean dialect nation language to emphasize that the word *dialect* is actually a misnomer, rife with the linguistic and cultural biases of Western imperialism and racism. He further differentiates between nation language and dialect, clarifying that dialect "carries very pejorative overtones. Dialect is thought of as . . . 'inferior' English. Dialect is the language when you want to make fun of someone. Caricature speaks in dialect. Dialect has a long history coming from the plantation where people's dignity was distorted through their languages and the descriptions that the dialect gave to them" (266).

Brathwaite underscores how the dialect of plantation culture acted to denigrate the enslaved. He implicitly recalls the "small" variant between *Negro* and *nigger*, a change made by traversing the path from English to dialectical English, which was used to distort enslaved Africans' collective self-perception and self-worth. *Negro* is the Spanish word for black. *Nigger*, in contrast, has the pejorative denotation and connotation of African dehumanization under chattel slavery. Dialect and its epithet for the African are theoretically and semantically opposed to an African-based cultural system that is the language of "Ashanti, Congo, Nigeria, from all that mighty coast of western Africa" (261). With his use of the word *mighty* to describe the cultures and countries of West Africa, Brathwaite interpellates the import of ancient African civilizations to and for the West. This region was the home of the former Ghana, Songhai, and Mali empires—kingdoms as renowned for their wealth as for their highly advanced civilizations, which included well-established networks of nautical trade among Africa, Europe, and Asia; international centers of religious and scholarly study, of which Timbuktu (in Mali) was just one; and highly developed political and social systems that, like much of the ancient world, included systems of servitude (Shinnie 56–85; Murphy 270–73).

Brathwaite further illustrates nation language's African roots by demonstrating that the hostile plantation environment forced African languages and cultural practices to "submerge themselves, because officially the conquering peoples—the Spanish, the English, the French, and the Dutch did not wish to hear people speaking Ashanti or any of the Congolese languages—So there was a submergence of this imported language. Its status became one of inferiority. Similarly, its speakers were slaves. They were conceived of as inferiors—nonhuman—in fact" ("Voices" 261–62). Here Brathwaite demonstrates the crucial link between Western theory and praxis. European slave owners and colonizers implemented the predominant eighteenth- and nineteenth-century racist doctrines on the material level within the environs of New World plantations, and Western ideologues conceived of Africans as subhuman. Africans' linguistic expression, though not deemed a formal language, was still communication and a potential threat to the slave system's survival. For this reason it had to be suppressed.

Western plantation owners' punitive suppression of African rituals is well documented.[2] Nation language's continued existence and entrenchment reflect the enslaved Africans' will to resist Western hegemonic domination, which confirms that nation language "invokes an affirmative ground for community. . . . Brathwaite eschews a narrative history of victimhood for the energy that a history of struggle creates" (Hitchcock 65). Nation language's power reflects the vernacular tradition's connection to New World resistance. Just as James's *The Black Jacobins* documents that African rites and Vodun chants engendered a sense of unity and catalyzed mass action among San Domingo's enslaved proletariat, Brathwaite's nation language compels its speakers to view themselves "as a people linked by the historical experiences of rupture, removal to the New World and organization into new . . . living relationships" (Nielsen 227).

SHATTERING THE PENTAMETER

"History of the Voice" explicates a struggle for linguistic primacy in the West. Braithwaite outlines the dimensions of this contest by discussing the dissimilarities between the "Ashanti and Congolese" languages of West Africa (261–62), which employ the kaiso (or calypso) dactyl, and the English of empire, which uses the pentameter, itself the syllabic embodiment of imperialist domination in the Americas (265). Aurally and metrically the pentameter predominates in most Anglo-Western literary productions,[3] leading Brathwaite to explain, "[Nation language] does not employ the iambic pentameter. It employs dactyls. It therefore mandates the use of the tongue in a certain way, the use of sound in a certain way. . . . In the Shakespeare . . . the voice travels in a single forward plane toward the horizon of its end. In the kaiso . . . we have a distinct variation. The voice dips and deepens to describe an intervallic pattern" (272). Consequently, on a syllabic level, a struggle for primacy of native expression takes place because the pentameter's forward and finite movement, according to Brathwaite, also "carries with it a certain kind of experience, which is not the experience of a hurricane. The hurricane does not roar in pentameter" (265).

Nation language's kaiso rhythms, on the other hand, better articulate and approximate the Caribbean's natural occurrences, like the hurricane, like the sun's rays dancing on a turquoise sea. With this exposition Brathwaite insists that only a more indigenous[4] linguistic and cultural system can communicate the native Caribbean experience. As the linguistic representation of imperial rule, the pentameter has robbed Caribbean people of "the syllabic intelligence, to describe the hurricane, which is our own experience; whereas we can describe the imported alien experience of snowfall. It is that kind of situation that we are in" (263). The syllable as a unit of oral intelligence is crucial to Brathwaite's thesis, for what more diminutive unit of speech more fully encapsulates the enormity of Western cultural imperialism? In the historical context of deracination and dispersal the syllable becomes shibboleth, a password unlocking a world of reclamation and resistance on the battlefield of linguistic discourse.

Brathwaite continues to contrast imperial English to nation language in his description of the latter's distinctly vernacular traits in which word and song constitute meaning. This meaning may be thoroughly communicated through orature as opposed to literature because

> it is from "the oral tradition." . . . The poetry, the culture itself, exists not in a dictionary but in the tradition of the spoken word. It is based as much on sound as it is on song. That is to say, the noise that it makes is part of the meaning, and if you ignore the noise (or what you would think of as noise, shall I say), then you lose part of the meaning. When it is written, you lose the sound or the noise, and therefore you lose part of the meaning. Which is, again, why I have a tape recorder for this presentation. I want you to get the sound of it, rather than the sight of it. (271)

Brathwaite stresses the orality of sound and song as these reflect a cultural tradition that is rooted in the voice. This cultural meaning is then opened in the voice and its varied tonal interpretations. Hearing sound and song means understanding meaning, and this is why he took taped recordings of nation language to his talk. Theorizing nation language solely on the page would be antithetical to its praxis and expression, so to explain nation language, he engaged his audience on the level of sound—not only the sound of his voice, tinged with Bajan nation language, but with the voices of many people, whose oral participation attests to nation language's communality.

Exemplifying Brathwaite's point that nation language voices the nexus between sound and meaning is the Jamaican patois pronunciation of the word *cyan*. In English it means *can*, but if one were to draw out the intermediary vowel sounds to "cy-y-a-a-an" the meaning actually becomes its opposite: *can't*. This is the sound that determines meaning itself, the sound and meaning Brathwaite urges his audience and readers to carefully consider.

THE VOICE AS HISTORY

Simon Gikandi comments on the voice and nation language theory's larger historical significance: "The voice . . . signifies shape and consciousness of that which has not, and cannot, be institutionalized," and the aim of Brathwaite's theory is to "create a space in which oral forms of history can be authorized as the true depositories of black cultures" (20). The voice and the orature it animates become living embodiments of a people's historical legacy. Unlike most institutionalized histories of the West, Africana orature stands as a counterhegemonic discourse in its valuation of Africana history and cultural heroes.[5] This is evinced in three particular stories that are oral in origin: *Sundiata*, the epic of old Mali;[6] the tales of John the slave; and the legend of John Henry (Hurston, "Characteristics" 16; Abrahams 13–14). As evinced by *Sundiata*, Africana orature has not expunged the medieval African contribution to Western civilization, nor has it dehumanized the African slave into the servile, infantile Sambo, as the tales of John the slave demonstrate. Neither has Africana orature denied the pivotal role of African American labor power in the development of American industrialization, as the legendary exploits of John Henry the steel-driving man also attest.

Similar to Fanon's chapter "The Negro and Language," Brathwaite's theory of nation language reveals the manner in which Western discourse's attendant doctrines of racism and imperialism demean indigenous Afro-Caribbean language and culture. He outlines the soul-killing effects of colonial education on Caribbean natives in terms similar to Fanon's Antillean schoolchildren learning of their "ancestors the Gauls." Brathwaite concurs that the ideological state apparatus of the English colonial educational system acted to

> recognize and maintain the language of the conquistador—the language of the planter, the language of the official, the language of the Anglican preacher—. It insisted that not only would English be spoken in the anglophone Caribbean, but that the educational system would carry the contours of an English heritage. . . . Shakespeare, George Eliot, Jane Austen, the models that were intimate to Great Britain, that had very little to do, really with the environment and the reality of the Caribbean—were dominant in the Caribbean educational system. People were forced to learn things that had no relevance to themselves. (262–63)

Thus, like the colonized Martinican subjects in Fanon's *Black Skin, White Masks*, colonized Bajans are stripped of their native identity and indoctrinated into the cultural symbology of a foreign European history that has no fundamental relation to the native Caribbean experience, other than that of the ideological enforcer of Western hegemony. Degraded and disremembered are the tales of Queen Nanny of the Maroons and glorified are the exploits of Robin Hood in Sherwood Forest (263). For Brathwaite, the colonial system's ideological state apparatuses—the educational system, local government, and churches—consistently devalue native culture and deny Afro-Caribbean orature's historical and cultural significance.

DETHRONING THE QUEEN'S ENGLISH

This same point of convergence between Brathwaite and Fanon also becomes a point of divergence. While Brathwaite explains the interposition of empire on native institutions, he continues with another analysis that challenges the typical narrative of imperial language imposition and native cultural subordination. He posits nation language as the linguistic system that subsumed imperial English rather than vice versa:[7] "English it may be in terms of its lexicon, but it is not English in terms of syntax. And English it certainly is not in terms of rhythm and timbre, its own sound explosion" ("Voice" 266). The vernacular's irrepressibility is precisely why nation language has evolved and changed, even altering the way the languages of European empire were spoken. Brathwaite posits that nation language's submergence

> served an interesting intercultural purpose, because although people continued to speak English as it was spoken in Elizabethan times and on through the Romantic and Victorian ages, that English was nonetheless, still being influenced by the underground language, the submerged language that the slaves had brought. . . . [Nation language] was moving from a purely African form to a form that was African, but which was adapting to the new environment and to the cultural imperatives of the European languages. And it was influencing the way in which the French, Dutch, and Spanish spoke their own languages. So there was a very complex process taking place which is now beginning to surface in our literature. (262)

Brathwaite's contention that English from the sixteenth century onward was being influenced by nation language is extremely significant for it reveals how an African-based linguistic system significantly altered the European languages of empire. Equally important is his larger theoretical proposition. By revealing how nation language moved from its traditional African form to an adapted Afro-Caribbean language that is spoken among descendants of African slaves, European slave owners, and European laborers, Brathwaite argues that nation language theory inverts the paradigm of European linguistic imposition and African cultural subordination. For nation language has become the dominant form of linguistic expression in the Anglophone Caribbean.

"The language of the slaves and labourers" (260) became the principal colloquial language in the colonial and postcolonial Caribbean. The irony is rich, for the West African cultural and linguistic system that European colonizers attempted to eradicate came to be the identifying marker of Euro-Caribbean and Afro-Caribbean linguistic expression. Brathwaite's position on nation language's (or Caribbean Creole's) impact on English from the Elizabethan era to the present day is supported in the work of other critics. According to Barbara Lalla and Jean D'Costa, the English spoken by whites in Jamaica and Barbados during the seventeenth century "bore many features of sound, morphology, and syntax directly relevant to Jamaican Creole" (16). Thus, in the Anglophone Caribbean, English slave owners as well as Irish and Scottish indentured servants came to speak an English whose meter, tone, and syntax pulsed with the inflections of western Africa. Nation language's submergence, then, became the simultaneous occasion for its adaptation, as it resurfaced by imprinting itself onto the European languages of empire. What is more, nation language is African-based orature, and, as such, it is the dialectic counterpoint to English, the language of Western hegemony in the Anglophone Caribbean. Linguistic discourse consequently becomes political discourse in the New World colonies, a political discourse that centers on using the Afro-Caribbean language of nation to define the Caribbean experience. In this regard nation language's metric rebellion is not solely based on subverting the linguistic meter of empire; it also utilizes a New World language system of African origins to describe and define the indigenous Caribbean experience itself.

Nation language's syntactical and tonal variations within English effectively voice the native Afro-Caribbean experience by itself and for itself. Since it is the only surviving language system indigenous to both Africa and the Caribbean, it also becomes a Caribbean cultural and linguistic system whose meter, tone, and diction are attuned to the Africana New World experience. This African-based language, with its own distinct syllabic and metrical pattern, comprises, according to Brathwaite, "the body work of the language" ("Voices" 264) that sounds out the Caribbean experience: "It is nation language in the Caribbean that, in fact, largely ignores the pentameter. Nation language is the language that is influenced by the African model, the African aspect of our New World Caribbean heritage" (265–66). This linguistic and cultural legacy was irrevocably shaped by the exigencies of chattel slavery and empire, historically "violent ruptures" through which unprecedented forms of expression and "collective meaning" (J. Gordon 10) were wrought.

NATION LANGUAGE AS ONTOLOGICAL AND PHENOMENOLOGICAL EXPRESSION

In the Heideggerian sense it may be said that nation language represents the linguistic expression of political and ontological self-determination since "the *phenomenon* of communication must be understood in an ontologically broad sense. Communication. . . . is grasped in principle existentially. . . . The communication of the existential possibilities of attunement, that is, the disclosing of existence, can become the true aim of poetic speech" (Heidegger 151–52). For enslaved Africans in the Americas the disclosing of their existence was certainly the aim of nation language's poetic speech. They voiced folktales and songs to reaffirm their humanity and articulate their existence as a cultural collectivity using what Brathwaite terms "total expression."

The total expression of nation language dissolves the divide between orature and literature, speaker and audience, individual and group. The spoken word *is* the literature of an enslaved community for whom the penalty against reading and writing was severe punishment or death. The voice becomes pen and paper, writer and reader. The distinction between speaker and audience dissolves in the call-and-response practice, wherein an unbroken circle of communication obviates any predetermined roles. The individual and group merge as stories and songs are given voice alternately by the one and the many. In this chorus of voices nation language becomes a communal activity in which a community itself is born. This is what Brathwaite identifies as total expression:

> Nation language is . . . part of what may be called *total expression*. Reading is an isolated, individualistic expression. The oral tradition, on the other hand, makes demands not only on the poet but also on the audience to complete the community: the noise and sounds that the poet makes are responded to by the audience and are returned to him. Hence we have the creation of a continuum where the meaning truly resides. And this total expression comes about because people live in

the open air, because people live in conditions of poverty, because people come from a historical experience where they had to rely on their own breath. . . . They had to depend on *immanence*, the power within themselves. ("Voice" 273)

Here Brathwaite provides the most compelling argument for Africana orature as a cultural manifestation of collective ontology or immanence. The continuum of meaning intrinsic to nation language reaffirms its participants' collective will and intent through call and response. In this communal circle the voice is used to articulate a collective totality of Being (Robinson 168–71) that is affirmed and indeed celebrated in the story's human animation. The gathering of enslaved Africans, their exchange of Anancy and other trickster tales, the singing of songs gave birth to a New World Africana community and culture. Enslaved Africans were strengthened and emboldened in this communal exercise that vivified their culture and reclaimed their collective humanity, despite the slave system's efforts to destroy it.

Through nation language their collective voice communicates and animates meaning, giving it life and renewed purpose. Meaning lives as the participants live: through the breath, in the voice, on the air. The storyteller and the audience become the tale or song that exists as living history. History and culture become tangible; they are immediate and, most important, alive in this life-affirming circle of expression. In nation language we may apprehend the possibility of ontological totality paradoxically wrought from the rupture of enslavement. Thus nation language acts as a theoretical and cultural discourse that may offer a collective totality of Being, thereby acting as a corrective to Western domination and dehumanization.

NATION LANGUAGE'S THEORETICAL ROOTS

Nathaniel Mackey is quite right in asserting that the seeds of Brathwaite's nation language theory lay in his 1971 historical study, *The Development of Creole Society in Jamaica 1770–1820*. Mackey argues that for Brathwaite "a struggle for turf is taking place in language" ("Other" 57). To illustrate this point he cites the following passage of Brathwaite's *Creole Society*: "It was in language that the slave was perhaps most successfully imprisoned by his master; and it was in his (mis-)use of it that he perhaps most effectively rebelled. Within the folk tradition language was (and is) a creative act in itself; the word was held to contain a secret power" (Brathwaite 237).

In *Creole Society*, Brathwaite identifies the enslaved African's resistance to imperial language imposition as both material and semiotic, yet he does so by categorizing this recalcitrance as a creative act. Through the humorous tale of Quashie, the ubiquitous Caribbean slave,[8] Brathwaite offers a striking example of agential self-determination. Quashie is baptized and adopts the Christian name Thomas to signify his spiritual rebirth. Quashie/Thomas has outstanding debts that he refuses to pay, rationalizing, "Me is new man now; befo me name Quashie, now me Thomas, derefo Thomas no pay Quashie debt" (Phillipo qtd. in Brathwaite 237). With Brathwaite's citation of Quashie's religious conversion as a creative act, one may grasp the development of nation language theory from these earlier stages in *Creole Society* to its refinement in "History of the Voice."

Though Brathwaite does not state that Quashie's use of what he then termed Jamaican Creole represents a linguistic and ideological challenge to slavery and empire, he does designate Quashie's (mis)use of language as a form of political rebellion. I would argue that both political *and* existential resistance is reflected in Quashie's speech. To illustrate this point Fanon's position on language bears repeating: "The phenomenon of language . . . should provide us with one of the elements in the colored man's comprehension of *the other*. For it is implicit that to speak is to exist absolutely for the other" (*Black Skin, White Masks* 17). When Quashie speaks, he exists for the English slave owner or colonizer. However, by choosing to address the slave owner or colonial administrator in the Jamaican Creole that affirms his African heritage and refusing to affect the Queen's English, Quashie takes a political and existential stand: he refuses to exist absolutely for the English colonizer, so he communicates subversively in the language that affirms his own African identity. What is more, Quashie strategically uses the religious instruments of empire to his advantage, so although he ostensibly submits to the hegemonic religious conversion of imperial rule, he concomitantly rebels against imperial economic exploitation by refusing to pay his debts.

In terms of nation language's existential relevance, Brathwaite's position on its expression of immanence bears repeating: "[Nation language] comes about . . . because people come from a historical experience where they had to . . . depend on *immanence*, the power within themselves" ("Voice" 273). For Quashie and countless others, the material reality of chattel slavery forced an existential awareness of their own innate power to resist imperial domination. Quashie resists by using the "language of slaves and laborers" to assert his African New World identity. He thereby privileges the cultural system of his own oppressed class over that of the ruling English slave-owning class. The actualization of slave resistance in and through language is also supported by Lalla and D'Costa, who demonstrate the manner in which Caribbean slaves alternately used Jamaican Creole or English acrolect depending on their social circumstances and their audience (42; see Abrahams 10). In this manner Quashie's decision to respond in nation language instead of the Queen's English may also be read as an act of protest against empire.

Brathwaite's specification that nation language emerges from a collective ontological source of immanence mirrors that of other nation language theorists, particularly as nation language articulates the Africana experience of Western oppression and the subsequent existential response. In discussing the work of the Black English theorist Geneva Smitherman,[9] George Yancy writes, "To best articulate that Black existential space where the *real* world . . . is filled with pain, struggle, blood, tears, and laughter—where death follows a minute of joy, where so much is improvisatory and surreal . . . requires fluency in the language that partly grows out of the nitty-gritty core of the epistemology and ontology of that space" (276). Yancy defends the use of nation language to distinguish among several ideological and cultural tropes that prompt an inherently existential awareness within the Black subject: the real, material world of anti-African racism versus the idealized, abstracted Western world of universal equality; the Africana response of improvisation and adaptation to the hostile, racist world; and mainstream language born of the idealized, abstracted world versus nation language born of the epistemology and ontology of Black existential space. Both Yancy and Brathwaite identify nation language as the tongue most capable of communicating what Fanon refers to as the lived experience of racism because, as Brathwaite illustrates, nation language emerged out of the very history of African racialized slavery (and racism) itself.

RACIAL ESSENTIALISM VERSUS AFRICAN SURVIVALS

Perhaps it is nation language theory's implicit conflation of ontological totality, collective immanence, and cultural memory that has caused several critics to label Brathwaite's work reductionist at best and essentialist and crude at worst (Edmonson, "Race, Tradition" 114; Hulme 74). These characterizations are inaccurate since Brathwaite explicitly

names both European and American colloquial influences that inspired
West Indian writers to use nation language in their literary texts. He
also identifies the European theoretical antecedents that preceded his
conceptualization of nation language theory.[10] In order to problematize
the essentialist categorizations of his theory, we must first examine the
debate surrounding the interrelated concepts of racial essentialism and
African cultural survivals (or retentions). To do this I will put forth two
critical interpretations of essentialism as these apply to Brathwaite's
work: the first and most commonly held analysis is that of bell hooks;
the second and comparatively less cited one is that of Diana Fuss. hooks
correctly argues that Western discourse has disseminated essentialist
theories that propagated "colonial imperialist paradigms of black identity which represent blackness one-dimensionally in ways that reinforce and sustain white supremacy. This discourse created the idea of
the 'primitive' and promoted the notion of an 'authentic' experience,
seeing as 'natural,' those expressions of black life which conformed to
a preexisting pattern or stereotype. Abandoning essentialist notions
would be a serious challenge to racism" (2482). hooks's essential, one-
dimensional black primitive is mirrored in the portrayals of savage
Africans found in sixteenth- and seventeenth-century travelogues,
which had a significant impact on the development of Enlightenment
racial science and racial hierarchies, as I detailed in chapter 1. She is
also correct in her assertion that an anti-African racial essentialism lies
at the core of hegemonic models of black identity and that notions of
nonessential blackness would seriously weaken the philosophical basis
of Western racism. She reinforces this point by calling for not only the
repudiation of essential notions of blackness but more nuanced readings of how the Africana historical experience of struggle has created
various black identities: "There is a radical difference between a repudiation of the idea that there is a black 'essence' and recognition of the
way that black identity has been specifically constituted in the experience of struggle and exile" (2483).

hooks's contention that more useful critiques of racial discourse
should include examinations of black identity formation that address
the historical experiences of struggle and exile is extremely relevant.
Her call for a more nuanced reading of Africana subjectivity urges less
focus on essentialism and more on the historical circumstances that
have created Africana identities and cultures. This argument is similar to that of Tiffany Patterson and Robin Kelley, who pose the following questions that have preoccupied scholars of Africana history

for centuries: "Were the so-called cultural survivals simply the most effective cultural baggage Africans throughout the world used in their struggles to survive? Or were they created by the very conditions under which they were forced to toil and reproduce?" (18). hooks and Patterson and Kelley raise important issues; nevertheless it must be acknowledged that African cultural retentions—like the West African trickster tales that find their varied forms in Bre'r Anancy of the West Indies and Bre'r Rabbit of the United States—functioned to create a distinctly New World Africana culture that was fundamentally opposed to chattel slavery.[11] Perhaps the question should not be one of cultural survival versus cultural adaptation but rather *how* Africans in the New World used their native cosmology to understand and envision their continued existence in hostile, foreign plantation environments.

Brathwaite's and Lalla and D'Costa's historical and textual documentation of African linguistic and cultural survivals in the Americas demonstrates that African cultural expressions survived in the New World plantation environment through simultaneous submergence and adaptation. Similarly Richard Wright argues, "If the American Negro retained, in part and for a time, remnants of his background of traditional African attitudes, it was because he couldn't see, feel or trust (at that moment in history) any other system of value or belief that could interpret the world and make it meaningful for him to act and rely upon it" (296). Thus the pertinent issue, as both Brathwaite and Wright stress, is not whether African survivals exist, but *why* they exist. They exist because enslaved Africans had to make sense of their deracination, bondage, and degradation. One way of creating this adaptive logic was through the articulation of cultural memory that gave voice to stories, songs, and music, an orature that then created a community itself defined by resistance and resilience.

In contrast to hooks's antiessentialist stance is Fuss's exploration of essentialism's broader discursive functions. Fuss introduces her primary argument in *Essentially Speaking* with the following claim: "Essentialism is neither good nor bad, progressive nor reactionary, beneficial nor dangerous. The question we should be asking is not 'is this text essentialist (and therefore 'bad')?' but rather, 'if this text is essentialist, *what motivates its deployment*?'" (xi). Her challenge is progressive, for not only is this practice uncommon among some of Brathwaite's critics,[12] but Fuss makes the argument that critics' adherence to essentialism need not be unequivocally essentialist itself: "To insist that essentialism is always and everywhere reactionary is . . . to buy into essential-

ism in the very act of making the charge; *it is to act as if essentialism
has an essence*" (21). Fuss logically and semantically implicates critics
in the very act and purpose of their own criticism—charging essentialism while using the same essentialist strategies that necessarily obviate
deeper analysis of a text's essentialist methodology. Indeed Fuss compels readers to consider "that essentialism can be deployed effectively
in the service of both idealist and materialist, progressive and reactionary, mythologizing and resistive discourses" (xii). With this determination she clarifies that essentialism serves varied and indeed opposing
discursive functions. Her insistence that the political ideology at work
behind essentialism must also be considered is especially relevant to
Brathwaite's theory of nation language. The progressiveness of that
theory's perceived essentialism lies in Brathwaite's counterhegemonic
revelation that nation language has actively reversed the historical paradigm of imperial cultural dominance, because its African-based cosmological system privileges the poetics and music of orature and it has
effectively replaced the language of empire as the predominant form of
English spoken in the Anglophone Caribbean.

BRATHWAITE'S PRESENT ABSENCE IN VERNACULAR THEORY

Fuss's argument for teasing out essentialism's uses in a text is quite
instructive; nonetheless her textual examples in *Essentially Speaking* are
somewhat problematic. The fifth chapter, "'Race' under Erasure? Post-
structuralist Afro-American Literary Theory," presents an examination
of Henry Louis Gates's and Houston Baker's theoretical (dis)engage-
ment with the oral tradition. Yet Fuss makes no mention of Brathwaite's
"History of the Voice," which predates both Gates's and Baker's work on
Africana orature by several years. Perhaps Fuss's combined use of the
Caliban[13] trope in her reading of James Baldwin's "Everybody's Protest
Novel" and her detailed analysis of Fanon's "The Negro and Language"
led me to expect a reading of Brathwaite as a postcolonial critic engaged
with the vernacular tradition. Alas, she neither mentions Brathwaite nor
discusses the import of nation language to vernacular theory. Her theoretical models on the use of Africana orature in literary criticism are
limited to Gates[14] and Baker. Baker's *Blues, Ideology and Afro-American
Literature* engages African American literature at the level of sound and
music in terms strikingly similar to Brathwaite's, as Baker calls on scholars of African American literature to "situate themselves inventively and
daringly at the crossing sign in order to materialize vernacular faces"

(202). Ironically the crossing sign that he invokes is the place where orature and literature meet, the site of critical valuation of all Africana cultural productions. This is the theoretical crossroads where Brathwaite's
nation language has been positioned since 1976, when "History of the
Voice" was first presented orally, and since 1979, when it was first published. Thus Baker's vernacular faces in *Blues* are those that appear at the
level of sound in and throughout Brathwaite's nation language theory
five years before Baker dared to envision them.

In *Blues*, Baker proclaims that if scholars incorporate aspects of the
oral tradition's improvisatory and creative force into their work, then a
font of creative expression will spring forth:

> If scholars are successful, their response to literature, criticism, and
> culture in the United States will be as wonderfully energetic and
> engrossing as the response of the bluesman Sonny Terry to the injunc-
> tion of his guitar-strumming partner Brownie McGhee. Brownie
> intones: "Let me hear you squall, boy, like you never squalled before!"
> The answer is a whooping, racing, moaning harmonica stretch that
> takes one's breath away, invoking forms, faces, and places whose signif-
> icance was unknown prior to the song's formidable inscriptions. (203)

Baker's image of call and response between these two blues musicians
recalls nation language's total expression. Brownie McGhee's call for
Sonny Terry to squall evinces a communality and community through
music that Brathwaite has identified as the total expression of nation
language, both in "History of the Voice" and his earlier essay, "Jazz
and the West Indian Novel." Baker's harmonica stretch and its musical
intonation of community that was nameless prior to its birth through
breath also reflect the creationist drive behind Brathwaite's nation language. Baker's call for theorists to mimic the improvisatory nature of
the blues is precisely what limits his own analysis, for he examines Africana orature and the blues only through a U.S.-centered critical framework. Eschewing improvisation that would have been possible with
greater diasporic analysis of Brathwaite's work, Baker focuses only on
African American cultural productions in the United States. As a result
his silence on Brathwaite's nation language theory is deafening.

In this regard Fuss's closing comments on Baker's and Gates's work are
extremely telling as they seemingly highlight the fundamental reason for
Brathwaite's present absence in Baker's (and Gates's) text. Fuss contends:

> What we see in the work of both Gates and Baker is a romanticization
> of the vernacular. As their detractors have been all too quick to point

out, each of these critics speaks *about* the black vernacular but rarely
can they be said to speak *in* it. . . . A powerful *dream* of the vernacular
motivates the work of these two Afro-Americanists, perhaps because,
for the professionalized literary critic, the vernacular has already
become irrevocably lost. What makes the vernacular . . . so powerful a
theme in the work of both Gates and Baker is precisely the fact that it
operates as a phantasm, a hallucination of lost origins. (90)

While Fuss's comments appear true for Baker and Gates, they represent the uninformed critical opinions that prompt Brathwaite to lament
that: "There don't seem to be any PhD or other cultural workers at work
on my work right now" (qtd. in Williams, "Kamau Brathwaite Talks"
309).

Brathwaite is the very embodiment of a literary critic who keeps
the oral tradition alive, in both poetry and theory. Orature is a living presence that is voiced over and over again, and that is precisely
Brathwaite's aim: to keep the oral transmission of African and African
diasporic history and culture alive. Peter Hitchcock stresses this very
point: "While there are other Caribbean poets who have embodied this
spirit, as living voices or vessels of history . . . Brathwaite has used it to
complicate one's sense of poetic space so that the nation might reside
in it" (77). In Brathwaite's nation language, poetic space and theoretical
space are one and the same: the voice carries the verse, which is mined
as a living theory of the nation and diaspora. Sound and song become
literature, just as orature becomes an African diasporic discourse.

THE VOICE OF NATION AND DIASPORA

In nation language the power of the voice lies in its dynamic conflation
of Africana orature, literature, *and* discourse. And while some critics view Brathwaite's theoretical project as one that is simply "oriented
toward writing back to the West" (Simpson 830), I believe that in nation
language we may witness the critic as griot, who not only writes back
to the West but also recites back to his audience, his theoretical progenitors, and the revolutionary ancestors who died actualizing Freedom in the Americas. Through nation language's merging of orature
and literature Brathwaite recites back to the forebears of James's *Black
Jacobins*, who—under Mackandal, Boukman, and finally Toussaint—
found strength in African and Vodun chants to fight for liberation in
seventeenth- and eighteenth-century San Domingo. Brathwaite also
harkens back to the forebears in early nineteenth-century South Caro-

lina, who had heard of Toussaint's Haitian Revolution, found inspiration in Gullah Jack's powerful African conjuring, and organized under Denmark Vesey's leadership for their own American rebellion. His nation language hails the same ancestors whose songs of lamentation drove Frederick Douglass to weep even decades after first hearing them (*My Bondage and My Freedom*, 71–72; *Narrative of the Life*, 262–63). By emphasizing the equal and interrelated significance of Africana orature and literature, nation language brings us to the source of all Africana cultural productions in the West: the breath, the word, and the song.[15]

Brathwaite posits language itself as political discourse. He uses theory as a Trojan horse, for inside the literary construct of the lecture cum essay he designates orality as the African cultural tradition that has transmitted and shaped New World Africana culture. This is exactly where he breaks with his predecessors. Where Douglass, Du Bois, and James credit the oral tradition for creating an indigenous African American culture of resistance, Brathwaite goes even further by illuminating how nation language itself is the oral articulation of Freedom. The nation language stories, songs, and music in Africana folktales and songs reveal Freedom as a tangible reality, attainable through its total expression, in its articulation and exercise among the enslaved masses. Thus, in the telling of tales and singing of songs, Freedom continues to exist as a process of actualization that is instantiated through oral expression. They gathered, often risking grave punishment or death, to experience and maintain a sense of community. Their Freedom was vivified in these gatherings, in their will to resist the subjection of the chattel slave system and dare to exist as a unified collective. Nation language then becomes another manifestation of their innate human Freedom.

BRATHWAITE'S DIASPORIC JAZZ NATION

In addition to presenting a New World cultural and theoretical critique, nation language theory also interpellates and imbricates two related conceptualizations in Western and Africana history and literature: the nation and the African diaspora. This diasporic analysis first necessitates readings of LeRoi Jones's *Blues People* and Brathwaite's "Jazz and the West Indian Novel," which presents the seeds of nation language theory. On the level of linguistic and auditory aesthetics, Brathwaite prompts us toward an understanding of nation language as sound and music, a language of music with "its own sound explosion" that "may be English, but often it is an English which is like a howl, or a shout, or a machine-gun, or the wind, or a wave. It is also like the blues. And sometimes it is English and African at the same time" (266). The howl that is nation language may be heard in Bob Marley's signature wail, the machine gun in Mutabaruka's and Linton Kwesi Johnson's dub poetry, the wind and wave in Miss Lou's (Louise Bennett) nation language poetry, and the blues in Don Drummond's plaintive, syncopated ska trombone. Brathwaite hears and conceptualizes nation language at the most visceral levels of sound and music, for nation language "is a place formed by the interrelationship of speech and music, both natural and human compositions" (Hitchcock 68).

With Brathwaite's inclusion of the blues in nation language, he links this Afro-Caribbean language to a larger cultural discourse of resistance in the African diaspora, for as both he and LeRoi Jones/Amiri Baraka have shown, blues is a music of protest that reflects the Negro American experience of anti-African racism in the West (Jones 28, 29, 50–59, 66; Brathwaite, "Jazz" 55). Rather tellingly "Jazz" encapsulates a brief introduction to the theory of nation language elaborated in "History of the Voice." Brathwaite "attempt[s] to show that the connection between native musical structures and the native language is very necessary to the understanding of nation language. That music is, in fact, the surest threshold to the language that comes out of it" ("Jazz" 270).

Brathwaite's assertion that nation language is born of Africana music is a critically innovative proposition, for he implies that musical production should be deemed the primary source of semiotic exchange for enslaved Africans in the Americas. With this he privileges music in a manner that breaks with his predecessors' critical inquiries. This is perhaps the most innovative feature of his nation language theory: music is not deemed subordinate to literature as a form of cultural production. To strengthen his position on Africana music as discourse and a mode of social protest, he opens "Jazz" with a summary of Jones's argument in *Blues People*: "[The blues] is . . . the artistic expression of a particular kind of Negro—the Negro slave and his descendants under the geographical and social conditions of the American South. . . . Jazz, on the other hand, is not 'slave' music at all. It is the emancipated Negro's music" (55). Later he writes, "Jazz then is a music of protest. It is also in many ways a music of protection: a shield of sound behind which the individual and the group have been able to protect their spirit" (58). Brathwaite's interpretation of blues and jazz as musical forms of protest and spiritual barriers reveals his concern with African diasporic cultural productions as forms of dissent. What is more, he issues a theoretical challenge, clarifying that his concern with the connections among Africana music, language, and literature "is not with the problems of Negro expression, but with the (British) West Indian contribution to the general movement of New World creative protest of which I regard jazz to be the archetype" (62).

Like the seeds of nation language that Brathwaite detects in the West Indian novels of the 1960s, jazz reflects a larger Africana expression of dissent against empire and Western hegemony while still, ineluctably, reflecting the influence of Western and Africana culture. Despite his explicitly stated goal of identifying common areas of New World creative protest, some critics have categorized "Jazz" as promoting an "orthodoxy of blackness" and "an ambiguous, ambivalent, hopelessly enmeshed critique."[16] Brathwaite furthers nation language's African diasporic thrust by linking its emergence in 1960s and 1970s Caribbean poetry to the cultural impact of Caribbean and American musical and lyrical forms. Citing the poem "Blues" by Derek Walcott, he writes that the poem "is a connection of Caribbean and Harlem/New Orleans which Buddy Bolden and Congo Square knew about, which McKay was to carry forward, and which in this poem, among some others . . . Derek Walcott continues. And it is this connection which brings in the influences of Langston Hughes for instance, and Imamu Baraka, and Sonia Sanchez, and Miles Davis, which further erodes the pentameter" (296). Brathwaite's polemic designation of nation language as an African diasporic discourse connecting the Caribbean to New Orleans's Congo Square and to Claude McKay's Harlem reflects his larger discursive project: linking the connected Africana cultures of creative protest in the United States and the Caribbean. Thus he identifies the thrust of Walcott's poem as the force of African diasporic articulation. This may be seen in his insistence that Walcott's "Blues" reflects a cultural sensibility that is also present in the works of several African diasporic poets. He situates the poem in relation to Claude McKay, whose sonnet "If We Must Die" symbolizes the militancy of the New Negro movement.[17] He also avers that Walcott's "Blues" recalls a musical tradition evinced in the blues and jazz music of Congo Square. Walcott's "Blues" represents a continuum in African diasporic oral and musical expression, as it recalls the influences of noted Black arts movement poets (Baraka and Sanchez), jazz musicians (Davis), and the Harlem Renaissance poet who most vocally and discursively sought to amplify the connections among jazz, poetry, and orality: Langston Hughes. So in his diasporic critique of Walcott's "Blues," Africana cultural expression in the Americas comes full circle. Deracination and dispossession become the occasions for survival and resistance. The African's survival in the New World is actualized through nation language's poetic and musical expression. The circle is the African diaspora, for nation language has resonance in the poetry of the St. Lucian author Walcott, just as it does in the jazz of New Orleans and in the African American poetry of Hughes and Sanchez.

Brathwaite's invocation of Harlem is also significant in terms of what Harlem has come to represent for him and other Africana writers the world over. James de Jongh has theorized that in the 1960s and 1970s Harlem was the principal meeting ground for poets from the African diaspora because they:

> were developing a consciousness of the fundamental unity of the Africana experience. The motif of black Harlem, which many Africana poets outside of the United States associated with the Civil Rights movement, as well as with the ghetto uprisings of the 1960s across America, was seen as a shared emblem of the common aims and actualities of black life. Harlem, to them, became a symbol of the destiny of Africana peoples to arise renewed, in spite of the unrelenting cultural, social, and political interposition by the European West. (183)

De Jongh's designation of Harlem as a sociopolitical and counterhegemonic trope for African diasporic poets is reflected in Brathwaite's theory of nation language just as it is in Brathwaite's poetry. De Jongh further holds that "Brathwaite includes Harlem as one of several microcosmic locales in the geographic dispersal of the African diaspora ... concluding with [Harlem's] characteristic employment as a landscape of the resurgent spirit of Africanadom" (188). Harlem as a potent symbol for Brathwaite is made clear in his critique of Walcott's "Blues." These diasporic connections among New Orleans jazz, Harlem Renaissance and Black Arts movement poetics, and Walcott's own nation language also represent aspects of Brathwaite's related conceptualization of tidalectics.

The tide in Brathwaite's tidalectics is not only moving to and fro between Africa and the Caribbean. The tide is also moving to and fro within the Americas, between the Caribbean and the United States as Brathwaite's writings on nation language, the blues, and jazz confirm. That he stresses the cyclic motion of the tide is significant, for a cycle implies a circle, and one may easily apprehend a circle among the disparate regions of Africa, the Caribbean, and the United States. This circle/cycle of diasporic connections is present in his lengthy treatise on nation language in "History of the Voice" and briefly in its introductory stages in "Jazz." He defines his concept of tidalectics as "dialectics with my difference. . . . Instead of one-two-three Hegelian, I am now more interested in the movement of the water backwards and forwards as a kind of cyclic, I suppose, motion, rather than linear" (qtd. in Mackey, *Paracritical Hinge* 9–10). With this we see how Brathwaite employs the recurring paradoxical trope of Western epistemology in his counterhegemonic project. Hegelian discourse presents a totalizing, racist view of Africa, Africans, and their enslaved descendants in the Americas. And like Douglass and Fanon before him, Brathwaite confronts the specter of Hegel, yet this discursive summoning serves to foreground Brathwaite's own reinscription and theoretical revision of Hegelian dialectics with the very ideological and polemical discourse that Hegel deemed impossible for African people. His tidalectics subverts the Western episteme of dialectics while acknowledging its enduring presence and highlighting its seeming paucity of relevance for Brathwaite's liberated consciousness and that of the like-minded Africana subject. Where Fanon mines the Hegelian dialectic of recognition and violent struggle to underscore the colonized subject's quest for liberation, Brathwaite confronts Hegel's Eurocentricity with the announcement of his own philosophical insurrection: You do not deem me human; therefore I must refashion your dialectic in a manner that allows my identity and intelligence to shine. Or, in the resistive and emphatic diction of nation language: "Ah yuh me ah talk, Hegel. Yuh cyaaan't define me wit yuh dialectics. I-man define miself wit mi own tidalectics. 'Ow yuh like dat?"

The Hegelian paradox in tidalectics is also manifest in nation language's dual interpellation of the nation and the African diaspora, for as Brathwaite's focus on nation language's diasporic manifestations attests, nation language also situates the nation within the historical and ideological framework of the African diaspora. Thus Brathwaite's designation of Afro-Caribbean language as the language of nation and diaspora represents a paradoxical element in Western discourse because the African diaspora

> holds a subversive resonance when contrasted with that of the nation-state. At the same time that European powers constructed national dialogues, African slaves were being uprooted from . . . various parts of the African continent and scattered about the New World like fragments from a shaven gem. Africans and their distant relatives in the

New World have abided by and sometimes revolted against, the myth
of national borders ever since. Embedded in the tale of diaspora is a
symbolic revolt against the nation-state, and for this reason the diaspora holds considerable significance. (Hanchard 238)

Hanchard is quite right to tie the emergence of the European nation
state to the quest for empire. It was during the nineteenth century that
the expansion of Western empire in Europe and the United States led
to new genealogies and myths of the Western nation, centered on the
Western nation-state's ineluctable presence and its disposition—both of
which were defined by an imperialist "civilizing" mission and the attendant discourses of Manifest Destiny and social Darwinism (Kelley 4).

Despite the predominant nineteenth-century historical discourses
that justified social Darwinism and the Western nation-state's imperialist drive, there are two striking parallels between Brathwaite's
nation language and Benedict Anderson's notion of national orature.
Anderson holds that the nation "is an imagined political community.
It is *imagined* because the members of even the smallest nation will
never know most of their fellow members, meet them or even hear of
them, yet in the minds of each lives the image of their communion"
(6). Similarly nation language unites its speakers through the communality of orature's total expression, its lived history, and its psychic
communion.

NATION LANGUAGE'S (RE)IMAGINED COMMUNITIES

The spiritual communion of the nation is most immediate in my own
childhood experience of the West African and West Indian Anancy
trickster tales. While my siblings and I were growing up, my parents
bewitched us with stories of the tiny yet indomitable spider Bre'r Anancy,
who always outsmarted bigger and stronger animals. In Anancy's
exploits my parents emphasized the struggles of our enslaved Jamaican
ancestors who triumphed over nearly impossible odds. Their parents
had told them the very same stories, just as my great-grandparents had
told these tales to my grandparents. I felt connected to this long line of
history; I felt joined to an entire culture and nation of forebears and
descendants who sat, chins cupped in hands, waiting to find out how
Anancy had bested them all. For Anderson, for Brathwaite, and indeed
for me, the communion of the nation lies in this very type of connection between the present and the past, between youth and elders. For
although I never met my great-grandparents, in hearing and experienc-

ing the Anancy stories we became one, and I did envision, as Anderson calls it, "the image of [our] communion" (6).

Brathwaite establishes nation language's generational and temporal continuum through its submergence, adaptation, and continuous voicing. It is "an English . . . of the submerged, surrealist experience and sensibility . . . which has always been there" ("History of the Voice" 266). In this eternal nation language, he foretells one of Anderson's more metaphysical descriptions of language as an ancient repository of national culture: "First, one notes the primordialness of languages. . . . No one can give the date for the birth of any language. Each looms imperceptibly out of a horizonless past. . . . Nothing connects us effectively to the dead more than language. . . . Second, there is a special kind of contemporaneous community which language alone suggests—above all in the form of poetry and songs" (144). Here Anderson, like Brathwaite, highlights orature's inimitable role in defining a national community through vocal communion. The poetry and songs of the nation act as a living bridge between past and present, between the living and the dead, through the nation's constant revoicing.

Given that Anderson's *Imagined Communities* is primarily concerned with the emergence of the nineteenth-century European nation-state, it is somewhat ironic that his theorization on national orature mirrors Brathwaite's own African diasporic theorization of nation language. For in Anderson's historiography of the imperialist Western nation-state, we find the African diaspora wrought from the rupture of chattel slavery and imperialism, and in his national orature we find Brathwaite's nation language: Africana poetry and songs that create Anderson's "contemporaneous community," orature that in its timelessness invokes the history of the voice as a form of primordial, originary language and as a valued repository of culture and history. In this way Brathwaite's theory of nation language simultaneously problematizes the discourse of the nation-state. Certainly his theory of nation language rebels against a nation defined by geography; however, the African diaspora itself offers an ephemeral, yet global national community in which nation language is voiced. Nation language's diasporic thrust, then, reveals a paradox in theories of the nation-state that bespeaks Africana diasporic resistance against Western domination in theory and praxis.

Brathwaite's placement of nation language within the African diaspora also suggests the equation of language and home, for he unites Africa, the Caribbean, and the United States in the space of the nation, in the sound of the voice, in the ideological construct of the African diaspora. All of these spaces then become a home in the classic sense of diaspora: "The 'African diaspora' . . . adheres to many elements considered to be common to the three 'classic' diasporas (the Jewish, the Greek, and the Armenian): in particular, an origin in the scattering and uprooting of communities, a history of 'traumatic and forced departure,' and also the sense of a real or imagined relationship to a 'homeland,' mediated through the dynamics of collective memory and the politics of 'return'" (Edwards, "Uses of Diaspora" 52). Indeed, for Africana people the history of traumatic and forced departure recalls the deracination and dispossession of the European slave trade and Western slavery; the spiritual bond is the ancestral home of Africa that is tied to the collective cultural memory evinced in nation language.

Sophia Lehmann concludes that among a diasporic people language is more than a form of communication; it becomes the cultural marker of a shared historical experience:

> Colonialism . . . conspired to create a legacy of global displacement,
> in which people are robbed of their homeland and the language in
> which their culture has been formed. Disparate diasporic communities
> are now faced with the shared struggle of articulating a cultural iden-
> tity in which history and home reside in language. . . .
>   In diaspora, language works both to define and to create this sense of
> commonality between people who share history and experience. (101, 103)

For a people (dis)connected to their homeland, language is at once that site of ancestral understanding and the locus of present illumination. Lehmann's focus on the cultural connections that arise out of a people's diasporic consciousness is particularly relevant to nation language, for in Brathwaite's homeland of Africa and the African diasporic language of its nation he traces lines of historical and cultural commonality among the bordered geographic regions of Africa, the United States, and the Caribbean.

In Brathwaite's view there is no Bajan nation language that is distinct from African American nation language, just as there is no Jamaican blues that is separate from African American blues. These areas of cultural commonality are perhaps best evinced in one of the closing paragraphs of "History of the Voice," where Brathwaite begs readers to hear the voice of Miss Queenie, a Kumina[18] queen:

> Without hearing her, you would miss the dynamics of the narrative—
> the blue notes of that voice; its whispers and pauses and repetitions and

stutters and elisions; its high pitch emphases and low pitched trails; and that hoarse quality which I suppose you know from Nina Simone. With Miss Queenie we are in the very ancient dawn of nation language, and to be able to come to terms with oral literature at all our critics must be able to understand the complex forces that have led to this classical expression. (298)

By equating the blues tones of the Jamaican Kumina priestess Miss Queenie, who invokes African ancestors and gods, to the famed African American blues and jazz singer Nina Simone, Brathwaite confirms one of nation language theory's central claims: that the voice is the carrier of African memory, history, and culture. Both women give voice to the African New World creative protest tradition through voice. Miss Queenie calls on African gods and the ancestors in a voice that dips and pauses with the cadence of nation language, and Simone sings "Four Women"[19] in a similar voice that also resounds with the rhythms and timbre of nation language. Geographically speaking, these women are regions apart, but in their total expression of nation language, in their same blues tones, their voices occupy a creative space of resistance that has shaped Africana culture in the Americas since the sixteenth century.

Brathwaite's disruptions of and challenges to hegemonic discourse mark a chasm in Western theory in the same way that the works of Walker, Douglass, Du Bois, James, and Fanon do. Yet Brathwaite departs from his predecessors in his designation of Africana music as the originary source of a New World linguistic and cultural discourse of resistance against Western chattel slavery and against Western hegemony as a whole. His theoretical intent is clear, yet it is concomitantly informed by the seemingly paradoxical specter of Western influences. This is unavoidable, for Brathwaite, like all of his predecessors, is still a part of the very Western tradition that his work forcefully destabilizes. Through this contentious discursive paradigm, I posit that in Kamau Brathwaite we find the Africana theorist as griot, oral historian, and trickster. The trickster is the West African god of duality, the spiritual embodiment of opposing forces, "disruption and reconciliation, betrayal and loyalty, closure and disclosure, encasement and rupture" (Gates, *The Signifying Monkey* 6). While embodying these forces, the trickster should not be reduced to either half of its many binaries. The trickster exists as all at once. In the same manner Brathwaite's theory of nation language binds the hegemonic forces of Western empire to the resistive, creative forces of New World liberation. He engages in counterhegemonic discourse while still acknowledging Western discourse's ineluctable influences on his own radical formulations. Therefore nation language is of the West just as it is of Africa and the African diaspora. And with nation language theory we may apprehend the conundrum of progressive Africana scholars: We are forever bound to the very Western discourse that negates us; we seek to subvert the intellectual tradition of which we have become a part. We use "individuality, satire, parody, irony, magic, indeterminacy, open-endedness, ambiguity . . . [and] chance" (Gates, *The Signifying Monkey* 6) to continually announce our historical, philosophical, and epistemological relevance.

We are tricksters leaving our mark in the world of Western letters.

Conclusion

I consider this study a beginning and a continuation. It marks the beginning of my career as an academic author, and it also represents a continuation of the discursive resistance and existential probing present in the works of the thinkers who have inspired me. The works of David Walker, Frederick Douglass, Carter G. Woodson, W. E. B. Du Bois, C. L. R. James, Aimé Césaire, Frantz Fanon, Kamau Brathwaite, Cheikh Anta Diop, Toni Morrison, Angela Davis, Sylvia Wynter, Ngũgĩ wa Thiong'o, Molefi Asante, Cedric Robinson, Martin Bernal, Lewis Gordon, Paget Henry, Maghan Keita, and others prove that Western discourse has been indelibly marred by Eurocentricity. These thinkers' works led to my own path of intellectual discovery and growth; it is one that I hope my students and others will be moved to embark upon, for we are living in very serious times.

The nature of knowledge production and dissemination in the United States is becoming increasingly problematic. This is best evinced by the absent presence of Africana historical figures in film and popular culture. In November 2012 part 1 of the PBS documentary *The Abolitionists* premiered. The work covered the pre–Civil War abolitionists, yet David Walker's *Appeal*, the most incendiary antislavery treatise written, published, and disseminated in the late 1820s, was not even mentioned. It was as though Walker had ceased to exist. And for all intents and purposes, with this documentary PBS had effectively written his remarkable legacy out of (media) history. This practice continued when, in the same year, the feature film *Lincoln* received critical acclaim yet made no mention of the crucial roles that both Frederick Douglass and Harriet Tubman played as advisors to the former president. What is more, the film failed to hint at *any* agential action on the part of the enslaved masses in the evolution of their own liberation. Once again Africana people were depicted as a helpless collectivity in need of the benevolent racial paternalism of white Americans to decide their political destiny. The sweeping historical epic *Les Miserables* was no better in its supposed adherence to historical realism. What of the French parliamentary debates on slavery in San Domingo? What of the incipient slave rebellions that were waged and then squelched prior to Toussaint's rise? What of Toussaint himself? And in the Ridley brothers' decision to cast European actors as Egyptian royalty and African actors as servants and thieves in the 2014 film *Exodus*, the filmmakers maintained the Hollywood tradition of "whitewashing" the Bible and, knowingly or not, adhered to the American school ethnologists' specious claims of a European-Egyptian ruling class (Baden and Moss n.p.). Baden and Moss raise important points about Hollywood's perpetuation of Western chauvinism in biblical films. However they fail to mention Douglass's and other vindicationists' findings on the ancient Egyptians' African racial identity, which refuted nineteenth-century racist thought promulgated in the American school ethnologists' oeuvre.

Given the far-reaching appeal of Hollywood films as quick-fix educational tools, it is no surprise that the American public believes that African people and history are completely separate from Western historical developments. For the average American, or Westerner, the color of Freedom, the human actualization of Freedom, and the cradle of human civilization are racially white and culturally European. The Freedom struggles outlined in *The Abolitionists*, *Lincoln*, and *Les Miserables* and the perpetuation of the American school ethnologists' Eurocentric historiography in *Exodus* makes this painfully clear—that and the fact that the academic consultants on these projects provided an inaccurate accounting of historical events. At the same time that these incomplete interpretations of Western history are being passed off as universalist, ethnic studies departments are being collapsed into global studies, as though the particular histories, cultures, and experiences that constitute the discipline's discrete fields are somehow interchangeable. Equally disconcerting is the fact that ethnic studies departments often face the looming threat of budget cuts and the misguided ire of conservative administrators and pundits. It is crucial that progressive scholars continue to unite to ensure accuracy and integrity in academic knowledge production, and the society and culture at large.

If the seminal works of the thinkers included in these pages were included in more educational curricula and studied alongside mainstream canonical works, a more balanced and catholic accounting of global historical and intellectual developments would become part of the Western academic experience, thereby creating a fully integrated intellectual space where true dialogue about the power dynamics among people of color and Europeans might occur. Imagine the stimulating classroom discussion that would arise in a course on nineteenth-century Great Books that paired Douglass's *Narrative of the Life* with Hegel's *Phenomenology of Spirit*, in which he outlines his famous master-slave dialectic? Think of the great service to students if they had the opportunity to understand why Douglass should be considered a slave reborn as a philosopher? Such pedagogical innovation would compel students to recognize the Eurocentric biases intrinsic to Western thought, which would in turn foster a more realistic sociopolitical context to merge what we have been taught to see as disparate, unrelated discourses: mainstream narratives of modernity and the "alternative narratives of modernity" (Mills 172) that are antihegemonic, antislavery, anticolonial, and anti-imperialist. These discourses could then be understood as related and integrated instead of bound to separate and unequal theoretical realms (172).

Due to this institutional segregation, Douglass's work, like those of the other thinkers in this study, is afforded conditional relevance that bespeaks the general perception held by most Westerners: that these Africana works, and the histories they recount, represent a very particularized aspect of the human experience, one that has little if any bearing on the greater movement of Western thought, culture, and society. Recall the conflict between Cornel West and Larry Summers in 2002. It is the glaring reality of Western domination, canonical limitations, and disciplinary segregation in the academy that led the former president of Harvard University, Larry Summers, to inform Cornel West that Africana studies was not a legitimate academic discipline. This conflict reflects the persistent fact that Africana letters garner only marginal canonical recognition.

It is my hope that this study will encourage even more interdisciplinary scholarship in critical race studies, in which academics continue to highlight the interstices among eighteenth- and nineteenth-century historical and philosophical texts whose interrelated tenets of scientific racism and Western hegemony acted to solidify institutional racism in the nineteenth, twentieth, and twenty-first centuries.

As just one small contribution, this book is my wish for a more free, just, and equal academy where Americans of all races may see the totality of their ancestors' legacies reflected in educational curricula and, accordingly, in society as a whole.

INTRODUCTION

1. While several scholars agree that the modern period in Western history begins with the European Renaissance, this study is primarily concerned with the Enlightenment, an era often denoted as the period in which modernity reaches its maturity. See Goldberg 3; Dussel et. al. 469–73; Eze, *Race and the Enlightenment*, 4.

2. I am using the term *racist discourse* in contrast to the more benign term *racialist discourse*. While both make distinctions among different racial groups, the former is defined by scientific racism's principal claim of the inherent racial superiority of Europeans and the innate inferiority of non-Europeans, which served as the justification for the latter's enslavement and oppression. Racialist discourse, in contrast, centers on racial classification—shared physical and cultural characteristics—and may not necessarily espouse unjust treatment for particular racial groups. See Valls, *Race and Racism* 5; Bernasconi, "Who Invented the Concept of Race?" 11; Goldberg 29.

3. Wheatley's ambivalence, both toward her captors and her racial identity, has been remarked upon by a broad range of scholars, including Drake 118; Gates and McKay 214–15; Baraka 313. Wheatley's ambivalence is plainly reflected in the contrasting thematic content of two of her most widely anthologized poems, "On Being Brought from Africa to America" and "To the Right Honourable William, Earl of Dartmouth."

4. Mills, "Kant's Untermenschen," 170–171; Goldberg, *Racist Culture*, 26–29; and Gordon *Introduction to Africana Philosophy*, 33–35.

5. For examples of prominent works of French scientific racism, see *Complete Works of Voltaire*, vol. 14 (cited in Bernasconi, "Who Invented the Concept of Race," 20–21) and Comte de Gobineau's *Inequality of the Human Races*. On Hume's, Kant's, and Hegel's influence on racist discourse and philosophical thought in general, see Eze, *Race and the Enlightenment* 5, 7–8; Henry, "Between Hume and Cugoano" 129, 133–38; Mills 173; Gordon, *Introduction to Africana Philosophy* 30–31,196–97; Schrader 33. On Jefferson's influence, see Jordan 429; Diggins 206–8.

6. Davis 130–31; Gordon, *Existentia Africana*, 41–67; Gates and McKay 386–87.

7. Although this tradition is commonly referred to as the Black vindicationist tradition in order to denote Africana historiographical agency, several Europeans and European Americans also contributed to this ideological movement. See Gates, "Preface to Blackness" 149–52.

8. Drake 32; West and Martin 311; Lynch 10–53; Levine, *Martin Delany* 62–65; Moses 34–37.

9. Asante 112–13; Keita, *Race and Writing History* 44–45; Lynch 19, 55–57, 81–82.

10. Keita, *Race and Writing History* 48. Keita pointedly notes that Chapin recognized Williams's genius due to Chapin's own adherence to degeneracy theory. Chapin states that Williams's genius was the result of his not being "a full-blooded African" (n17).

11. Throughout this work *ontology* and *ontological* are used to denote the branch of philosophy concerned with the concept and "problem" of human existence, particularly as these pertain to the Africana experience of Western racism. See Gordon, *Existentia Africana* 8–9; Schrader 34–36; McDonald; Blackburn 260.

12. While the term *proletariat* denotes paid wage laborers, I am using it in the same way that Du Bois and James do, to highlight the pivotal role that enslaved African labor played in Western capitalist accumulation. Du Bois uses the term *black worker* throughout *Black Reconstruction*; see especially the first chapter, "The Black Worker," 3, 5, 7, 9, 13, 15, 16. James uses the term *modern proletariat* in *Black Jacobins*, 85–86.

13. Arendt 211. On Arendt's own racist views see Gines 13, 22–23, 25–29, 77–92.

14. Stanton, 50–51, 70–72; Du Bois, *World and Africa*, 99; Diop 45, 50–51; Gordon, *Introduction to Africana Philosophy*, 25–26.

15. See all three of Douglass's autobiographies: *Narrative of the Life, My Bondage and My Freedom, Life and Times*. In addition to Du Bois's *Souls of Black Folk* and *Dusk of Dawn*, see *World and Africa*, "Message" 261.

16. For an in-depth discussion of Douglass's role as a philosopher and the reticence among Western thinkers to acknowledge that role, see Butler 1–8 Gordon, *Existentia Africana* 42–61.

17. Among the texts that address this intertextuality are Wellek and Warren 111–24; Sartre, *Literature and Existentialism* 44–45; Lamarque 2–4; Gates, *Signifying Monkey* xxii, xxiv; Henry, *Caliban's Reason* 90–153; Morrison 3–28; Wynter, "On Disenchanting Discourse" and "Ceremony Must Be Found."

18. See Gilroy, *Black Atlantic* 171 on the unfavorable critical reception that Richard Wright's philosophical novel *The Outsider* received. See also Johnson 12–15, 28, 31, 35 for detailed analyses of the phenomenological dimensions of Wright's *Native Son* and *Outsider*.

19. *Facticity* refers to the actuality of the human experience. See Fanon, *Black Skin, White Masks* 109–40; Schrader 23–25.

1. BEING APART

1. Central to this chapter's focus is the refinement of racist thought in some of the most prominent Enlightenment thinkers' works. For a detailed discussion on the major ideological differences between the radical (Transatlantic) Enlightenment and the moderate (American) Enlightenment, see Israel, *Revolution of the Mind*, 1–91. For an analysis on the manner in which the commodification of print culture led to the widespread dissemination of contemporary ideas within Europe, and among its disparate social classes, see Outram, *Enlightenment*, 10–25.

2. Although some critics argue that Linnaeus's system of human classification is nonhierarchical, others emphasize that its implicit hierarchy is based on racial descriptions, some of which were informed by European travelogues. These critics also note that the Linnaean system's theoretical foundation is reliant on the Great Chain of Being, which itself is unmistakably hierarchical. For works that note the hierarchical nature of Linnaean classification, see Bernasconi, "Who Invented the Concept of Race?" 15; Popkin 86; Eze, *Race and Enlightenment* 5. For a work that comments on its nonhierarchical formulations, see Jordan 221.

3. Bernasconi, "Who Invented the Concept of Race?" 17–21; Immerwahr 482; Popkin 84–85, 90–91; Ward 82–86.

4. Bernasconi, "Who Invented the Concept of Race?" 15; Eze, *Race and Enlightenment* 5; Hudson 252; Popkin 86.

5. See Outram 58–60 for an analysis of Enlightenment travelogue writers' depiction of Asian Pacific Islanders as members of a peaceful yet highly sexual Utopian society.

6. Bruce 689–90; Keita, *Race and Writing History* 25–26, 164; Bernal 244; Sanders 524–25; Van Sertima 109–10; Diop 27–28.

7. While philosophical racism represents a dominant strain in Enlightenment writings on racial difference, two Western thinkers, James Beattie and Johann Herder, critiqued the European chauvinism of Hume and Kant, respectively. For Beattie's critique of Hume's "Of National Characters," see

Immerwahr 483–85; Eze, *Race and Enlightenment* 34–37. For Herder's critique of Kant, see Eze, *Race and Enlightenment* 65–78. For Herder's critique of the Enlightenment's inherent philosophical and political contradictions, see Outram 65–66.

8. Anderson 37–46; Tyrell 1015; Keita, "Africans and Asians" 4.

9. Building on Hume's footnote on innate African racial inferiority, Long's text includes a lengthy polygenetic explanation of the professed inferior evolution of Africans as justification for their enslavement. See Popkin 262–63; Ward 85–88; Bernasconi, "Kant as an Unfamiliar Source of Racism" 145.

10. Valls, "'A Lousy Empirical Scientist'" 131, 135–39; Eze, "Hume, Race, and Human Nature" 696.

11. Henry, "Between Hume and Cugoano" 129, 133, 135, 142; Immerwahr 485–86; Popkin 262–66; Valls, "'A Lousy Empirical Scientist,'" 132–34.

12. Qtd. in Popkin 253–54. Hume's original footnote establishes the innate inferiority of all non-European races; nevertheless it is important to mention that the revised footnote lacks mention of "all other species of men." By focusing solely on the "Negro" race, Hume thereby strengthens the force of his anti-African racism. See Immerwahr 484–86.

13. Kant 58; Popkin 263; Ward 87–88.

14. Williams, *Capitalism and Slavery* 99–107; Allen 161. This point is further explored in relation to the American and European economic systems in chapter 2 in my analysis of Du Bois's *Black Reconstruction* and James's *Black Jacobins*.

15. The intertextuality of Enlightenment discourse that Eze has observed may be found in Kant's *Physical Geography*, excerpted in Eze, *Race and Enlightenment* 61–62; Jefferson, *Notes* 128–29. Both Kant and Jefferson offer scientific explanations of the reticular skin membrane as the source of Africans' dark pigmentation, as well as their residence in hot climatic zones.

16. Diggins partially acknowledges the impact of Linnaean classification and the Great Chain of Being on Jefferson's belief in racial hierarchies; however, he does not stress Jefferson's allegiance to racist thought as the major reason for his inability to conceptualize Africans as equal to Europeans. Instead Diggins argues that the opposing strains in Enlightenment thought between empiricism and the mind's ability to "impose its rational will and moral imagination on the environment" are to blame for Jefferson's privileging of whites over blacks. See Diggins 228.

17. Eze notes that Jefferson's original manuscript for *Notes* included the following line, which clearly echoes Hume: "But never yet . . . as far as I have heard, has a black excelled in any art, in any science." See Eze, *Race and Enlightenment* 99n1.

18. Drescher 416–28; Juengel 899; Dubois and Garrigus 159–62.

19. It is now commonly known that Jefferson fathered several children with his slave mistress, Sally Hemings. See Gordon-Reed.

20. Although Stuckey 122–35 characterizes Walker's *Appeal* as the earliest encapsulation and expression of a black nationalist ethos, Hinks challenges this claim by explaining that Walker's text eschews cultural nationalism that defined the work of Martin Delany and instead emphasizes interracial cooperation. In Hinks's estimation this proves that the *Appeal*'s identification as the literary template for black nationalism is overstated. However, Hinks himself lists myriad black nationalist issues that Walker's *Appeal* does address; thus his insistence on the *Appeal*'s absence of a cultural nationalist bent becomes insignificant when compared to its focus on black political nationalism. See Hinks 198–99, 249–50. A thorough reconciliation of these opposing views may be found in Asukile 17–21.

21. On the *Appeal*'s application of Enlightenment doctrines, see Duran 159–63. On the *Appeal*'s radical typography's mirroring of Walker's philosophically emphatic message of African equality, see Dinius 55–68. On the *Appeal*'s prefiguration of modern Black nationalist issues and problems, see Asukile 17–21; Stuckey 122–35.

22. See Wright's introduction to Douglass's *My Bondage and My Freedom*, xii; Levine, *Martin Delany* 71. Though not directly stated, Douglass's discursive reaction against the Fugitive Slave Laws is also suggested in Gordon, *Existentia Africana* 48.

23. Douglass, *My Bondage and My Freedom* 271–72; Douglass, *Life and Times* 259–61; Stuckey 225.

24. The ontology of blackness is reinterpreted and reinvigorated in the existentialist writings of Frantz Fanon, which I discuss at length in chapter 3.

2. THE AFRICAN DIASPORIC PROLETARIAT

1. On Pan-Africanism in the francophone African diaspora see Edwards, *Practice of Diaspora* 69–119, 276–305. On Pan-Africanism in the Anglophone and Hispanophone African Diaspora see W. James 185–232.

2. On Du Bois's gradual disillusionment with liberalism see Robinson 200–203, 228; Bogues 75–77. On James's self-identification as a Trotskyite, see Grimshaw 7–12.

3. James explains the indelible impression Du Bois's radical historiography had on his own theoretical development in "Lectures" 86–91.

4. See Robinson 185–208, 228–40, 270–28 for Du Bois's and James's significance in the context of the Black radical tradition. See also Gilroy, *Black Atlantic* xi, 193, 197–98, 221 on their inauguration of Black Atlantic studies.

5. Du Bois, *Black Reconstruction* 7; James, *Black Jacobins* 360–62. See Robinson 184; Bogues 80, 85 for brief discussions of Being and Freedom in Du Bois's and James's texts.

6. While *Black Reconstruction* seemingly presents an overall critique of Marxism's limitations with respect to Western slavery as a racial institution,

Du Bois does cite several correspondences written by Marx and members of Marxist organizations to stress Marx's antislavery stance. See *Black Reconstruction* 23–24, 89–90, 218, 353–54, 357, 360.

3. FRANTZ FANON

1. On Fanon's disenchantment with the Negritude movement see Caute, *Frantz Fanon,* 21–24; Gendzier 43–44; Kebede 543; Martin 394–96.

2. Gendzier 199; JanMohamed 60–63, 85; Nursey-Bray 137–38.

3. Fanon, *Black Skin, White Masks* 27–30, 41, 87, 115–22, 138–40, 160–65, 175, 180–82; Gendzier 53–56.

4. Regarding my contextualization of Fanon, I am not answering Gates's call in "Critical Fanonism" to "historicize" Fanon as a means of neutralizing conflicting contemporary critical interpretations of Fanon's legacy in postcolonial theory. Rather I am attempting to show how Fanon's engagement with the sociopolitical and philosophical tomes of the Western canon enabled him to radically expand their previously Eurocentric parameters. See Gates, "Critical Fanonism" 457–65, 469–70.

5. Although Fanon is rather firm in his introduction (14) that *Black Skin, White Masks* is specifically pertinent to the colonial world of the French Antilles, the remainder of the text makes numerous references to the colonial subject in general.

6. On the cover of the Grove Press 1967 edition of *Black Skin, White Masks,* the *Newsweek* reviewer describes Fanon's work as "a strange, haunting mélange of existential analysis, revolutionary manifesto, metaphysics, prose poetry and literary criticism."

7. I am making the distinction between dialectics and materialism because Fanon does. He applies Hegelian dialectics to the colonial setting in a manner that is distinct from his application of Marx's historical materialism to the same.

8. The connected issues of imperial language appropriation, cultural imperialism, and mental colonization are explored in great detail in Ngũgĩ 1–30.

9. One such existential implication is the project of transforming language so as to transform one's reality. See Gordon, *What Fanon Said* 10–12.

10. Fanon explores the connection between epistemic violence and physical violence further in *Wretched of the Earth*, 35–106.

11. Chapter 4 of *Black Skin, White Masks* is devoted to debunking O. Mannoni's theory of an innate dependency complex among the colonized, whose manifestations actually predate colonial rule. Fanon refutes Mannoni's thesis with evidence of a learned inferiority or dependency complex following the institutionalization of colonial systems of culture, power, and knowledge.

12. Although Fanon engages quite vigorously with Hegel's *Phenomenology of Mind*, he does not mention Hegel's excision of Africa from the stage of world

history. In fact Fanon takes several theoretical jabs at his mentor Aimé Césaire's Negritude philosophy by insisting that the discovery of ancient African kingdoms would not dispel colonial alienation. See Fanon, *Black Skin, White Masks*, 34, 225, 226.

4. BRATHWAITE'S NATION LANGUAGE THEORY

1. As evidence of Brathwaite's commitment to orature, he first introduced his theory of nation language at the 1976 Carifesta, an annual Caribbean writers conference, where "History of the Voice" was given as an oral presentation. Thus he first theorized on nation language through the spoken word instead of choosing to publish his findings in a written text. This speaks to his ongoing theoretical project of decentering the written word as the primary cite of cultural, historical, and ideological discourse.

2. Abrahams and Szwed 332–34; Blassingham 125–26, 130–33, 135, 138, 160–61, 180–81, 220–21, 419–20, 507, 616; Patterson 73; Gates and McKay xxxix.

3. To properly contextualize the pentameter's centrality in Western linguistic expression, Brathwaite traces its development in English poetry from its initial eighth-century appearance in *Beowulf* to its pinnacle in the sixteenth-century works of Shakespeare ("Voice," 264–65, 272).

4. Since the Arawak Indians of Jamaica and Barbados were exterminated by the sixteenth century, I am using the term *indigenous* in a relative sense. European extermination of these indigenous peoples was the principal catalyst for the subsequent importation of enslaved African labor. Thus sixteenth-century nation language, with its West African base, comes closest to what may be identified as an indigenous New World language system.

5. I am using *cultural heroes* in the same way that Hurston uses the term to describe the principal trickster figures in West African and Africana folktales ("Characteristics of Negro Expression" 36–37).

6. Abrahams (10, 18) charges that the "bardic forms of epic" were completely lost in the Africans' adaptation to the New World; however, this claim seems to contradict his position that enslaved Africans still held fast to the West African cultural practice of eloquent oratory and ornate speechmaking. This focus on orality is the drive behind the West African griot's recitation of ancestral genealogies and epics.

7. Although Abrahams (xvi) does establish the African slaves' incorporation of European words into their own West African languages, he maintains that this linguistic conflation resulted in New World dialects of European languages. Unlike Brathwaite (and Lalla and D'Costa), he does not consider the significant impact of African languages on the European languages themselves.

8. See Patterson 57, 96 for an explanation of how the name Quashee, an Akan word for "Sunday," came to signify the stereotype of the "shiftless" slave, much like the Sambo figure of the southern American plantations.

9. Smitherman's work on Black English is a major contribution to vernacular theory; however, she focuses more on Black English as an African American linguistic system and mentions diasporic articulations only briefly (2–15). For diasporic expressions of Black English, see 5–6, 8–9. However Yancy's article on Smitherman does recognize Brathwaite as a nation language theorist whose theoretical contributions must be noted (295).

10. Brathwaite locates Caribbean nation language within a larger historical and cultural tradition that identifies the fourteenth- and fifteenth-century European national languages and literatures movement begun by Dante's *De vulgari eloquentia*. He also openly acknowledges the impact of hearing T. S. Eliot's radio broadcast readings of *Prelude* and *The Waste Land* for inspiring him to hear the musical link between orature and jazz. And he credits the BBC cricket commentator John Arlott's expressive Hampshire "burr" for stirring within West Indian writers an excitement about the English vernacular and their own vernacular in particular ("Voice" 267–71, 286n34).

11. As early as 1934 Hurston designated the trickster-hero of West Africa an African American culture hero, found in the form of Bre'r Rabbit, the fox, the bear, and the lion ("Characteristics of Negro Expression"36). For a description of the West Indian Bre'r Anancy, see Hurston, *Tell My Horse* 25.

12. Here I use *uncommon* in the broad sense, as most literary theorists who have written on Brathwaite's work seem to take a pro-essentialist position or an antiessentialist position, rarely teasing out the deployment of essentialist methodology itself. While Edmonson certainly engages with Fuss's argument in "Black Aesthetics" (93–34), she fails to apply this argument to a substantive analysis of Brathwaite's work in her later (1994) article, "Race, Tradition and the Construction of the Caribbean Aesthetic" (110, 113–15). See also Moore-Gilbert 195 for a brief discussion of Brathwaite's use of essentialism as a critique of hybridity theory.

13. For works that discuss the import of Shakespeare's Caliban to Caribbean discourse see Henry, *Caliban's Reason* 4–5, 12; Retamar 6–16, 39–45, 46–55.

14. Though Gates's *Signifying Monkey* centers on the African American vernacular's inscription within the literary tradition, I will analyze aspects of Baker's *Blues* since its inclusion of music offers striking parallels to Brathwaite's nation language theory.

15. Here I take my cue from Brathwaite the college professor. In class he often reminded us that enslaved Africans came to the New World with nothing but breath and memory.

16. Edmonson, "Race, Tradition" 114, 118. Edmondson constructs an argument against Brathwaite's use of a jazz aesthetic for critiquing West Indian literature on the grounds that his theorization of a jazz aesthetic does not give due consideration to indigenous Caribbean musical forms. Nevertheless Brathwaite explains that indigenous Caribbean musical forms, like calypso

and ska, are not directly connected to a protest tradition in the same way that jazz is ("Jazz" 59–60).

17. On the connection in "If We Must Die" to the New Negro movement and the Harlem Renaissance see Huggins 70; Gates and McKay 1003–7.

18. Brathwaite describes Kumina as "a memorial ceremony for calling down ancestral spirits and African gods and is similar to, say, *vodun*, in Haiti" (*The Development of Creole Society* 224).

19. Nina Simone wrote the song "Four Women" and performed it in the early years of the Black power movement, on July 1, 1967, at the Newport Jazz Festival. The song describes four women who evoke four different historical tropes of African American womanhood: the mammy, the tragic mulatta, the jezebel, and the ghetto avenger.

Abrahams, Roger D., ed. *Afro-American Folktales: Stories from Black Traditions in the New World.* New York: Pantheon Books, 1985. Print.

Abrahams, Roger D., and John F. Szwed, eds. *After Africa: Extracts from British Travel Accounts and Journals of the Seventeenth, Eighteenth, and Nineteenth Centuries Concerning the Slaves, Their Manners, and Customs in the British West Indies.* New Haven: Yale University Press, 1983. Print.

Allen, Theodore. *The Invention of the White Race.* Vol. 1: *Racial Oppression and Social Control.* New York: Verso, 2012. Print.

Althusser, Louis. *Lenin and Philosophy.* New York: Monthly Review Press, 1971. Print.

Anderson, Benedict. *Imagined Communities: Reflections on the Origin and Spread of Nationalism.* London: Verso, 1983. Print.

Arendt, Hannah. *The Origins of Totalitarianism.* New York: Harcourt, Harvest Books, 1966. Print.

Asante, Molefi. *Kemet, Afrocentricity, and Knowledge.* Trenton, NJ: Africa World Press, 1990. Print.

Asukile, Thabiti. "The All-Embracing Black Nationalist Theories of David Walker's *Appeal*." *Black Scholar* 29 (1999): 16–24. *Academic Search Complete.* Web. 21 Jan. 2013.

Baden, Joel, and Candida Moss. "Does the New 'Exodus' Movie Whitewash the Bible?" CNN.com. Web. 19 Dec. 2014.

Baker, Houston A. *Blues, Ideology and Afro-American Literature: A Vernacular Theory.* Chicago: University of Chicago Press, 1984. Print.

Baraka, Amiri. "The Revolutionary Tradition in Afro-American Literature." 1980. *The Jones/Amiri Baraka Reader*. Ed. William Harris. New York: Thunder's Mouth Press, 1993. Print.

Baucom, Ian. "Frantz Fanon's Radio: Solidarity, Diaspora, and the Tactics of Listening." *Contemporary Literature* 42 (2001): 15–49. JSTOR. Web. 30 May 2007.

Benitez-Rojo, Antonio. *The Repeating Island: The Caribbean and the Postmodern Perspective*. Trans. James E. Maranis. Durham, NC: Duke University Press, 1996. Print.

Bergner, Gwen. "Who Is That Masked Woman? Or, the Role of Gender in Fanon's *Black Skin, White Masks*." *PMLA* 110 (1995): 75–88. JSTOR. Web. 30 May 2007.

Bernal, Martin. *Black Athena: The Afroasiatic Roots of Classical Civilization*. Vol. 1: *The Fabrication of Ancient Greece 1785–1985*. New Brunswick, NJ: Rutgers University Press, 1987. Print.

Bernasconi, Robert. "Kant as an Unfamiliar Source of Racism." *Philosophers on Race: Critical Essays on Race*. Ed. Julie Ward and Tommy Lott. Oxford: Blackwell, 2002. 145–66. Print.

———. "Who Invented the Concept of Race? Kant's Role in the Enlightenment Construction of Race." *Race*. Ed. Robert Bernasconi. Oxford: Blackwell, 2001. 11–36. Print.

Bhabha, Homi. *The Location of Culture*. London: Routledge, 1994. Print.

Birt, Robert. "Existence, Identity, and Liberation." *Existence in Black: An Anthology of Black Existential Philosophy*. Ed. Lewis R. Gordon. London: Routledge, 1997. 203–13. Print.

Blackburn, Simon. *Oxford Dictionary of Philosophy*. Oxford: Oxford University Press, 1994. Print.

Blassingham, John W., ed. *Slave Testimony: Two Centuries of Letters, Speeches, Interviews, and Autobiographies*. Baton Rouge: Louisiana State University Press, 1977. Print.

Bobb, June D. *Beating a Restless Drum: The Poetics of Kamau Brathwaite and Derek Walcott*. Trenton, NJ: Africa World Press, 1998. Print.

Bogues, Anthony. *Black Heretics, Black Prophets: Radical Political Intellectuals*. London: Routledge, 2003. Print.

Brathwaite, Kamau. *Ancestors*. New York: New Directions Books, 1987. Print.

———. *The Arrivants*. Oxford: Oxford University Press, 1998. Print.

———. *The Development of Creole Society in Jamaica 1770–1820*. Oxford: Oxford University Press, 1971. Print.

———. "History of the Voice." *Roots*. Ann Arbor: University of Michigan Press, 1993. Print.

———. *Islands*. Oxford: Oxford University Press, 1969. Print.

———. "Jazz and the West Indian Novel." *Roots*. Ann Arbor: University of Michigan Press, 1993. Print.

———. *Middle Passages*. New York: New Directions Books, 1992. Print.

Brown, Vincent. "Social Death and Political Life in the Study of Slavery." *American Historical Review* (2009): 1231–49. *JSTOR*. Web. 12 Mar. 2011.

Bruce, Dickson D. "Ancient Africa and the Early Black Historians, 1883–1915." *American Quarterly* 36.5 (1984): 684–99. *JSTOR*. Web. 17 Dec. 2006.

Buhle, Paul. *C. L. R. James: The Artist as Revolutionary*. London: Verso, 1988. Print.

Butler, Broadus. "Frederick Douglass: The Black Philosopher in the United States. A Commentary." *Philosophy Born of Struggle: Anthology of Afro-American Philosophy from 1917*. Ed. Leonard Harris. Dubuque, IA: Kendall/Hunt, 1983. 1–8. Print.

Cabral, Amilcar. *Unity and Struggle: The Speeches and Writings of Amilcar Cabral*. New York: Monthly Review Press, 1979. Print.

Carr, David. *Time, Narrative, and History*. Bloomington: Indiana University Press, 1988. Print.

Caute, David. *Frantz Fanon*. New York: Viking Press, 1970. Print.

Césaire, Aimé. *Discourse on Colonialism*. Trans. Joan Pinkham. New York: Monthly Review Press, 1972. Print.

Chaney, Michael. "Picturing the Mother, Claiming Egypt: *My Bondage and My Freedom* as Auto(bio)ethnography." *African American Review* 35 (2001): 391–408. *JSTOR*. Web. 21 Jan. 2013.

Christian, Barbara. "The Race for Theory." *African American Literary Theory: A Reader*. Ed. Winston Napier. New York: New York University Press, 2000. 280–89. Print.

Clarke, John Henrik. *Africans at the Crossroads: Notes for An African World Revolution*. Trenton, NJ: Africa World Press, 1991. Print.

Cooper, Wayne. *Claude McKay: Rebel Sojourner in the Harlem Renaissance*. Baton Rouge: Louisiana State Press, 1987. Print.

Cox, Oliver C. *Capitalism as a System*. New York: Monthly Review Press, 1964. Print.

Davis, Angela. "Unfinished Lecture on Liberation II." *Philosophy Born of Struggle: Anthology of Afro-American Philosophy from 1917*. Ed. Leonard Harris. Dubuque, IA: Kendall/Hunt, 1983. 130–36. Print.

de Jongh, James. *Vicious Modernism: Black Harlem and the Literary Imagination*. New York: Cambridge University Press, 1990. Print.

Diggins, John. "Slavery, Race, and Equality: Jefferson and the Pathos of the

Enlightenment." *American Quarterly* 28 (1976): 206–28. *JSTOR*. Web. 20 July 2007.

Dinius, Marcy. "'Look!! Look!!! At This!!!!' The Radical Typography of David Walker's *Appeal*." *PMLA* 126 (2011): 55–72. Print.

Diop, Cheikh Anta. *The African Origin of Civilization: Myth or Reality*. Trans. Mercer Cook. New York: Lawrence Hill, 1974. Print.

Douglass, Frederick. "The Claims of the Negro Ethnologically Considered" 1854. *The Life and Writings of Frederick Douglass*. Ed. Philip Foner. Vol. 2. New York: International, 1950. Print.

——. "Lecture on Slavery No. 1." *The Life and Writings of Frederick Douglass*. Ed. Philip Foner. Vol. 2. New York: International, 1950. Print.

——. "Lecture on Slavery No. 2." *The Life and Writings of Frederick Douglass*. Ed. Philip Foner. Vol. 2. New York: International, 1950. Print.

——. "Letter to His Old Master." 1848. Rpt. in *My Bondage and My Freedom*. 1855. New York: Washington Square Press, 2003. 323–30. Print.

——. *Life and Times of Frederick Douglass*. 1892. New York: Collier Books, 1962. Print.

——. *My Bondage and My Freedom*. 1855. New York: Washington Square Press, 2003. Print.

——. *Narrative of the Life of Frederick Douglass*. 1845. *The Classic Slave Narratives*. Ed. Henry Louis Gates Jr. New York: Penguin, 1987. Print.

Drake, St. Clair. *Black Folk Here and There*. Los Angeles: UCLA Center for Afro-American Studies, 1987. Print.

Drescher, Seymour. "The Ending of the Slave Trade and the Evolution of European Scientific Racism." *Social Science History* 14 (1990): 415–50. *JSTOR*. Web. 12 Feb. 2013.

Dubois, Laurent, and John Garrigus, eds. *Slave Rebellion in the Caribbean 1789–1804: A Brief History with Documents*. New York: Bedford-St. Martin's Press, 2006. Print.

Du Bois, W. E. B. *Against Racism: Unpublished Essays, Papers, Addresses, 1887–1961*. Ed. Herbert Aptheker. Amherst: University of Massachusetts Press, 1985. Print.

——. *Black Reconstruction in America 1860–1880*. 1935. New York: Atheneum, 1962. Print.

——. *Dusk of Dawn: An Essay towards an Autobiography of a Race Concept*. New York: Schocken, 1968. Print.

——. *The Souls of Black Folk*. 1903. *Three Negro Classics*. New York: Avon, 1965. Print.

——. *The World and Africa*. 1946. New York: International, 1965. Print.

Duran, Jane. "Walker's *Appeal*: An Exercise in the Extension of Enlightenment Thought." *Philosophia Africana* 12 (2009): 159–65. *Academic Search Complete*. Web. 21 Jan. 2013.

Dussel, Enrique, et al. "Europe, Modernity, and Eurocentrism." *Nepantla: Views from the South* 1 (2000): 465–78. *Project Muse*. Web. 12 Feb. 2013.

Eagleton, Terry. *Ideology: An Introduction*. London: Verso, 1991. Print.

———. *Literary Theory: An Introduction*. Minneapolis: University of Minnesota Press, 1996. Print.

Edmonson, Belinda. "Black Aesthetics, Feminist Aesthetics, and the Problems of Oppositional Discourse." *Cultural Critique* 22 (1992): 75–98. *JSTOR*. Web. 22 Jan. 2008.

———. "Race, Tradition and the Construction of the Caribbean Aesthetic." *New Literary History* 25.1 (1994): 109–20. *JSTOR*. Web. 14 Jan. 2008.

Edwards, Brent Hayes. "Dossier on Black Radicalism: The 'Autonomy' of Black Radicalism." *Social Text* 19.2 (2001): 1–13. *JSTOR*. Web. 30 May 2007.

———. *The Practice of Diaspora: Literature Translation, and the Rise of Black Internationalism*. Cambridge: Harvard University Press, 2003. Print.

———. "The Uses of Diaspora." *Social Text* 19.1 (2001): 45–71. *JSTOR*. Web. 30 May 2007.

Erickson, Peter. "Representations of Blacks and Blackness in the Renaissance." *Criticism* 35.4 (1993): 499–527. *JSTOR*. Web. 30 May 2007.

Eze, Emmanuel."The Color of Reason: The Idea of 'Race' in Kant's Anthropology." *Anthropology and the German Enlightenment: Perspectives on Humanity*. Ed. Katherine Faull. Lewisburg, PA: Bucknell University Press, 1995. 200–241. Print.

———. "Hume, Race, and Human Nature." *Journal of the History of Ideas* 61.4 (2000): 691–98. *JSTOR*. Web. 14 July 2013.

———, ed. *Race and the Enlightenment: A Reader*. Oxford: Blackwell, 1997. Print.

Fanon, Frantz. *Black Skin, White Masks*. 1952. Trans. Charles Lam Markmann. New York: Grove Press, 1967. Print.

———. *A Dying Colonialism*. 1959. Trans. Adolfo Gilly. New York: Grove Press, 1967. Print.

———. *The Wretched of the Earth*. Trans. Constance Farrington. New York: Grove Press, 1963. Print.

Flynn, Thomas. "Sartre and the Poetics of History." *The Cambridge Companion to Sartre*. Ed. Christina Howells. Cambridge: Cambridge University Press, 1992. 213–60. Print.

Foner, Philip, ed. *The Life and Writings of Frederick Douglass*. Vols. 1 and 2. New York: International, 1950. Print.

Forbes, Jack D. *Africans and Native Americans: The Language of Race and the*

Evolution of Red-Black Peoples. Urbana: University of Illinois Press, 1993. Print.

Fuss, Diana. *Essentially Speaking: Feminism, Nature and Difference.* New York: Routledge, 1989. Print.

———. "Interior Colonies: Frantz Fanon and the Politics of Identification." *Diacritics* 24.2–3 (1994): 19–42. *JSTOR.* Web. 20 July 2007.

Gates, Henry Louis, Jr. "Critical Fanonism." *Critical Inquiry* 17.3 (1991): 457–70. *JSTOR.* Web. 30 May 2007.

———. "Preface to Blackness: Text and Pretext." *African American Literary Theory: A Reader.* Ed. Winston Napier. New York: New York University Press, 2000. 147–64. Print.

———. *The Signifying Monkey: A Theory of African American Literary Criticism.* New York: Oxford University Press, 1988. Print.

Gates, Henry, and Nellie McKay, eds. *The Norton Anthology of African American Literature.* 2nd ed. New York: Norton, 2004. Print.

Gendzier, Irene. *Frantz Fanon: A Critical Study.* New York: Random House, 1973. Print.

George, G. M. James. *Stolen Legacy.* New York: Philosophical Library, 1954. Print.

Gikandi, Simon. "E. K. Brathwaite and the Poetics of Voice: The Allegory of History in *Rights of Passage.*" *The Critical Response to Kamau Brathwaite.* Ed. Emily Allen Williams. Westport, CT: Praeger, 2004. 15–24. Print.

Gilroy, Paul. *The Black Atlantic: Modernity and Double Consciousness.* Cambridge: Harvard University Press, 1993. Print.

———. *Postcolonial Melancholia.* New York: Columbia University Press, 2005. Print.

Gines, Kathryn. *Hannah Arendt and the Negro Question.* Bloomington: University of Indiana Press, 2014. Print.

Goldberg, David. *Racist Culture: Philosophy and the Politics of Meaning.* Oxford: Blackwell, 1993. Print.

Gordon, Jane Anna. *Creolizing Political Theory: Reading Rousseau through Fanon.* New York: Fordham University Press, 2014. Print.

Gordon, Lewis R., ed. *Existence in Black: An Anthology of Black Existential Philosophy.* New York: Routledge, 1997. Print.

———. *Existentia Africana: Understanding Africana Existential Thought.* New York: Routledge, 2000. Print.

———. "Existential Dynamics of Theorizing Black Invisibility." *Existence in Black: An Anthology of Black Existential Philosophy.* Ed. Lewis Gordon. New York: Routledge, 1997. 69–79. Print.

———. *An Introduction to Africana Philosophy.* Cambridge: Cambridge University Press, 2008. Print.

———. *What Fanon Said: A Philosophical Introduction to His Life and Thought.* New York: Fordham University Press, 2015. Print.

Gordon-Reed, Annette. *Thomas Jefferson and Sally Hemings: An American Controversy.* Charlottesville: University of Virginia Press, 1997. Print.

Gramsci, Antonio. *Selections from the Prison Notebooks.* Ed. and trans. Quintin Hoare. New York: International, 1971. Print.

Grimshaw, Anna, ed. *The C. L. R. James Reader.* Oxford: Blackwell, 1992. Print.

Hall, Stuart. "New Ethnicities." *Stuart Hall: Critical Dialogues in Cultural Studies.* Ed. David Morley and Kuan-Hsing Chen. New York: Routledge, 1996. 441–49. Print.

Hanchard, Michael. "Identity, Meaning, and the African-American." *Dangerous Liaisons: Gender, Nation, and Postcolonial Perspectives.* Ed. Anne McClintock, Aamir Mufti, and Ella Shohat. Minneapolis: University of Minnesota Press, 1997. 230–39. Print.

Hegel, Georg Wilhelm Friedrich. *Lectures on the Philosophy of World History.* 1857. Trans. H. B. Nisbet. Cambridge: Cambridge University Press, 1975. Print.

Heidegger, Martin. *Being and Time.* 1953. Trans. Joan Stambaugh. Albany: State University of New York Press, 1996. Print.

Heinemann, F. H. *Existentialism and the Modern Predicament.* New York: Harper & Row, 1958. Print.

Henry, Paget. "Between Hume and Cugoano: Race, Ethnicity, and Philosophical Entrapment." *Journal of Speculative Philosophy* 18 (2004): 129–48. *JSTOR.* Web. 9 Aug. 2012.

———. *Caliban's Reason: Introducing Afro-Caribbean Philosophy.* New York: Routledge, 2000. Print.

Hinchman, Lewis P., and Sandra K. Hinchman. "In Heidegger's Shadow: Hannah Arendt's Phenomenological Humanism." *Review of Politics* 46.2 (1984): 183–211. *JSTOR.* Web. 19 July 2007.

Hinks, Peter. *To Awaken My Afflicted Brethren: David Walker and the Problem of Antebellum Slave Resistance.* University Park: Pennsylvania State University Press, 1997. Print.

Hitchcock, Peter. *Imaginary States: Studies in Cultural Transnationalism.* Chicago: University of Illinois Press, 2003. Print.

hooks, bell. "Postmodern Blackness." *The Norton Anthology of Theory and Criticism.* Ed. Vincent B. Leitch. New York: Norton, 2001. 2478–84. Print.

Hudson, Nicholas. "From 'Nation to Race': The Origin of Racial Classification in Eighteenth-Century Thought." *Eighteenth-Century Studies* 29 (1996): 247–64. *JSTOR.* Web. 20 Jan. 2013.

Huggins, Nathan Irvin. *Harlem Renaissance*. London: Oxford University Press, 1971. Print.

Hulme, Peter. "The Locked Heart: The Creole Family Romance of *Wide Sargasso Sea*." *Colonial Discourse/Postcolonial Theory*. Ed. Francis Barker, Peter Hulme, and Margaret Iversen. New York: Manchester University Press, 1994. 72–88. Print.

Hume, David. "Of National Characters." 1741. *Selected Essays of David Hume* Oxford: Oxford University Press, 1998. Print.

Hurston, Zora Neale. "Characteristics of Negro Expression." 1934. *African American Literary Theory*. Ed. Winston Napier. New York: New York University Press, 2000. 31–44. Print.

———. *Tell My Horse: Voodoo and Life in Haiti and Jamaica*. 1938. New York: Harper & Row, 1990. Print.

———. *Their Eyes Were Watching God*. 1937. Chicago: University of Illinois Press, 1978. Print.

Immerwahr, John. "Hume's Revised Racism." *Journal of the History of Ideas* 53 (1992): 481–86. *JSTOR*. Web. 9 Aug. 2012.

Israel, Jonathan. *A Revolution of the Mind: Radical Enlightenment and the Intellectual Origins of Modern Democracy*. Princeton: Princeton University Press, 2010. Print.

James, C. L. R. *Beyond a Boundary*. 1963. Durham, NC: Duke University Press, 1993. Print.

———. *The Black Jacobins: Toussaint L'Ouverture and the San Domingo Revolution*. 1938. New York: Random House, Vintage, 1963. Print.

———. *A History of Pan-African Revolt*. Washington, DC: Drum and Spear Press, 1969. Print.

———. "Lectures on the Black Jacobins." *Small Axe* 8 (2000): 65–112. *Project Muse*. Web. 20 May 2007.

———. *Notes on Dialectics*. 1948. London: Allison & Busby, 1980. Print.

———. *Wilson Harris: A Philosophical Approach*. St. Augustine, Trinidad: University of West Indies, 1965. Print.

James, Winston. *Holding Aloft the Banner of Ethiopia: Caribbean Radicalism in Early Twentieth-Century America*. New York: Verso, 1998. Print.

Jameson, Fredric. *Marxism and Form: Twentieth-Century Dialectical Theories of Literature*. Princeton: Princeton University Press, 1971. Print.

JanMohamed, Abdul. "Economy of Manichean Allegory: The Function of Racial Difference in Colonialist Literature." *Critical Inquiry* 12 (1985): 59–87. *JSTOR*. Web. 30 May 2007.

Jefferson, Thomas. *Notes on the State of Virginia*. 1785. New York: Barnes & Noble, 2010. Print.

Johnson, Charles. *Being and Race: Black Writing since 1970*. Bloomington: Indiana University Press, 1988. Print.

Jones, LeRoi. *Blues People*. New York: Morrow Quill Paperbacks, 1963. Print.

Jordan, Winthrop. *White over Black: American Attitudes toward the Negro, 1550–1812*. Chapel Hill: University of North Carolina Press, 1968. Print.

Jorgensen, Carl. "The African American Critique of White Supremacist Science." *Journal of Negro Education* 64 (1995): 232–42. JSTOR. Web. 21 Jan. 2013.

Juengel, Scott. "Countenancing History: Mary Wollstonecraft, Samuel Stanhope Smith, and Enlightenment Racial Science." *ELH* 68 (2001): 897–927. JSTOR. Web. 11 Feb. 2013.

Kant, Immanuel. *Observations on the Feeling of the Beautiful and the Sublime and Other Writings*. 1764. Ed. Patrick Frierson and Paul Guyer. Cambridge: Cambridge University Press, 2011. Print.

Kebede, Messay. "The Rehabilitation of Violence and the Violence of Rehabilitation: Fanon and Colonialism." *Journal of Black Studies* 31 (2001): 539–62. JSTOR. Web. 14 Oct. 2007.

Keita, Maghan. "Africans and Asians: Historiography and the Long View of Global Interaction." *Journal of World History* 16 (2005): 1–30. *Project Muse*. Web. 5 Aug. 2013.

———. *Race and the Writing of History: Riddling the Sphinx*. Oxford: Oxford University Press, 2000. Print.

Kelley, Robin D. G. "'But a Local Phase of a Global Problem': Black History's Global Vision, 1883–1950." *Journal of American History* 86.3 (1999): 1–37. JSTOR. Web. 18 Oct. 2005.

Kennington, Richard. "Rene Descartes." *History of Political Philosophy*. Ed. Leo Strauss and Joseph Cropsey. Chicago: Rand McNally, 1963. 379–98. Print.

Kocklemans, Joseph. "Phenomenology." *Cambridge Dictionary of Philosophy*. Ed. Robert Audi. Cambridge: Cambridge University Press, 2009. 664–66. Print.

Lalla, Barbara, and Jean D'Costa. *Language in Exile: Three Hundred Years of Jamaican Creole*. Tuscaloosa: University of Alabama Press, 1990. Print.

Lamarque, Peter. *The Philosophy of Literature*. Oxford: Blackwell, 2009. Print.

Lehmann, Sophia. "In Search of a Mother Tongue: Locating Home in Diaspora." *Melus* 23.4 (1998): 101–18. JSTOR. Web. 18 Oct. 2005.

Le Sueur, James D. *Uncivil War: Intellectuals and Identity Politics during the Decolonization of Algeria*. Philadelphia: University of Pennsylvania Press, 2001. Print.

Levine, Robert. *Martin Delany, Frederick Douglass, and the Politics of Repre-

sentative Identity. Chapel Hill: University of North Carolina Press, 1997. Print.

———. "Road to Africa: Frederick Douglass' Rome." *African American Review* 34 (2000): 217–31. *JSTOR.* Web. 19 June 2012.

Long, Edward. *A History of Jamaica.* 1774. Quebec: McGill-Queen's University Press, 2002. Print.

Lubiano, Wahneema. "Mapping the Interstices between Afro-American Cultural Discourse and Cultural Studies: A Prolegomenon." *African American Literary Theory: A Reader.* Ed. Winston Napier. New York: New York University Press, 2000. 643–52. Print.

Lynch, Hollis. *Edward Wilmot Blyden: Pan-Negro Patriot, 1832–1912.* London: Oxford University Press, 1967. Print.

Lyon, Arabella. "Interdisciplinarity: Giving Up Territory." *College English* 54.6 (1992): 681–93. *JSTOR.* Web. 19 July 2014.

Mackey, Louis. "Philosophy of Literature." *The Cambridge Dictionary of Philosophy.* Ed. Robert Audi. Cambridge: Cambridge University Press, 1995. 677–79. Print.

Mackey, Nathaniel. "Other: From Noun to Verb." *Representations.* 39 (1992): 51–70. *JSTOR.* Web. 18 Oct. 2005.

———. *Paracritical Hinge: Essays, Talks, Notes, Interviews.* Madison: University of Wisconsin Press, 2005. Print.

Martin, Tony. "Rescuing Fanon from the Critics." *African Studies Review* 13.3 (1970): 381–99. *JSTOR.* Web. 30 May 2007.

McClintock Anne. "'No Longer in a Future Heaven': Gender, Race, and Nationalism." *Dangerous Liaisons: Gender, Nation, and Postcolonial Perspectives.* Ed. Anne McClintock, Aamir Mufti, and Ella Shohat. Minneapolis: University of Minnesota Press, 1997. 89–112. Print.

McDonald, Henry. "American Literary Theory and Philosophical Exceptionalism." *Rhetoric Review* 22.2 (2003): 138–53. *JSTOR.* Web. 21 July 2014.

Mills, Charles. "Kant's *Untermenschen.*" *Race and Racism in Modern Philosophy.* Ed. Andrew Valls. Ithaca: Cornell University Press, 2005. 169–93. Print.

Moore-Gilbert, Bart. *Postcolonial Theory: Contexts, Practices, Politics.* New York: Verso, 1997. Print.

Morrison, Toni. *Playing in the Dark: Whiteness and the Literary Imagination.* New York: Random House-Vintage, 1993. Print.

Moses, Wilson. *The Golden Age of Black Nationalism, 1850–1952.* Oxford: Oxford University Press, 1978. Print.

Mudimbe, V. Y. "African Gnosis Philosophy and the Order of Knowledge: An Introduction." *African Studies Review* 28.2–3 (1985): 149–223. *JSTOR.* Web. 30 May 2007.

Murphy, E. Jefferson. *History of African Civilization*. New York: Dell, 1972. Print.

Ngũgĩ wa Thiong'o. *Decolonizing the Mind: The Politics of Language in African Literature*. Portsmouth, NH: Heinemann, 1986. Print.

Niane, D. T. *Sundiata: An Epic of Old Mali*. 1960. Trans. G. D. Pickett. Edinburgh: Pearson, 2006. Print.

Nielsen, Aldon. "Ancestors and Words Need Love Too." *The Critical Response to Kamau Brathwaite*. Ed. Emily Williams. Westport, CT: Praeger, 2004. 225–36. Print.

Nixon, Rob. "Caribbean and African Appropriations of *The Tempest*." *Politics and Poetic Value*. Ed. Robert von Halberg. Chicago: University of Chicago Press, 1987. 185–206. Print.

Nursey-Bray, Paul. "Race and Nation: Ideology in the Thought of Frantz Fanon." *Journal of Modern African Studies* 18.1 (1980): 135–42. *JSTOR*. Web. 30 May 2007.

Outram, Dorinda. *The Enlightenment*. Cambridge: Cambridge University Press, 2011. Print.

Patterson, Orlando. *Slavery and Social Death*. Cambridge: Harvard University Press, 1982. Print.

Patterson, Tiffany Ruby, and Robin Kelley,. "Unfinished Migrations: Reflections on the African Diaspora and the Making of the Modern World." *African Studies Review* 43.1 (2000): 11–45. *JSTOR*. Web. 15 Oct. 2008.

Plato. *Timaeus*. Trans. Francis M. Cornford. Indianapolis: Bobbs-Merrill Educational, 1959. Print.

Popkin, Richard. *The High Road to Pyrrhonism*. San Diego, CA: Austin Hill Press, 1980. Print.

Retamar, Roberto Fernandez. *Caliban and Other Essays*. Trans. Edward Baker. Minneapolis: University of Minnesota Press, 1989. Print.

Robinson, Cedric J. *Black Marxism: The Making of the Black Radical Tradition*. Chapel Hill: University of North Carolina Press, 1983. Print.

Said, Edward. *Culture and Imperialism*. New York: Random House-Vintage, 1993. Print.

Sanders, Edith. "The Hamitic Hypothesis: Its Origin and Functions in Time Perspective." *Journal of African History* 10 (1969): 521–32. *JSTOR* Web. 19 Feb. 2013.

Sartre, Jean-Paul. *Being and Nothingness*. 1943. Trans. Hazel E. Barnes. New York: Washington Square Press, 1992. Print.

———. *Critique of Dialectical Reason*. 1960. Trans. Alan Sheridan-Smith. New York: Verso, 2004. Print.

———. *Existentialism and Human Emotions*. New York: Philosophical Library, 1957. Print.

———. *Existentialism Is a Humanism*. New Haven: Yale University Press, 2007. Print.

———. *Literature and Existentialism*. New York: Citadel Press, 1962. Print.

Schrader, George Alfred. *Existential Philosophers: Kierkegaard to Merleau-Ponty*. New York: McGraw Hill, 1967. Print.

Shinnie, Margaret. *Ancient African Kingdoms*. New York: St. Martin's Press, 1965. Print.

Siemerling, Winifred. "W. E. B. Du Bois, Hegel, and the Staging of Alterity." *Callaloo* 24.1 (2001): 325–33. *JSTOR*. Web. 30 May 2007.

Simpson, Hyacinth. "'Voicing the Text': The Making of an Oral Poetics in Olive Senior's Short Fiction." *Callaloo* 27.3 (2004): 829–43. *JSTOR*. Web. 30 May 2007.

Smitherman, Geneva. *Talkin and Testifyin: The Language of Black America*. Detroit: Wayne State University Press, 1977. Print.

Snowden, Frank M. *Blacks in Antiquity: Ethiopians in the Greco-Roman Experience*. Cambridge: Harvard University Press-Belknap, 1970. Print.

Stanton, William. *The Leopard's Spots: Scientific Attitudes toward Race in America, 1815–59*. Chicago: University of Chicago Press, 1960. Print.

Stuckey, Sterling. *Slave Culture: Nationalist Theory and the Foundations of Black America*. New York: Oxford University Press, 1987. Print.

Tucker, Gerald E. "Machiavelli and Fanon: Ethics, Violence, and Action." *Journal of Modern African Studies* 16.3 (1978): 397–415. *JSTOR*. Web. 30 May 2007.

Tyrell, Ian. "Making Nations/Making States: American Historians in the Context of Empire." *Journal of American History* 86.3 (1999): 1015–44. *JSTOR*. Web. 25 Jan. 2007.

Valls, Andrew. "'A Lousy Empirical Scientist': Reconsidering Hume's Racism." *Race and Racism in Modern Philosophy*. Ithaca: Cornell University Press, 2005. 127–49. Print.

———. *Race and Racism in Modern Philosophy*. Ithaca: Cornell University Press, 2005. Print.

Van Sertima, Ivan. *They Came before Columbus: The African Presence in Ancient America*. New York: Random House, 1976. Print.

Volney, Constantin-François. *The Ruins, or Meditations on the Revolutions of Empires: And the Law of Nature*. 1807. Charleston, SC: Bibliobazaar, 2013. Print.

———. *Travels through Syria and Egypt VI in the Years 1783–1785*. 1788. Whitefish, MT: Kessinger, 2009. Print.

Walker, David. *Walker's Appeal In Four Articles; Together with a Preamble, to the Coloured Citizens of the World, but in particular, and very expressly, to those of the United States of America.* 1829. New York: Hill and Wang, 1965. Print.

Ward, Julie. "'The Master's Tools': Abolitionist Arguments of Equiano and Cugoano." *Subjugation and Bondage: Critical Essays on Slavery and Social Philosophy.* Ed. Tommy Lott. New York: Rowman & Littlefield, 1998. 79–98. Print.

Wellek, Rene, and Austin Warren. *Theory of Literature.* New York: Harcourt Brace, 1970. Print.

West, Michael, and William Martin. "A Future with a Past: Resurrecting the Study of Africa in the Post-Africanist Era." *Africa Today* 44.3 (1997): 309–26. JSTOR. Web. 10 July 2014.

Willett, Cynthia. "The Master-Slave Dialectic: Hegel v. Douglass." *Subjugation and Bondage: Critical Essays on Slavery and Social Philosophy.* Ed. Tommy L. Lott. New York: Rowman & Littlefield, 1998. 151–70. Print.

Williams, Emily Allen. "Kamau Brathwaite Talks with Emily Allen Williams about Four Decades of Critical Response." *The Critical Response to Kamau Brathwaite.* Westport, CT: Praeger, 2004. 294–314. Print.

Williams, Eric. *Capitalism and Slavery.* 1944. New York: Capricorn Books, 1966. Print.

Williams, Raymond. *Marxism and Literature.* Oxford: Oxford University Press, 1977. Print.

Wright, Richard. *Black Power: A Record of Reactions in a Land of Pathos.* 1954. New York: Harper Collins, 1995. Print.

Wynter, Sylvia. "The Ceremony Must Be Found: After Humanism." *Boundary 2* 12.13 (1984): 19–70. JSTOR. Web. 11 Aug. 2012.

———. "On Disenchanting Discourse: 'Minority' Literary Criticism and Beyond." *Cultural Critique* 7 (1987): 207–44. JSTOR. Web. 8 July 2014.

Yancy, George. "Geneva Smitherman: The Social Ontology of African-American Language, the Power of *Nommo*, and the Dynamics of Resistance and Identity through Language." *Journal of Speculative Philosophy* 18.4 (2004): 273–99. *Project Muse.* Web. 25 Jan. 2007.

INDEX